**Recent Titles in
Hip Hop in America**

Free Stylin'

Free Stylin'

HOW HIP HOP CHANGED THE FASHION INDUSTRY

Elena Romero

Foreword by Daymond John

Hip Hop in America
Juleyka Lantigua–Williams, Series Editor

 PRAEGER

AN IMPRINT OF ABC-CLIO, LLC
Santa Barbara, California • Denver, Colorado • Oxford, England

Library of Congress Cataloging-in-Publication Data

Romero, Elena, 1973–
    Free stylin' : how hip hop changed the fashion industry / Elena Romero ; foreword by Daymond John.
        p. cm. — (Hip hop in America)
    Includes bibliographical references and index.
    ISBN 978–0–313–38646–6 (hardback) — ISBN 978–0–313–38647–3 (ebook)
1. Fashion design—United States. 2. Hip-hop—Influence. 3. Clothing trade—United States. I. Title. II. Title: Free styling.
TT507.R656   2012
746.9′20973—dc23   2012000371

ISBN: 978–0–313–38646–6
EISBN: 978–0–313–38647–3

16 15 14 13 12   1 2 3 4 5

This book is also available on the World Wide Web as an eBook.
Visit www.abc-clio.com for details.

Praeger
An Imprint of ABC-CLIO, LLC

ABC-CLIO, LLC
130 Cremona Drive, P.O. Box 1911
Santa Barbara, California 93116-1911

This book is printed on acid-free paper ∞

Manufactured in the United States of America

This book is dedicated to my oldest daughter, Gabriela, a natural fashion diva who from the moment she could talk knew what she wanted to wear.

Contents

Foreword

Growing up in Hollis, Queens, I remember hearing the early sounds of hip hop from Spoonie Gee (credited for the origination of the term "hip hop" and "yes, yes y'all") and The Sugar Hill Gang's 1979 classic "Rapper's Delight."

I was about 12 years old when I fell in love with fashion. At first, I was into the labels that were popular at the time—Puma, Pony, Ellyse, and Kangaroos for sneakers; Lee's and Levi's for jeans; and sweatsuits by Le Coq Sportif. I remember the first hip hop artists wearing some really crazy outfits like Grandmaster Melle Mel and Afrika Bambaataa, wearing stuff like George Clinton, Parliament, and the Funkadelics on stage.

Hip hop attire on the streets was actually simple between the early to mid-1980s. Those of us who followed the music found a way to trick it out and make it special by customizing our wares. B-boys were a great example for practicality, function, and style. As dancers, their pants couldn't be too baggy so b-boys either tapered jeans by putting pin tucks or permanent creases down their legs or took shoe laces and stringed them up to their thighs. To stand out, sneakers could have dyed soles or checkerboard laces.

Each New York borough had its own unique flavor. As Queens guys, we wore Adidas shell-toes because of Run-D.M.C. and donned a BVD look, which consisted of a BVD short-sleeve T-shirt with a BVD tank top over it. We would head to Jamaica Avenue to the Colosseum Mall for sweatsuits and airbrushed gear by The Shirt Kings. Local Jamaica

Avenue shops like Mr. Lee's and Montego Bay would be regular shopping destinations. But no matter what borough you represented, you could count on all of us shopping on Delancey Street in the Lower East Side for outerwear and in Harlem for one-of-a-kind custom outfits at shops on 125th Street like A.J. Lester and Dapper Dan.

Growing up with LL Cool J, I'd go on hip hop tours with him, mostly on the eastern seaboard. I, like so many guys from around the way, would basically act as a roadie, security, assistant, or simply hang out. The tours included every major hip hop artist like Run-D.M.C., The Fat Boys, Eric B. and Rakim, Big Daddy Kane, Whodini, Salt-N-Pepa, MC Lyte, and Queen Latifah. When we headed out West, N.W.A. would be on the tour, and further down South, Luke Campbell and 2 Live Crew. In my early entrepreneur days, I'd stock up on merchandise that I'd purchase on Delancey Street and sell it to people in different states while on tour.

African American designer Willi Smith became the first to jumpstart what was coined "streetwear" with his brand Williwear, but it was Cross Colours that introduced the world to an explosive volume business. Cross Colours cleverly started making product in Kente colors with a denim feel. Just as Cross Colours was approaching $100 million in sales, Karl Kani made it big with his line of blue jeans. We, in our local hoods, could finally say we had something to call our own.

Years later, I decided to launch FUBU with my boys J. Alexander Martin, Keith Perrin, and Carl Brown. We seized what Cross Colours started in 1990 and took it to the next level. At best, we thought that we'd grow to own a boutique, where we would make clothes for our friends and family, and each make $30,000 to $40,000 a year. We never dreamed our company would become a $350 million dollar powerhouse.

Documenting our success as a company and as a segment of the fashion industry *was only a handful of key media vehicles.* Veejay Ralph McDaniels put us in his Phat Fashion shows, which he committed to highlighting the newest and hottest designers. Consumer magazines like *The Source* started placing our gear in its fashion pages. But on the trade publication level, it was the now defunct *Daily News Record (DNR)*, the men's fashion bible, that covered the urban market on a consistent basis.

The reporter responsible for that was none other than Brooklyn-born and raised Elena Romero. I didn't know at the time if her interest was coming from her personally or from the publication. I would soon discover that she, like me, grew up with hip hop in her heart and telling our stories was a natural fit. All of us in the industry felt comfortable talking to her. As a hip hop insider, Elena knew our struggles and progressions. She always made sure to give an accurate depiction of where we were, where we were going, and how it related to the fashion market overall.

Hesitant at first about possibly being pigeonholed as solely a hip hop fashion writer, Elena approached covering the urban fashion market with trepidation. Listening to her reporter's natural instinct, she began legitimizing an industry once looked upon as a fad. Her dedication to telling our stories made retailers and leading business executives take us seriously. As our businesses grew, Elena was right there giving the fashion industry the inside scoop.

Until now, our story had not been written. *Free Stylin': How Hip Hop Changed the Fashion Industry* is the first comprehensive book to share the story of how hip hop infiltrated the garment district. The tale is as historic as it is controversial. Many of us didn't necessarily go to college and didn't have a fighting chance coming out of the hood, but we created an industry. It's very important to understand that. As a CEO, I'm more seasoned than someone who left an Ivy League school. All this came from designing a shirt.

Utilizing her journalistic lens, Elena explores the transition from hip hop style to hip hop branding; why major departments stores such as Federated Department Stores, Saks, Inc., and Mervyn's, to Target and J.C. Penney incorporated urban to their floors; how celebrity endorsements pushed our brands into the mainstream; and how the fashion trends made their transitions from the hood to the international runway.

Despite the $58 billion in sales our industry generated by 2002, there are only a handful of books dedicated to this market bonanza. Unfortunately, most focus on specific areas such as "bling" and kicks. *Free Stylin': How Hip Hop Changed the Fashion Industry* is a significant contribution to this genre and will finally give our story the platform it deserves.

In essence, this book is a part of the conscious movement that I associate with our brand and could easily share the name For Us, By Us.

"The Shark" Daymond John
Co-founder, FUBU The Collection
Star of ABC's *The Shark Tank*
Author of *The Display of Power: How FUBU Changed a World of Fashion, Branding and Lifestyle* and *The Brand Within: The Power of Branding from Birth to the Boardroom (Display of Power)*

Author's Note

_____

For over 40 years, hip hop has made its mark on U.S. culture and on the world. Comprised of the MC (known today as the rapper), the deejay, graffiti artists, and b-boys/b-girls (break dancers), the culture has impacted people across the globe and unified youth of all colors from the ghettos to the suburbs.[1] Its most prevalent identification: a uniform known on the streets as urban gear or hip hop clothing.

As hip hop evolved so did the styles and trends it inspired. By the mid-1980s, it was the All-American youth brands that slowly began to feel the impact of this new fashion segment. The world started to witness a new fashion evolution called by different names and eventually christened "urbanwear"—apparel that spoke to the lifestyle of hip hop followers and enthusiasts by addressing their most immediate need—fit. Hip hop found a home in what was called the young men's fashion market. It had a segment of the market, a name in a viable area. Hip hop later fueled other segments of fashion, including women's and accessories which were also mimicked by couture and mainstream designers.

Early hip hop brands in their purist form originated with graffiti artists who needed another extension of their work. Unlike fashion entrepreneurs before them, who studied fashion or had relatives in the fashion industry to show them the ropes, many of these newcomers got their education from the "school of hard knocks" or life and used their street smarts and word-of-mouth to get their product around. Street savvy marketers would soon convert urban styles into full-fledged brands and prove success at retail. As manufacturing and sales veteran Dave Rowan puts it, "Not only was the shit fresh. Literally and aesthetically, it was what was being created on the streets by the innovators who were in all the videos and trendsetting. Now [urban] was available to the retailers who had the balls to embrace it or in some cases, actually began their retail careers with it. The consumer ate it voraciously." Savvy marketing, along with the popularity of hip hop music, would soon have select designers incorporating the urban look onto their runway. By the late 1980s and early 1990s, designer fashionistas from Issac Mizrahi to Karl Lagerfeld for Chanel would show collections inspired by hip hop on the runway. Sportswear designers would soon catch on and look to cash in on a movement in development. An eclectic style originally comprised of borrowed looks from designer and popular brands of the early 1980s, hip hop would eventually evolve into a worldwide fashion phenomenon with brand identifiers of its very own. The first early sightings of so-called urban labels started with youth brands like Major Damage, Get Used, and Troop. However, these fashions were made with the consumer in mind. In time, this new fashion category would have designer faces—brown faces—such as Karl Kani and later, Sean Combs—attached to the brands, which catapulted the style genre to new heights. Changing the specs (specifications) of apparel to accommodate a baggier, loose-fitting silhouette, young fashion entrepreneurs hustled their way into the fashion industry with their talent, a little luck, business sense, and a whole lot of game.

African American designer Willi Donnell Smith of Williwear died ahead of his time, but his legacy with his brand Williwear put streetwear on the map. Carl Jones and T. J. Walker, formerly of West Coast-based Cross Colours, put an ethnic spin to streetwear in 1990 as they captured urbanites with their message of unity and solidarity. Their wares spoke to the inner souls of hip hop fashion followers with clever messages on brightly colored head-to-toe garments. Costa Rican born Carl Williams, known to the world as Karl Kani (as in 'Can I'), would start the trend out East with his baggy jeans, oversized sweatshirts, and metal nameplate overalls. He later had his brand housed under the Threads 4 Life Corp. umbrella, which Cross Colours developed as the first conglomerate of urban fashion brands. Soon, Brooklyn's April Walker, founder of Walker Wear, would attempt to join the squad. Walker's relationship with Cross Colours was short-lived and although she did not know at the time, it would actually be a blessing in disguise. Cross Colours, the company that became overnight sensation, would soon need to liquidate. While Cross Colours did close to $100 million in sales prior to its downfall, the apparel company proved there was big money to be made if the market could be reached.

Cross Colours became a hub for great talent similar to how the Ralph Lauren brand jumpstarted the careers of many. It was no surprise to see that many people who were affiliated Cross Colours would go on to work for other urban fashion brands as salespeople, marketing experts, and stylists or start urban brands for themselves such as style guru June Ambrose; Tony Shellman, who co-founded Mecca USA, Enyce and Parish Nation; and Jeffrey C. Tweedy, who made his career building celebrity hip hop brands, most notably, Sean John.

The retail success of pioneering urban brands Cross Colours and later, Karl Kani became a rude awakening to the established fashion guard that had long lacked leading black designers. Black people in fashion were considered to be more behind the scenes and very few were upfront and center (or even majority stakeholders in ownership). Their message—at times subtle and other times obvious—was clear—gear for you by us, later brilliantly adapted by team FUBU with "For Us, By Us." I met the team behind FUBU in April 1996 and it was among the first urban companies I covered in-depth at the now defunct trade *Daily News Record (DNR)*. I could easily relate to "The Shark" Daymond John, J. Alexander Martin, Carl Brown, and Keith Perrin. All of us shared a lot of things in common—from our love of hip hop to our innate drive for success. An invitation to a Phat Fashion (founded by veejay Ralph McDaniels), hosted at the now defunct Supper Club in Manhattan, gave me the opportunity to see their line personally. FUBU was part of the runway lineup that also included Karl Kani, Tommy Jeans, Pepe Jeans (licensed to Tommy Jeans at the time), Adidas, and Speedo. At first, I was apprehensive about covering such an event for fear that my editors would label the event as not being newsworthy. But the key to winning them over became the celebrity and mainstream designers' angle.

Like many Generation Xers in the New York Tri-State area, the host of Phat Fashion veejay Ralph McDaniels, nicknamed Uncle Ralph by deejay Red Alert, was a very familiar face. McDaniels' video show, *Video Music Box* made its pre-cable debut on WNYC-TV (1984 to

1996) and pre-dated MTV in the 1980s. Moving to WNYE-TV (Channel 25) in 1996, the video show provided viewers with an insider's perspective on the world of hip hop through videos, interviews with rappers, and party coverage. I, like so many others, grew up on *Video Music Box*. McDaniel's viewers, including myself, were known to run out of school at 3:00 P.M. and take over the television by 3:30 P.M. to catch a glimpse of his music show. I first met him in 1989 while interning at WNYC-AM radio during my junior year of college. I bumped into him in the elevator of 1 Centre Street, introduced myself, and let him in on the fact that I was a friend of his younger brother, Bryan. (I didn't want to come off as a mere fan.) Ralph became heavily involved in the fashion business in 1993 with the launch of Phat Fashion and then with his clothing store, Uncle Ralph's Urban Gear in 1997, once located in the Crown Heights section of Brooklyn. FUBU was a brand all too familiar to McDaniels.

McDaniels met the FUBU guys in the early 1990s at the height of *Video Music Box*'s fame. As a TV host and accomplished music director, he would always have people come up to him on a set with gear—a hat, T-shirt, sweatshirt, jeans, whatever people had in their possession at the time with the hope of getting a product placement opportunity. The intent was always to have him wear the product on air or possibly include it in his next music video. McDaniels would always politely shrug them off by saying, "Yeah, no problem." That simply translated to: if he liked the product, he would wear it or place it in a video. That is how he met FUBU team as Daymond, Keith, J., and Carl were among the people who would approach him on a daily basis. At the time, McDaniels had not heard of the FUBU brand, but was familiar with West Coast-based lines like Cross Colours and Karl Kani. FUBU's message, "For Us, By Us," really was one that hit home for him. It also did not hurt that the guys were from Queens, which neighbored Long Island, his hometown. Since they hit it off from the start, McDaniels invited the FUBU crew to one of his weekend events in Virginia Beach, Virginia.

"There are gonna be a lot of artists there," McDaniels recalls saying to them. "Puffy's gonna be there. Tribe's [Called Quest] gonna be there. I had this basketball game I had to do with Puffy. Teddy Riley was hot at that time and a whole lot of basketball players were there." The FUBU guys decided to go and attempt to get their product in the eyes of 10,000 hip hop fans. According to McDaniels, one day that weekend he received a call from John. He told him that Puffy had taken the free FUBU product he had been given, but was not wearing it. He asked McDaniels if he could help him out. A brief conversation with Puffy to "give them a shot" would eventually help FUBU get their product on that particular Bad Boy.

McDaniels, like many others, including Queens native and music director Hype Williams, would lend a helping hand in an effort to support these brothers. Intrigued by a ghetto-fabulous FUBU fashion show performance I had seen at Phat Fashion, I decided to personally visit the FUBU showroom located inside the Empire State Building. I met team FUBU at their then small office, which they shared with Bear Force, an outerwear brand produced by Alliance Worldwide, a sibling of the FUBU parent company, Samsung. FUBU had barely enough space for a rack of clothes, a small conference table, and a few chairs for guests. The FUBU guys and I immediately clicked as they began telling me their rags-to-riches story in depth. They explained how they had the hottest booth at MAGIC International, one of the largest fashion trade shows located in Las Vegas twice a year. I would soon discover that this was in fact the case and that this newcomer would be the head decorator of the country's fashion landscape.

Brands such as FUBU, Maurice Malone, Pelle Pelle, and Ecko Unlimited began to open the minds of fashion critics as their fashions appeared on the prestigious 7th on Sixth runway in New York during Men's Fashion Week in 1997 all while having their tradeshow booths dominating the youth section the MAGIC show in Las Vegas. Once limited to local mom-and-pop specialty stores in the hood, today's hip hop wares can be readily accessed at your local Macy's department store in the United States and in a number of shops internationally. It took the hard work and talent of many to make this happen and believe me, it was no small feat.

My early reporting days as a market editor and later associate editor of the now defunct *DNR*, as well as my experience as contributing editor to *Women's Wear Daily (WWD)*, afforded me the opportunity to cover many of the brands and retail stores I have written about in this book. I was barely six weeks into my first full-time reporting position at *DNR*, when I decided to write about urban fashion. A telephone call from Dexter Wimberly, cofounder of August Bishop, a boutique public relations firm representing urban designer Maurice Malone at the time, planted the idea. That call led to my first hip hop fashion article at *DNR* entitled "Hip Hop Designers Go Mainstream." At the time, it seemed a bit of a stretch for the conservative trade daily newspaper to have me cover traditional men's fashion, obituaries, the industry party scene, in addition to the underexplored youth beat. But that particular story set a precedent for others like it in the immediate future. My gut feeling at that time told me I was onto something. I will admit that I was hesitant about making urban fashion too much a part of my beat for fear of being categorized as an ethnic expert (although that seemed inevitable because I was a young Latina urbanite). In fact, my gut was dead on with an emerging trend that would change the course of U.S. retail.

Another telephone call, this time a news tip from Peter Mintz, a 15-year fashion veteran and sales manager at Mecca USA at the time, gave me lead one of my biggest urban fashion stories at *DNR*. Just nine months into the job, I broke the story "Federated May Hop on Hip YM Trend" thanks to Mintz. The story detailed how Federated (today Macy's Inc.), which housed Macy's and Bloomingdale's, was rumored to be making a big move into the urban business. There was a lot happening at the time that would make this notion a good idea. Trade shows such as MAGIC and NAMSB, Inc. (National Association of Men's Sportswear Buyers) were transformed into urban fashion spectaculars and hip hop was emerging as the U.S.'s new rock and roll. Most importantly, Federated saw an opportunity to make big money because of urban fashion's success at the mom-and-pop specialty store level. Up until Federated's bold move, the majority of mainstream department stores had opted to steer clear of this emerging cultural phenomenon. Such brands like Mecca USA and FUBU were considered underground, restrictive, and otherwise "ghetto," although this was never voiced out loud. Urban brands had no choice but to rely solely on urban retail specialists who recognized the need for oversized, baggy, logoed gear in sizes XL to 6XL. Federated did in fact move the urban business into a bigger distribution channel and subsequently created a domino effect in the youth department store business. Without realizing it at the time, that story was the start of the documentation of the hip hop fashion explosion.

My fashion journalism career grew parallel to the market that was exploding before my eyes. Since the history of urban fashion is still fairly young, I am fortunate that many of the urban fashion pioneers are alive and have the ability to give a firsthand account of how hip hop changed the fashion industry. Hence, I took an oral history approach to writing this book and personally interviewed many of the key people responsible for creating this dynamic business. My writing approach to telling the story of hip hop urban fashion is much more journalistic than it is academic. This was done intentionally. As a 1970s baby, the 1980s for me were a period of musical discovery. I listened to a little bit of everything, from pop and freestyle music to discovering hip hop thanks to my cousin Joey Torres from the Soundview section of the Bronx. Joey, a teenager at the time, had come to live with my grandmother and family in Brooklyn in mid 80s. I was about 10 years old when he introduced me to the boom box and played hip hop on my stoop. It was the same time I first saw hip hop film classics *Breakin'* and *Beat Street* on VHS that I rented from a local video store just walking distance from my home. Like many Generation X children, I fell in love with the music, attempted to break-dance, and wore the fashions that kept me from being made fun of. My mom did her best to please me and kept me up-to-date with the latest styles and brands, whether it was buying me Pro Keds or picking up my colored Lee jeans from the husky department (the section labeled specifically for overweight kids) of the local Freeman's apparel shop in Sunset Park, Brooklyn. My teenage style varied from my old-school looks of Le Tigre striped shirts, colored Lee jeans, a brass-buckled name belt, and shell-top/fat shoelaced Adidas sneakers to graduating to a more social-conscious way of dressing in my college days to the very brightly hued, oversized Cross Colours. While I have traded in my baggy jeans for a more age-appropriate look, my style will always have an urban flare and sophistication to it.

Free Stylin' documents urban fashion's roots, history, and the power moves that ultimately led to a pop culture phenomenon. This is the story of how urban style went from the hood to the runway—how pioneering brands such as Cross Colours and Karl Kani got their start to how Sean John, Rocawear, Phat Farm, and Ecko Unlimited created a $58 billion "urbanwear" industry by 2002.[2] The book begins by discussing what youth fashion was like before hip hop and also addresses the influence of the media, designer brands, and the individual stories of pioneering brands that competed with designer household names such as Tommy Hilfiger, Ralph Lauren, Nautica, Donna Karan, and Calvin Klein. My objective in taking this project was in part to highlight the inspirational stories about the people behind the hip hop brands, as well as to connect the dots as to the creation of this fashion subculture. This book is more than just the story of style. It tells the story of entrepreneurs, young people of color that created a movement, a force within fashion that was unexpected, challenged the status quo, and competed head on with the established fashion guard. Unfortunately, I was not able to include the story of every single hip hop brand in this book. I wish I could as it was never my intention to leave out any particular brand or individual out, but circumstances made it unavoidable. A number of things contributed to this, including brand and individual accessibility, timing, deadlines, and page count. Therefore, the story of urban fashion is told through the unique lens of select brands in an attempt to tell the general story of how an industry came into being. For the purpose of this book, I will use the term "urban" to categorize the apparel of hip hop fans once derived from urban areas. The word in the apparel industry has been received with mixed reviews. The term "urban," as it pertains to fashion, has been loosely used to categorize a fast-growing diverse segment of fashion that very few really understand. In this book, "urban" refers to clothing inspired by hip hop culture, which originally stemmed from a style worn in urban cities. "Urban," as it relates to fashion, became used by garmentos and mainstream fashion executives in the early 1990s after trading in past fashion jargon such as "ethnic" and "black" in the 1980s during its first wave of these fashions. The word, to some in the fashion industry, carries a stigma similar to the derogatory word "nigger." Some feel that the use of the word "urban" to categorize a type of teen style was created by the mainstream as a way of pigeon-holing a fashion style worn, at first, by African American and Latino teens across the country. Others, including myself, recognize the need to take ownership of this style, which is an extension of hip hop and record its growth and consumer buying power.

Despite those who disagree with the extreme looks of the style—from U.S. President Barack H. Obama to entertainer Bill Cosby—there is no question that the contributions of urban designers should be acknowledged and celebrated. *Free Stylin'* shares their stories in hopes of chronicling how fashion was truly changed by young and talented people of color. It is time to set the record straight and tell the story behind this U.S. fashion phenomenon.

Acknowledgments

This book could not have been possible without the support and encouragement of my family, friends, colleagues, students, and advocates of hip hop. I will forever be indebted to my parents, Aida and Jesus, for everything they have done for me; my sister, Tina, who has taught me invaluable lessons throughout the years; my nieces Leann and Hope, whom I love dearly; and a special thanks to my two children, Gabriela and Gionna. I do everything with them in mind. My daughters are truly my life's joy and inspiration.

I have been very fortunate in my life to build long-lasting friendships that are as strong as family bonds. A special thank you to my dearest friend Shinoa and her husband Julio, for their encouraging words and wisdom; to the Carrillo family, for treating me and my daughters as extended members of their families and babysitting countless times while I was writing and editing this manuscript; to my dearest friends Jessica Rodriguez and Nakita Vanstory, both of whom pitched in to help me with this project whether it was tape transcriptions or proofreading; and to Alex B. Wright, for always encouraging me to be the best.

Some of my closest friends have worked alongside me over the years. This book was just an idea in 2002, and I was lucky to have people believe in me back then. I must start off by thanking my former Fairchild co-worker and now FIT colleague Lynda Johnson; without her, I would have never been able to start my college teaching career.

She has always served as an exemplary role model, colleague, and friend. My career transition started with her words of encouragement over lunch and I will be eternally grateful. I want to also thank my first book interns Annette Martinez, Sandy Sanay, and Katherine Guerra; these ladies from the very beginning encouraged me to write this book and provided essential preliminary research.

I have been very lucky to have mentors who have pushed me to reach for my dreams. I want to thank my college mentor and friend, Allen McFarlene, assistant vice president for Student Diversity and Programs and Services at NYU, for his countless years of support and encouragement. You truly made a positive difference in my life. Thank you for always being so supportive and willing to strive for initiatives with change in mind.

It's tricky to mix business and friendship, but I have been very fortunate to do so with several individuals. Thank you my honorary Boricua brother Neil Mossberg, my sidekick in so many ways. I've always been able to count on you whether it's been researching a fashion trend, getting into the most exclusive clubs, or simply organizing my industry parties. Thank you for always making me look good. A special thanks to my dear friend and publicist Serena Muñiz, founder of Media Guru Public Relations. From the moment we met, we were able to see each other's lives transcend. Thank you for being my number-one cheerleader and helping me promote this book. We always dreamed of the day we could work together and we finally did it. I couldn't have done it without you.

Thanks also goes to Shara McHayle of Bounce Media, Marlynn Snyder of Black Tree Marketing and Paul Estevez of The Americana Group for their marketing efforts behind this book. Shara, it's been great to see each other grow professionally and personally over the years. Thanks for all those empowering pep talks while this book was in production. Marlynn, thank you for being by my side when I've needed a friend the most. Thanks for being part of my support team. Paul, thanks for taking the lead in building my strategic marketing plan for this book. Thank you for all your hard work on this project and seeing the potential of my work beyond the pages of this book. Thanks also goes to Harold Tamara of KXM, who spearheaded the video part of my book project. Thanks for helping me bring some of the fashion stories found in this book to life on the web. Thanks is also in order to my legal counsel and friend Tony Dunlop. Thanks for having my back. I've been fortunate to work with several talented creative directors over the course of my career. I'd like to first thank creative director extraordinaire Phillip Shung of Sundree, can you believe it? Thank you for all your support and help during the ideas stage of this book all the way through its completion. Without you, I would not be able to execute this book's visual branding or visual presentation. I want to also thank creative director Arthur Medina, for his design support in developing my early promotional materials. I couldn't have teased my book in Las Vegas without your postcard design. Certainly, I cannot forget photographer Darius Vick and make-up artist Leora Edut for their effortless work in developing my publicity headshot image. Thanks for capturing my beauty from the inside out.

The photos found inside this book would not have been possible without the renowned photographers who have documented the hip hop experience as a part of their life's body of work. First and foremost, I want to thank photographer and fellow Brooklynite Jamel Shabazz. From the moment we spoke and met, he saw my vision. He believed in my project and became the first photographer to commit to working with me. Brother Jamel, thank you from the bottom of my heart. I will be forever in your gratitude. I also wouldn't have been able to tell the story of hip hop fashion without the work of the legendary Ernie Paniccioli. I want to especially thank you and your lovely wife, Angela, for welcoming me into your home to view your extensive archives. You are a true pioneer and it was an honor to work with you. Thank you so much for helping me fulfill my dream. In addition, I'd like to thank photographer lifestyle Ronnie Wright, whom I have had the pleasure of knowing since my *DNR* days. Wright was among a handful of photographers who covered all the urban fashion events in the 1990s and having his work in my book was very important to me. Thanks for being part of my project.

I want to personally thank my students and academic colleagues at both the Fashion Institute of Technology (FIT) Department of Advertising and Marketing Communications (AMC) and the City College of New York (CCNY), especially at the Division of Interdisciplinary Studies at the Center for Worker Education (CWE). At FIT, a special thanks to Roberta Elins, who gave me my teaching break and has always been very supportive of me and my work;

Richard Balestrino and Al Romano, chair and assistant chair, respectively; and Gina Mackey and Shalaia Craddock, who have made my teaching experience very pleasant. A special thank you goes to Mark-Evan Blackman, chairperson of Menswear, for always lending an ear and believing in me and my book idea. Also, to the FIT library staff; without their help, research for this book would have been much more difficult. A very special thanks to FIT Chief Archivist Karen Cannell, who embraced my donation of audio tapes, transcripts, and research materials for a special collection devoted to hip hop fashion.

At CCNY, Acting Senior Vice President for Academic Affairs and former Provost now Dean Juan Carlos Mercado, for being a supportive boss and Kathlene McDonald, CWE chairperson, for always being an advocate of my work and encouraging me to grow professionally. In addition, I want to thank the staff and faculty at CWE, especially John Calagione, Deborah Edwards-Anderson, and Warren Orange. John, thank you for the great job lead. It was truly one of the best decisions I've ever made; Deborah, you have been a phenomenal colleague and friend. Thank you for being by my side. A very special thank you to my colleague and honorary brother, Warren Orange, for helping me figure out a title for this book and all his encouragement throughout this project. I will never forget the countless hours we spent reminiscing about hip hop and sharing our stories, our history. We founded the City College of New York (CCNY) Is Hip Hop History? Conference in 2010 and the CCNY Reading Hip Hop Lecture Seies in 2011. I hope both continue to serve as a platform for hip hop scholars to discuss the vitality of hip hop and its impact on our community. I want to also thank CWE's librarian, Seamus Scanlon, for his assistance in acquiring vital research for this book. A special thanks also goes to the CWE faculty, especially Martin Woessner, CCNY assistant professor of History and Society, for providing feedback on the early stages of this manuscript.

To my former students turned editorial volunteers on this project, especially Katharine Nieves (interviews transcriber), Tichelle Porter (who helped me with initial research for this book and provided tremendous encouragement and support through the writing process and Sheila Romero (interviews transcriber), no relation. Thanks is also due to Tiffany Murchison, Julia Macfall, Mary Eustace, Afryea Deas-Marina, Triscott St. Kitts and Jessica Lebron. All of your excitement and enthusiasm for this book really served as a great inspiration when writing this book seemed too much of a complicated task.

Thanks to the fashion industry professionals, publications, and leaders that have been advocates of my work, hip hop, and emerging trends. A special shout-out to designer Marc Ecko, Seth Gerszberg, Jeffrey Tweedy, and Daymond John, who provided the foreword for this book. Daymond, thank you for friendship and support. You're a living legend and your story is truly a remarkable one. I feel fortunate to be among the few who documented your work and shared your tale with the world. I want to also thank Peter Mintz, Barney Bishop and Dexter Wimberly (August Bishop), Tiffany Ellzy, Jennifer Bartok (Celebrity Catwalk), April Walker, Karl Kani, Russell Simmons, Myorr Janha, Rueben Campos, Dick Baker (deceased), Antonio Gray, Israel Sandoval, David Wolfe and Tim Bess of The Doneger Group; Carrie Harris, *WWD*, the defunct *DNR*, *Vibe*, *Urban Latino*, *The Source*, *XXL*, Bernadette Odoms, Leslie Short, Marvet Britto (The Britto Agency), Sandra Guzman, Barry Bookhard, Ben Murray, Gary Williams, W. Zak Hoke, Bryan Adams (Fab Communications), Uncle Ralph and Bryan McDaniels, Carlito Rodriguez, Christopher Blomquest, *Sportswear International*, *MR*, *WWD*, MAGIC International, Emil Wilbekin, Richard "Zulu" Zuluaga, Jennifer Maguire, Cel Garay (Xcel Photo), Phil Colon, Rafael Jimenez (Republica Trading Co.), Raquel Cepeda, Rokafella, Shawn Newman, Sonya Magett, Lloyd Boston, George Chinsee, Harriet Cole, Willie "Esco" Montanez, and Keith Clinkscales.

To the entire staff at Praeger, especially former acquisitions editor, Daniel Harmon, who was excited about this project from the very beginning. Thank you for taking on this project and providing hip hop fashion a platform. A special thanks to Jane Messah, who took on this project in its final editing stages. To Valentina Tursini, editorial assistant at Praeger, thanks for all of your help. Last, but certainly not least, to Juleyka Lantigua-Williams, whom without this book would not have been possible. Thank you for believing in me, my idea and for being the person to make this book a true reality.

CHAPTER I
A Century of Style

Fashion has always served as an indicator of the times. What we wear depends on who we are and most importantly, what we listen to. This has been especially true of the youth. From the beginning of the nineteenth century, adult men's clothing was traditionally manly, and young men's dress generally followed suit.

Suits, neckties, and hats were the uniform of choice for musicians in the beginning of the twentieth century. Many of the performers were poor gentlemen and their look was Sunday's best. This look could be seen in ragtime and early country music as well as in early New Orleans groups. In 1900, Americans owned only 8,000 cars, and the automobile became a wildly fashionable fad by the end of the decade. Both popular music and popular dress followed in the wake of the automobile's stampede into society. By 1904, Sak's and Co. had developed a 270-page catalogue of motoring apparel.

From 1910 to 1920, tango fever was at its peak and bright colors were all the rage. Orange, for example, was referred to in fashion circles as tango. Most popular musicians dressed in accordance with the fashion of the times, which included creased trousers, slimmed-down suits, and big-soled U.S. shoes. Silent film star Charlie Chaplin made floppy hats and short-fitted, hip-hugging jackets with narrow sleeves and wide-peaked lapels fashionable. It was during this decade that young people entered a period of cultural flux. Hemlines rose, music got faster and jazzier, and parties got wilder. While "jazz babies" or "shebas," as young women were called, wore silk stockings, short skirts, and bobbed hair, their "sheiks" experimented with new styles. Climbing out of roadsters or doing the Charleston with his girl at a party, the young hep cat of the twenties wore huge, flapping pants called oxford baggies, which appeared in 1925, and knickers, also called plus fours. Other fads that the young jazz-party crowd displayed

1

were long raccoon coats, sweaters with wild, busy prints, and "patent-leather hair" parted down the center and slicked down with pomade.

By the 1930s and 1940s, the beanpole look was out, and men wanted a look that emphasized their physique. They began selecting garb that would showcase their broad chests and athleticism. This would give rise to the incredible popularity of the double-breasted suit. Long, broad lapels emphasized a square shoulder look. The striped suit became a standard in male dress. American film dancer, singer, and actor Fred Astaire often wore double-breasted pinstripe suits, a look that made him appear dashing and, at the same time, natural. Many male stars dressed themselves with the help of their tailor. This was quite a different picture for Hollywood actresses, who were required to wear costumes chosen by a designer.

During this same time, the zoot suit became popular for both blacks and Mexican Americans. The term "zoot" was in circulation within the urban jazz culture. Zoot meant something worn or performed in extravagant style. To pull off such outfits, the wearer had to exert tremendous assertiveness. Outrageously padded shoulders and trousers dramatically tapered at the ankles became the signature look. Pachucos, who were Mexican American youths, made zoot suits their signature style and spoke their own slang called Caló. The term "*pachuco*" probably originated in the twentieth century. There are various theories that explain its origins. One is that it is Mexican slang for a resident of the cities El Paso, Texas, and Juárez, Mexico. Another theory is that is derived from Pachuca, the name of the city in the Mexican state of Hidalgo where Mickey Garcia, who some say is the originator of the zoot suit, befriended a local. Another theory is that it derives from *pocho*, a derogatory term for a Mexican born in the United States who has lost touch with Mexican culture. Pachucos often wore zoot suits on special occasions, like a dance or birthday party.

In the 1940s, the zoot suit was associated with celebrities like Thelonious Monk with his beret and Kid Creole. More than an extravagant style or costume, the zoot suit was interpreted as a cultural gesture. It was, in the most direct and obvious ways, an emblem of ethnicity and a way of negotiating an identity. Black jazz bandleaders like Cab Calloway and Louis Jordan helped popularize the loose-fitting zoot suits. People often referred to these musicians as the "Gentlemen of Harlem" because of their debonair appearance. With wartime (World War II) rationing in 1942, zoot suits were effectively forbidden by new government regulations that attempted to limit the use of wool. The demand for zoot suits did not decline, however, so bootleg tailors in Los Angeles and New York met the demand.

The conditions of war brought about racial paranoia. In Los Angeles, there was an unprecedented population explosion of Mexicans and laborers of color. Couple that with the fact that women and people of color filled military industry jobs once held by white men who now were off to war did not help ease social tensions. Simultaneously, young people of color were becoming fascinated with jazz, whose fashion attire became affiliated hoodlums, criminals, and gangsters. The murder of José Diaz in August 1, 1942, whose case is commonly referred to as the Sleepy Lagoon Murder, is considered a precursor to the zoot suit riots of 1943. Diaz, who was born in Mexico but raised in the United States, was attending a party when a rumble broke out. He became an innocent casualty and was stabbed, beaten, and then killed. Los Angeles Gov. Cuthbert L. Olson used the incident to promote his call to action—an attempt to end juvenile delinquency. To find those responsible for the murder, the Los Angeles Police Department (L.A.P.D) rounded up 600 youth, mostly Mexican Americans who were singled out as being zoot suiters.

In the end, 22 youths were put on trial and identified as members of the 38th Street Boys gang. Their intense trial was followed by the zoot suit riots months later. The contempt for the zoot suit attire and what it symbolized had European sailors and Marines attack zoot suiters who were predominately Mexican youths (African Americans and Filipino Americans were also attacked) in Los Angeles because the clothes were deemed unpatriotic. The riots would soon follow in other major cities like San Diego, Detroit, Philadelphia, and New York. Not solely confined to the United States, the zoot suit initiated a similar style of dress in France. Soon, the American Swing movement would also affect fashion as well as behavior, ways of walking, speaking, and dancing.

The 1950s marked the emergence of marketing to the teenage culture. During this decade there was a glaring disparity between parents/adults and their children/young adults. Teen boys had two distinct looks: a greaser look, like that of actor Marlon Brando in the 1953 outlaw biker film *The Wild One* and The Fonz (played by Henry

Winkler) in the hit 1970s television series *Happy Days* or a more clean-cut look, like that associated with the role of Richie Cunningham also in *Happy Days*. Greasers, or the bad boys of the 1950s, followed a more rebellious look, donning leather motorcycle jackets, white cuffed t-shirts, and denim jeans and were synonymous with riding motorcycles. The preppie look was about being neat and well groomed. Guys wore button-front shirts while teen girls donned pin curls and wore scoop-neck blouses, tapered pants, and poodle skirts.

It was becoming apparent to marketers that this rock-and-roll generation had its own music, culture, and style. Television in the United States was growing in popularity as teens glued themselves to the screen to catch Dick Clark's musical variety show *American Bandstand* for a glimpse of the latest dance moves and popular fashion fads. Big bands and sock hops, which were informal dances at high schools, were all the rage. Even then, teens bragged about their wares, such as Carl Perkins' "Blue Suede Shoes" (1956). When teens were not able to catch their fashions from music shows, it was about following the careers of teen idols like Fabian and the grown-up Mickey Mouse Musketeer Annette Funicello on the silver screen. Older generations feared the worst—that their innocent children would fall victim to juvenile delinquency due to the rebellious undertones of the music.

The 1960s brought Beatlemania to the United States and the mod style associated with them. Gone were the clean-cut teen looks and in were the styles more reminiscent of London. Tailored suits like those of Pierre Cardin, skinny ties, rounded haircuts, and Vespa motor scooters became common. Out were the greasers and in were the Beatniks, another group of rebellious teenagers, who popularized the color black and wore turtlenecks, dark shades, and French berets. Female counterparts were known for wearing pencil skirts, slacks with stirrups, and cowl collars. This decade went from dull to extreme psychedelics towards the end. By the middle of this decade came the space age attire of go-go boots and fashions *a la* Twiggy.

The 1960s were also the era of the African American civil rights movement. At this time, the United States was divided by racial discrimination and inequality. Television brought the debate into the homes of Americans who watched a young and vibrant Reverend Martin Luther King, Jr. deliver powerful speeches like "I Have a

Dream" in 1963 or Fanny Lou Hamer's electrifying delivery of the "Is this America?" speech.[1] Her speech on voting rights was on behalf of the Mississippi Freedom Democratic Party (MFDP) and was presented at the 1964 Democratic Convention in Atlantic City. A "black is beautiful" spirit was on the rise, and for African Americans, there was no better way to represent being "black and proud" than getting in touch with their roots. This movement brought about the donning of African-inspired garb like dashikis (a brightly-colored loose-fitting pullover) and African fabrics such as kente cloth.[2] The Black Panther Party, like the Young Lords of Chicago and New York, preached self-empowerment; their uniform of leather and berets became symbolic identifiers of power. During this time, African Americans began to embrace their natural beauty and allow their hair to go *au natural*; the growing of Afros became both a fashion statement and a political symbol. The times were changing and fashion was an obvious way of expressing allegiance to a culture and way of being.

The 1970s represented a mishmash of fashion styles. The hippie movement brought unisex looks, unrestrictive garments in bold prints, and more ethnic garb into a person's wardrobe. Bell-bottom pants, flower shirts, fringe suede vests and jackets, long straight hair, and the no-makeup look (for women) came to the forefront as young people empowered themselves with a "make peace, make love" attitude. It seemed the more ethnic the dress code, the better. Nehru jackets, kimonos, and muumuus with origins from India, Japan, and Hawaii respectively, were all extremely popular. The look seems to have coincided with the music of the period. On the one hand, the style was rebellious, like the sounds of Janis Joplin, Santana, Sweet Water, The Grateful Dead, The Who, and Jimi Hendrix. Yet, dressing up was also part of the norm as disco music brought partying into full swing. Partying brought about the miniskirts, maxi dresses, halter neck cat suits, and hot pants. The fashion could not have been better portrayed than in the 1975 Motown film *Mahogany* starring Diana Ross and Billy Dee Williams.

Polyester suits were made famous by a young John Travolta, who played Tony Manero in the iconic film *Saturday Night Fever*. The "tighter the better" was the motto for those who donned designer jeans by Calvin Klein, Jordache, and Sergio Valente. Tight-fitting clothes became a virtual uniform for rock and roll in the 1970s. Rod Stewart wore leopard-skin tights that took the idea of a close fit to a new level. During the glitter rock era, David Bowie wore dashes of makeup across his face in the shape of a lightning bolt and Kiss never came out in public without their masks on which were their signature black/white makeup. David Bowie's stardom led to the glam rock movement in Great Britain. It had even the most butch rockers, Sweet and Slade, wearing glitter, eyeliner, and high-heeled boots.

Punk clothing became a fashion statement birthed by the punk rock counterculture of the 1970s. Sid Vicious became a poster child of the punk look. Hairstyles became an integral part of this look, often dyed black and teased into spikes or a mohawk. Some hair was bleached white, but most striking were hairstyles in neon, orange, green, or blue. In 1971, Vivienne Westwood and her partner Malcolm McLaren launched Let It Rock, a successful apparel boutique on King's Road in London. Her clothes emphasized a link between fashion and music with ripped safety pin clothing mimicking the pierced, mutilated bodies of punk rock stars. Many punk rockers shopped at thrift stores or street vendors for used, distressed, and mostly black clothing. Key accessories were metal studded belts, black t-shirts, and earrings; the black leather metal studded jacket was emblematic of this look. The punk movement lasted 16 years after Westwood opened her store in London.

For blacks in the United States, the 1970s marked a new era in popular music.[3] The three most distinct black popular styles were funk, disco, and later, rap.[4] Black youths were influenced by the styles of the funk doctor James Brown with his ruffled shirts, bell-bottom pants, and leather outfits. The emergence of disco pushed both expensive and extravagant styles from Halston dresses and Diane Von Furstenberg's signature wrap dress for the ladies to polyester shirt jackets and suits for the gentlemen. There was also a movement in the popularity of reggae, made most famous by Rastafarian Bob Marley, whose distinct comfortable style consisted of dreadlocks, tank tops, untucked button-down shirts, jeans, dashikis, and tricolor garb sporting the colors of the Ethiopian flag.

Latinos also followed the popular sounds and fashion trends of the times, but New York Latinos, especially, had a look and sound of their own. Prior to salsa, it was old Cuban music that dominated Latino households.[5] By the 1960s, a new wave of music eventually recognized as salsa in the 1970s was booming in New York barrios and would make its way on screen in *West Side Story* (1961). The music called for dressing sexy and dressing up to impress the ladies. The big-band sound of Tito Puente, Machito and his Afro-Cubans, and Tito Rodriguez kicked this genre into full swing, and the Fania All-Stars made salsa a household name by 1975 with its largest New York salsa concert held at Yankee Stadium.

Hip hop grew out of the cross-fertilization of African American and Caribbean cultures, the catalyst being when Clive "Kool DJ Herc" Campbell moved from Kingston, Jamaica to 168th Street in the Bronx.[6] The devastation in the South Bronx in the 1970s, caused in part by the advent of intentional and unintentional fires, helped inspire a new musical outlet that would much later be called hip hop. With the commercial success of rap music and its appeal in popular culture, fashion would be the easiest way to identify who was down with the new sound.

"With fashion before hip hop, you had two options. It was either a classification or collections business," explains Carrie Harris, former vice president of men's and children clothing at forecasting agency Directives West.[7] Back then, the denim sold was primarily by Levis. "That could represent 10 percent of the business," Harris says. The "collections business" is a term used for branded attire and it came out of Seattle with popular brands like Unionbay, Generra, and Bugle Boy. In the late 1970s and early 1980s, fashion for young men was split between the West Coast and East Coast. The West Coast brought harem pants to life, thanks in part to the singers MC Hammer, Bobby Brown, and Vanilla Ice.

In the East, however, Michael Jackson's 1982 "Thriller" video inspired teens to wear ankle-cut jeans, a single-sparkling glove, glittery socks, and the wet-look hairstyle featured in the videos "Beat It" and "Billy Jean." The 1980s symbolized all things preppie. To follow the style and lifestyle meant being popular, smart, and wealthy. For kids in the hood, this was a grass-is-greener-on-the-other-side moment. Those who captured the look included Richie in the film *Pretty in Pink* or Alex P. Keaton from the television sitcom *Family Ties* or even Ferris in *Ferris Bueller's Day Off*. Unlike the punk rockers who wore black, ripped clothes and were against the establishment, preppies embraced conformity and smart dressing, which consisted of loafers, khakis, polo, and rugby shirts in colors like pink and green. L.L. Bean was a big proponent of the look as was the classic Ralph Lauren. The release of *The Preppy Handbook* in 1981 gave fashionistas a point-by-point guide to the look and lifestyle.

This preppie movement set the stage for urban youth and their re-interpretation of the look. Sweat suits, shell-toed sneakers, and personalized hooded jackets could be seen at popular New York City clubs like The Roxy, Disco Fever, Sparkle, Savoy Manor Ballroom, Ecstasy Garage, Club 371, T-Connection, The Crow's Nest, The Tunnel, Danceteria, and Studio 54. Emcees began bragging about their clothes in lyrics, and fans followed accordingly. In 1985, Run-D.M.C. released "My Adidas," and shortly after they negotiated a deal with the manufacturer to produce a line of Run-D.M.C. sneakers and accessories. This was the beginning of hip hop fashion entrepreneurship. Apparel manufacturers began to make clothes and market to hip hop fans. This would mark the beginning of what we have come to know as hip hop fashion.

This book attempts to put this unique fashion category into perspective. The approach was to tell the multidimensional story of hip hop fashion from every angle—from the designers who invented it to the retailers who carried the brands. By no means will it be the only authoritative book on the subject, but it is my hope that it will invoke further discussion on the topic and serve as a starting point for referencing hip hop fashion in context to fashion history.

CHAPTER 2
Fresh Dressed

Hip hop music presented a soundtrack and people needed a wardrobe to wear [with it]. When the stars started becoming stars, and needing more outfits, and the music videos became more important, they gave people something to emulate and something to copy.
—Emil Wilbekin, former editor in chief, *Vibe* magazine

Fashion has always had a significant value for young people in large urban centers, aka the hood. It has pretty much served as an identifier to differentiate those who have from the ones who have not. Those who are frontin' or rather perpetuating to have more than they do in order to fit in with the status quo, use wardrobe as a way to assimilate with peers. The more recognized the label or style, the better the recognition or "props" from their peers. Author, activist, and political analyst Bakari Kitwana, who once served as executive editor of *The Source*, pointed out in his book, *The Hip Hop Generation: Young Black and the Crisis in African American Culture* (2003) that the so-called hip hop generation shares a common consciousness very distinct from the generation before it.[1] Kitwana states that the umbrella term "hip hop generation" covers black people (and also includes Latinos) born from 1965 to 1984, and the perspective of this generation is diverse and reflect its understanding of the complexity of surviving the "hard-knock life." The group War sang in 1973, "The World is a Ghetto," and that notion has always resonated with black and Latino youth, no matter what hood they represent.

No matter the label or status brand chosen to wear, the objective by hip hop aficionados has been to make sure the gear is stylish enough to stand out in a crowd. It is part of the set norms deriving from hip hop culture, which also has certain ideas, ideals, values, knowledge, and ways of knowing. Knowing how to dress is part of any cultural knowledge base and is no different with the generation born out of hip hop. From the haircut to footwear, each element of dress has to make a statement on its own. Ideas of always being neat, clothes pressed, and shoes extra clean are just some of the psychographic attributes that come with the culture. This in part can be attributed to breaking stereotypes of the poor. Since fashion is a mode of self-expression and aspiration, much like music, it is a powerful weapon to symbolize social class, success, and wealth. "A lot of us came from poor neighborhoods and didn't have money to buy expensive clothes," recalls Terrence Byerson, an old-school hip hop head born in the Bronx and long-standing Harlem resident. "Many of us had hand-me-down clothes and at times then wore high waters. We were taught to not walk out the house with dirty sneakers. Looking neat and clothes ironed was part of our culture."

Success and wealth was associated with different people. In the hood, role models for some were the hustlers and celebrities who flaunted their riches by the clothes they wore and the cars they drove. Unattainable wealth and success was associated with white people. This was due in part to seeing success firsthand on the early celebrity reality TV show *Lifestyles of the Rich and Famous* hosted by English celebrity writer Robin Leach. "Money, Power, Respect" became the urban anthem long before Lil' Kim penned the song. Leach's signature line of "champagne wishes and caviar dreams" spoke volumes to urban youth aspiring to live the American dream.

The U.S. statistics of poverty, however, indicate that not much has changed over the course of three decades. In 1970, about 25.5 million people or 13 percent of the U.S. population were living below poverty level according to the U.S. Census Bureau's *Current Population Survey (CPS)*. The poverty rates for blacks (referred to as Negroes at the time) were more than three times that of whites. In 1980, 29.3 million people were listed below poverty level or 13 percent of the U.S. population. The median family income in 1980 was $21,900 for whites, $12,670 for blacks, and $14,720 for Hispanics. In 1990, persons living below the official government-defined poverty level were 33.6 million or 13.5 percent. It was not until 2000 that the poverty rate dropped to 11.3 percent with about 31.1 million people being listed as poor. However, the official poverty rate in 2009 jumped to 14.3 percent—up from 13.2 percent in 2008. This was the second statistically significant annual increase in the poverty rate since 2004. In 2009, 43.6 million people were living in poverty, up from 39.8 million in 2008—the third consecutive annual increase in the number of people in poverty. The real median household income for whites (not Hispanic) was $49,777 as compared to $32,584 for blacks and $38,039 for Hispanics.[2]

Coordination has always played a key part of the hip hop dress code. Color coordination, for example, has always been part of being fashionable in the hood. Combinations such as black and gray, brown and beige, light and dark blue were prevalent in the early seventies and still hold true today. Accessorizing has also been part of the hip hop look. Hats and watches are used to complete an ensemble. "It's just a very flamboyant lifestyle," says hip hop pioneering designer Karl Kani, referring to the styles worn in the hood. "It's just always been like that. It's always been about nobody being better than us. We should always want the best and want to be the best at what we do." There was a rhyme and reason to this thought pattern. The guys who dressed the best got the girls and attention. And if a guy was part of a crew that was doing music in addition to being best dressed, even more attention came his way.

Yet obtaining "the look" today is quite different than the early days of hip hop. Back in the 1970s and early 1980s, youth had to create their own outfits from what existed and what was accessible to them at the time. Many got their fashion cues from older siblings, relatives, and the local street hustlers they looked up to. Most importantly, where one shopped was not for common knowledge. Urban youth had to shop at Army/Navy stores and select sneakers to get what they were looking for. Shopping for unique fashion came with a high price tag and an extra-long commute. It was something that had to be strategically planned. Fashion was a mission and guys led it while girls were on their coattails. Almost an exact science, a person from the hood could easily tell where a guy was from just by the way he dressed. "That's not a myth," adamantly says Carlito Rodriguez, writer, producer, and former editor in chief of *The Source*. "Bronx dudes looked a little more grimy. Brooklyn dudes looked like stickup dudes. Manhattan dudes, uptown cats, were a little more dipped out. Lower East Side dudes were similar to Brooklyn."

Like the code of the streets, where a guy shopped for his clothes and footwear was kept top secret or under wraps. Each borough had its

Old-school Brooklyn guy wearing Gucci hat. (© Jamel Shabazz. Used by permission.)

shopping hot spots, while other stuff was just universal. "If you were dressed a certain way, you were saying something," says Rodriguez. "You would get challenged. There was a certain hardness [toughness] to the way you dressed. That was something you couldn't fake 'cause you would get robbed." That is not to say that hard dudes would not get robbed in Rodriguez's opinion. "If you get caught at the wrong place at the wrong time, you gonna get got. But it's just you knew that if I put on these sneakers and wear these pants and throw on this jacket or this sheepskin, I'm saying some shit. Either you were a square or you were one of us. If you were one of us, then you had to carry that shit."

At the 2010 "Is Hip Hop History?" Conference held at the City College Center for Worker Education, Rodriguez made it a point to stress that "one couldn't walk in a store and cop a hip hop starter kit." A term coined by his friend Panchi, the wild Comanche, from 183rd and Graham in the Bronx, the "hip hop starter kit" referred to particular wardrobe items needed to look and play the part of a true hip hop head. Simply put, an outfit could not be created by pulling what was featured on a mannequin. "We couldn't achieve a certain look based on what was in a window," recalls Rodriguez. From the fitted cap on the mannequin's head all the way down to the shoelaces on the sneakers, teens could not blend right in. There was no simple hook-up look at the time or a head-to-toe ensemble that mixed and matched like Garanimals, the children's clothing line.

To create a particular look or one's signature style, the idea was to search high and low for interesting fashion. It was a just like a free-style, which is a performance, improvisation, or routine intended to demonstrate an individual's special skills. In this case, that special talent revolved around fashion sensibilities. In essence, urban teens acted like professional personal shoppers who could easily put an outfit together to fit any occasion. Except the way one acquired such a skill set was based on one's fashion knowledge acquired on the streets, individual taste levels, and definitive style choices. For these urban trend-setters, the styling choices were free or unrestrictive. Over time, urban teens would develop a reputation (or rep) for being the best at something, like having the most unique sneakers or best hat collection.

Custom designer Guy Woods of 5001 Flavors, saw this firsthand. According to Woods, what hip hop teens lacked in funds, they made up for in creativity. "You got on a new pair of sneakers that you waited two months to get. That's why you roll your pants leg up so you can show your sneaker," says Woods. "Kids would put rubber bands at the bottom on the sneakers or pants so that they could keep the blue die off. Everybody couldn't have a Benz or a Beamer so the sneaker became the focal point or the eyeglasses or that dope shirt." The lack of funds made hip hop teens fashionable by default. Woods, like so many teens of the hip hop generation, would recall sitting down and thinking about what to wear days in advance. "It might be Tuesday and you are thinking about Friday 'cause there is a party in school," he says.

Queens' guys enjoyed shopping at the Colosseum Mall, which opened in 1984 as an indoor flea market similar to Brooklyn's mini-mall, Caesar's Bay Bazaar. Bronx guys, for example, shopped at "Jew Man's" in the Bronx, off Simpson Street and Westchester Avenue and right by the number 2 train. No one could ever recall the shop by its real name, but "Jew Man's" was not your ordinary shop. And it was not just guys from the Bronx that would go there, either; Manhattanites were also known to take the number 2 train to get their sneakers. The store resembled a warehouse as it stocked a variety of fashions in bulk; shoppers could find everything from sneakers to hoodies. The store was reminiscent of the many mom-and-pop stores in the hood at that time. Haggling was a big part of the shopper's experience and the shopper always left satisfied. "You could go in there with short money," recalls former customer, Byerson. "That wasn't common practice. It was like going to Delancey Street." Like the deejays that would wash off the labels of their records so other deejays would not see where they were getting their breaks from, the same could be said about those looking to obtain the most fashionable gear. Everything was like a b-boy battle in the sense that it was a competition to win the title "best-dressed" like the best dancer or MC.

However, the exact science behind shopping was not simple to figure out. There were several factores involved in which finances played a big role. The more disposable income one had, the better the chances of shopping for exclusive merchandise. For a tailored look, it was stores like Leighton's and the famous AJ Lester's on 125th Street in New York. Both carried exclusive merchandise—from alligator shoes in a variety of colors to tailored clothing like raw silk suits—for the sharp dressers and hustlers who could afford its wares. Harlem hustlers like Bat became known for his head-to-toe pink ensembles while guys like Small Paul built a reputation for owning an extensive sneaker collection. Athletic brands were carried throughout mom-and-pop specialty stores in urban areas such as Adidas, Pumas, Nike Cortez, and British Walkers. Frank's Sporting Goods on Tremont Avenue in the

Bronx was among the go-to stores for sneakers. Back to the mark of hood distinction, uptown guys would prefer to wear Super Pro-Keds with blue and red stripes on the side or the Pro-Keds 69ers with three lines across while the "average" kid in the hood wore Chuck Taylors.

Customization became another point of distinction. It could be the most distinct shirt found at an Army/Navy store off the beaten path or a plain pair of dungarees from VIM, one of the most popular discount denim retailers of the 1980s. Once purchased, it was up to the shopper, his/her talented graffiti writer friend, or a tailor to give it a personal touch. Customization was not limited to just casual clothes like T-shirts, sweatshirts, and caps. Tailored clothing too saw this trend with custom silk shirts and pants as well as tailor-made suits becoming part of the fashion status quo of urban trendsetters who went to custom tailor shops like Orrie's on 125th Street for their one-of-a-kind outfits. The legendary Dapper's Dan's Boutique would put its own spin to custom fashion as it specialized in making clothes in replica luxury fabrics. During the cold winter days, it was about wearing a sheepskin coat (in preferred colors like gray, beige, or navy), pea coats, and leather jackets. Manhattan's Delancey Street, also known as the bargain district for outerwear, was the hub for finding a leather jacket at a good price.

Haggling was the name of the game if you wanted to obtain the jacket at a price you could live with. The outerwear purchased usually was not brand specific, but rather the consumer focused on style. A good example of this was the "8-ball" or "stop light jacket," commonly referred to as the "stop jacket." In the early 1980s, these two distinctive styles were one-hit wonders. The "8-ball" jacket was based on the "money ball" in billiards with which the hip hop community resonated. In the game of pool, the ultimate object is to legitimately pocket the 8-ball after clearing the table. So the jacket, like the ball, symbolized winning or success. The color-blocked leather was based on at least three colors and featured an oversized 8-ball replica in the center of the jacket as well as on the elbow part of the sleeves. Popular color waves included black, purple, and white; red, white, and blue and yellow, red, and green made famous by Salt-N-Pepa. The stop light leather came in two variations primarily. Urban teens either gravitated to the traffic light version or its stop sign counterpart. Both revolved around taking precautions and heeding warning.

Outerwear brands became significant because of the styles they carried. There was the Stratojac coat, a three-quarter length wool car coat and Spain's Cortefiel jackets, known for their corduroy blazers and leather jackets. On the other hand, Triple F.A.T. (For Arctic Temperatures) goose-down bubble jackets reigned in the late 1980s. Hats were similar to outerwear in that certain styles were brand-driven while others were not. Hip hop classics included the velour "beaverskin" fedora, "godfather" homburgs, "stingy brims," bucket hats, rain hats, and Kangol caps made popular by LL Cool J.

G. Shabazz Fuller, former co-founder of early hip hop brand Shabazz Brothers Urbanwear, vividly recalls shopping in Harlem and wearing Lee's overstarched to perfection during his teenage years. His fashion statement consisted of either Swedish Knits (pants) or overlaps—dress pants with an outside seam with little flaps. When a guy walked, the overlaps would pop up and one could see the color underneath. The goal for guys was to match the rest of the gear to the different colors. Other common looks included plaid slacks, Chinese (which had buttons) or the Koman-branded ones. Footwear was classified into primarily two categories—dress shoes and sneakers. Dress shoes of the time (many imported from England) consisted of British Walkers, Playboys, and Hush Puppies while sneakers of choice were Puma, Adidas, 69ers, and later Nike; all with fat (thick) shoelaces. Colors were very important too like navy, burgundy, forest green, gray, chocolate brown, black, and red. Jewelry completed an outfit whether it was gold or silver St. Mary medallions, rope chains, and later, afro-centric medallions and beads.

Because hip hop is like a competitive sport, fashion has always been about being the first to have the new "joints" (the latest styles). Hip hop heads have always paid meticulous attention to detail as they sought out distinction from the crowd and individuality to be the best at it. Generally healthy competition, the need to have the latest fashion trends caused beefs (problems) back in the days and even today such as hating on another's flyness which could be caused by "accidentally" stomping on someone's foot. A mark of dirt on a pair of newly purchased footwear would be the equivalent to someone throwing the gauntlet down. This challenge could be handled a number of ways—from an actual fight to a b-boy battle. The fights could be just trash talking to others being much more serious and even resulting in injury.

B-boys on subway platform. (© Jamel Shabazz. Used by permission.)

Being robbed for the latest pair of sneakers or technology has also resulted in death.

Denim has always been a staple in the hip hop wardrobe. Levi's and Lee's were the early brands of choice for both boys and girls alike. Urban teens gravitated to Levi's for the classic look while Lee's provided the color options. It seemed that there was no color in the spectrum that Lee did not offer. Both brands were paired with shirt labels like LeTigre, Izod, or Chams de Baron. Rodriguez remembers wearing Tale Lord and Devils jeans, both featured characters such as racecar and a devil. For about one-third of the price, one would pay for designer Jordache; these jeans provided urban youth with the similar style sensibilities. The 1980s were also the decade of the designer jeans' craze *a la* Jordache, Sergio Valente, Gloria Vanderbilt, and Calvin Klein, which a 15-year-old Brooke Shields made famous with her "You want to know what comes between me and my Calvins? Nothing" television advertising campaign. At this time, teen urban girls were able to distinguish themselves from a crowd very much like the guys did early on. Tight bubble-gum jeans with polo shirts and baby hair slicked back into a pony tail while donning clear lip gloss was the everyday-around-the-way girl look for those ages 12 and up. In the 1980s, the preppy look came into play along with the excessive use of jewelry and adornment.

The big and baggy look often synonymous with hip hop was not always the case. The baggy pants origin is still up for debate. Early traces of baggy pants can be dated to the oxford baggies during the jazz age of the 1920s and the zoot suit era of the 1930s and 1940s, although the look typically associated with hip hop today has been linked to prisons. Incarcerated males have typically been given pants without belts to wear and many times larger than necessary. Others point to the need to accommodate body shapes and necessity to address fit. It is no secret that people of color have different body types than whites, who have served as models for fashion specifications. Shopping can be a daunting task for people of color who have more in the hips, thighs, and butt department. For children growing up, like myself, it meant either shopping in a husky department store or just going up at least one size to accommodate your fit. The true origins of the baggy style are probably somewhere in the middle.

T-shirts became a staple in every hip hop follower's closet like sneakers. B-boys were known to wear T-shirts, sneakers, and sweatsuits in cool colors because they had to move and bounce. The MC was the flashiest out of the bunch. He wore T-shirts and sneakers at first and later gravitated to Timbs and baggy jeans, but the MC always rocked a customized item whether a cross, a name plate, four-finger ring, or brass buckle belt with his name on it. Graffiti artists, like b-boys, had to wear clothes that were flexible. Due largely to their art, graffiti artists had to climb fences, walls, trains, and fire escapes. The best way to do this was not to sacrifice comfort. But make no mistake, that was accomplished without sacrificing style. The preppy movement promoted brands like Ralph Lauren, Tommy Hilfiger, and Nautica. Plaid shirts and rugby-striped shirts were among the wardrobe staples and were mixed with athletic attire like sweatshirts and Nike sneakers.[3] The West Coast rap scene put up front and center the *cholo* looks such as baggy khaki pants, plaid oversized shirts, bandanas, and baseball caps.

Birthed in the South Bronx, hip hop music and its styles did not penetrate Middle America until the late 1980s after MTV began playing heavily on rotation rap videos and launched *Yo! MTV Raps* in 1988. "Hip hop music presented a soundtrack and people needed a wardrobe to wear," says Emil Wilbekin, managing editor of essence.com who served as a style editor for *Vibe* in its early years of inception and later, as its editor in chief. "When the stars started becoming stars and needing more outfits and the music videos became more important, they gave people something to emulate and something to copy," he notes. With each of the four traditional elements of hip hop—the MC or master of ceremonies, the deejay, art (graffiti), and dance (b-boy, uprock, top rock, etc.)—they each had their own distinct style. The looks were a mix of New York and West Indian influences due to the fact that pioneering hip hop musicians paid homage to both. You had shearlings, leather bubble coats, and bomber jackets and then you had a West Indian influence like the Big Phat gold jewelry, name plates, and crease jeans with a bleach stripe down the side. It was also a mix of uptown and downtown (New York). Many teens from the Bronx as well as drug dealers would hang out at the downtown nightspots like Danceteria, The World, and Latin Quarters, so one could also see a mix of disco and hip hop. "It was about not looking like the next man," says Wilbekin. Hip hop style therefore was not a uniform as much as it speaks to personal style and "swagger."

The commercialization and success of hip hop artists in the 1990s made this the decade of bragging and luxury. During this same time, hip hop fashion entrepreneurs started venturing into launching their own brands. Prior to this the market had experienced success with urban brands like Get Used, Major Damage, and Troop. What drove consumers to these brands was product over marketing. Once the

LL Cool J wearing Kangol hat and Troop outfit. (© Ernie Paniccioli. Used by permission.)

market was introduced to "black-owned" and "black-designed" brands, the consumer gravitated instead to support those brands. A great example of this is what happened to Troop. The brand was strong for about five years until the rumor hit that the brand's name stood for "To Rule Over Oppressed People" and was secretly owned by the Klu Klux Klan (KKK). Although its owners were actually Jewish and

Baby and Lil Wayne wearing bling. (Ronnie Wright)

Korean, this rumor was hard to dispel. Rumors of racism would follow other mainstream brands over the years like Tommy Hilfiger, Liz Claiborne, and Timberland. The racism card is one that is hard to figure out. Let's take the love for construction work gear and footwear, for example. "One of hip hop's most enduring fashion statements thus comes from mostly white-ethnic construction workers, whose unions, ironically, are still notorious for excluding blacks."[4]

It would just be a matter of time before black-owned, operated, and/or designed brands would be launched like Cross Colours, Karl Kani, Walker Wear, and Maurice Malone. The mid-1990s would then see an emergence of hip hop lifestyle brands that would follow with labels such as Mecca USA, PNB Nation Clothing Co., FUBU, and Ecko Unlimited. By this time, both hip hop music and fashion would experience commercial success. Hip hop brands would demonstrate record-breaking annual earnings by the late 1990s/early 2000s such as FUBU ($350 million), Ecko Unlimited ($280 million), Phat Farm ($300 million), Sean John ($200 million), and Rocawear ($120 million) while newcomers such as Enyce and Akademiks earned under $100 million.

The year 1996 marked the height and golden age of hip hop. Bad Boy Entertainment and Death Row Records were on top and it was the same year Biggie Smalls and Tupac Shakur were killed. Ghetto fabulous was really in its prime. Will Smith rapped about "Getting Jiggy with It" and Cash Money Millionaires focused on "Bling Bling." The term "bling" in and of itself is up for debate. Puffy swears he invented the term and Andre Harrell says that he invented it. "It's about being able to wear head-to-toe designer gear and still keep it real and roll up in the hood with your people and hang out," says Wilbekin. Designer goods were now at the disposal of artists, due in part that design houses were no longer as reluctant to lend clothes for hip hop videos and magazine shoots.[5] Showing off their success meant bragging about wearing designer/luxury labels, donning expensive and custom-made jewelry, and driving expensive cars that symbolized the "good life."[6] In attempt to downplay the materialism being demonstrated by popular artists, more nation-conscious rappers such as X-Clan and the Native Tongue chose to replace gold jewelry with African leather medallions or other nongold adornments. Flashing their wares at times has come at a price.[7] Guru of Gang Starr was robbed of his Rolex watch at gunpoint outside a music studio in Queens and Mobb Deep's Prodigy was robbed of over $300,000 worth of jewelry at gunpoint near a recording studio near the Queensbridge Project.

According to Recording Industry Association of America (RIAA)'s 2000 Consumer Profile, rap/hip hop music buyers were the second largest segment of music purchasers. Driven largely by a successful series of releases in 2000, including Eminem's *The Marshall Mathers LP* (seven times platinum), Dr. Dre's *Dr. Dre 2001* (six times platinum), and Nelly's *Country Grammar* (five times platinum), the rap/hip hop genre leaped to second place among music consumers with 12.9 percent of the market. Rap/hip hop replaced country music as the number two genre, shifting the latter for the first time in a decade. Thanks to the advent of music videos, music television, and the growing importance of hip hop music, clothes would play a significant factor in the marketing of the hip hop artist. What was once a style solely designated for the hood would soon become part of a cultural phenomenon brought into every household via the mass media.

CHAPTER 3
The Revolution Will
Be Publicized

The celebrities made the trend. What they wore was what the people wanted to wear. We were the ones behind it. We, the stylists, were the ones doing it. If we liked it, we pulled it and placed it on [the artist.] If the artist wore it then, it became major.

—Roger McKenzie, formerly of *The Source* and *Mod Squad*

Music television did for hip hop in the 1980s what traditional television did for rock and roll in the 1950s: it gave a generation a voice and linked it with the one thing that united it. The music video brought elements of fantasy and reality to the screen. It became a direct link to record sales and, therefore, broadcasting videos provided artists of all music genres an additional promotional conduit.

When MTV made its debut in 1981, it did so with a rock state of mind. This left little to no place for black musicians to showcase their musical talents and therefore, hip hop was at an initial loss. While prior to 1987, MTV almost exclusively featured music videos, it would take the 24-hour music station two years to realize that black musicians tuned in a viable demographic. The year 1983 became a golden age for music television and the awakening year for MTV. Michael Jackson's "Billie Jean" hit, was added to MTV's rotation, which soon opened the door for other black videos to follow suit, especially those in the R&B category. The year also birthed several local music formatted shows on non-cable television. The legendary veejay Ralph McDaniels debuted *Video Music Box*, the first urban music show broadcasted on public television and WABC's *Hot Tracks*, which was initially hosted by WKTU DJ Carlos DeJesus. It would take Miami's all-request video show, *The Video Jukebox*, later called *The Box*, two years later to make its debut. Ironically, it would be acquired by MTV in 1999.

Thanks to McDaniels, a Trinidadian, urban youth were able to see a music show developed, produced, and hosted by someone that was one of them. A college-aged McDaniels, who was attending York Institute of Technology in Westbury, New York, had completed his last internship at WNYC-TV, Channel 31 located in downtown Manhattan, before MTV even existed. He had started to deejay and was watching a number of other deejays come up. McDaniels, who did not have the money to have the equipment that some of those guys owned, started to deejay in local schools. Upon graduation, he was given a job at WNYC as an engineer and soon questioned the programming at the station. "I would sit there for hours watching these TV shows, and be like, how come there's no producing on this channel?" McDaniels recalls. "This is public broadcasting. How come there's nothing on there for us? We're part of the public."

One day, according to McDaniels, something big came into the station by mistake. The videotapes had live performances of some R&B acts that were being played on the radio. They were relatively unknown acts and McDaniels never even knew these live acts existed; he came up with the idea of airing and putting them all together. That idea morphed eventually into what became *Video Music Box*. His show aired Monday through Saturday at 3:30 P.M. (right after school) and also at noon on Saturdays. Urban teens would run out of school to immediately take over their parents' television sets just to catch McDaniels introduce the latest hip hop artist, their videos, and hear local shout-outs on *Video Music Box*. "I'd like to give a shout-out to," began a famous opening line by local fans looking to acknowledge their friends, family, loved ones, their borough, or their affinity for an artist. Most of the shows were shot on-location at popular New York City spots from nightclubs to play yards. Airing on a public broadcasting station, McDaniels was well aware he had to proceed slowly in order to get station support. He made sure the show had both positive elements and was educational.

The success, power, and impact of the show did not hit McDaniels until 1984 when he aired the legendary Fresh Fest, hip hop's first money-making tour featuring Run-D.M.C., Kurtis Blow, Whodini, and the Fat Boys. "I had no idea how many people were even watching the show at that point," he says. "I just knew that we were growing and that it was a live concert from the Nassau Coliseum." The concert had made a big impact on the New York-viewing audience because they had never seen anything like that on television. (Remember that this was pre-cable.) McDaniels would partner with childhood friend Lionel "The Vid Kid" Martin, who originally studied prelaw at City College and went to school with hip hop empresario Russell Simmons. Martin would eventually switch his career path to film and television by obtaining his master's degree and joining McDaniels on *Video Music Box* as a freelancer. When Martin began working at Children's Television Workshop (CTW), he advised McDaniels that they should get into music videos. They did and their first video together became MC Shan's "Left Me Lonely."

From the inception of hip hop music videos, fashion played an important role as wardrobe became part of a hip hop artists' armor. "It's like showing up to a fight," says Vinnie Brown of the rap group Naughty by Nature. "If you look like you got it together, that's automatic intimidation. It sells the image and it sells the message that you are trying to get across. It makes people buy into you." In fact, fans would also start mimicking their favorite artists' style. Although the

Afrika Bambaataa and The Soul Sonic Force. (Leon Morris/Getty Images)

look of the artists varied from group to group, the idea behind wardrobe was the same—to be original and stand out in the crowd. Early groups like Afrika Bambaataa and the Soul Sonic Force focused on costume-like wardrobes while others like Melle Mel and the Furious Five focused their attention on wearing outlandish street attire.

In the early 1980s when crack and coke started hitting urban neighborhoods hard, two classes of street kids evolved and this became evident also in the type of artists that would emerge. The kids, who totally dove into the drug culture and benefitted from it, donned the jewelry, custom outfits, and extravagant fashions. The look was one that Eric B. and Rakim mastered. Then, there existed the conscious bunch, direct kids of the 1960s and the civil rights movement. They carried that into their culture, their music, and how they dressed. Enter the X-Clan and Native Tongue with Tribe Called Quest, Jungle Brothers, Queen Latifah, Monie Love, and a host of others, who promoted afrocentricity in their music and wardrobe with the donning of beads, African medallions, onyxes, and African-inspired garb.

Later groups like Run-D.M.C. would put the street look on the map with their trademark godfather hats, sweat suits, and Adidas shell-toe

X-Clan became known for its afrocentric style. (© Ernie Paniccioli. Used by permission.)

Run-D.M.C. (Michael Ochs/Getty Images)

sneakers. Their 1986 Madison Square Garden concert, which aired on MTV, epitomized their street look. Tens of thousands of fans holding their sneakers in the air during the performance of "My Adidas" made it clear that celebrities had the power to influence style. Adidas executives immediately signed the group to a $1 million contract, making Run-D.M.C. the first non-athlete to have a sneaker endorsement. Some acts like Jermaine Dupri's Kriss Kross, became famous more for their look than their music; they will forever be known for wearing their clothes backwards. This pint-sized Atlanta act's signature look became oversized baggy jeans and shirts, either polos or athletic jerseys. Although the look never quite caught on in the streets, it definitely made this group become most remembered for an unusual fashion statement. Other acts like MC Hammer and Vanilla Ice brought "Hammer pants," a baggy, parachute-like pant, center stage.

Kriss Kross. (© Ernie Paniccioli. Used by permission.)

According to McDaniels, fashion for hip hop videos in the early days had to be something that was going to last like a song. In the early 1980s, the artist usually went out and bought his/her clothes with his/her money. It might have been a custom outfit by Dapper Dan or something picked up from 125th Street or Delancey Street that nobody else had. That outfit would be used throughout the life cycle of an album. Therefore, the outfit would be used for promotional pictures and performances as well as the music video. Unfortunately, not every artist had a video. "When you made a video that was like, almost making a movie," says McDaniels. "It took a while before artists started getting videos for every single. Nowadays, there are 10 videos for an artist on the Internet that they make. But back in the days, you might've gotten just one shot—one video for your album, so you put everything that you could into that video."

In the early days, the look of the video was in the court of the artist since directors were not familiar with dealing with these types of artists. Hip hop music video directors were not as familiar with their style as they are today. "We knew that if a guy was hardcore, people usually wanted to see him in that kind of way," recalls McDaniels. Many rappers based their style (then and now) on what they were really into—either what they were wearing or what they saw being worn in the hood. Hustlers and drug dealers, who had the money, these were really the guys that created the styles. "Some artists were not as fashion-minded but got their influences from going to the hood and seeing the hustlers and drug dealers," says McDaniels. "These guys were getting money and jumping out of cars that [rappers] couldn't even name. [Rappers] didn't know of Gucci." A few artists like Big Daddy Kane had a different style than the status quo rapper of their era. Big Daddy Kane's style was closer to that of the Stylistics or Blue Magic. While Big Daddy Kane fans were accustomed to seeing him in his signature camouflage attire, he was easily recognized also for his dress look of silk suits or silk pants and shirt combos. Artists like Kane recognized the importance of developing their particular style as did rapper Kwamé. Always seen as being an eccentric guy through his music, this could also be said about Kwamé's style. He wore polka dots emphatically and even became part of the title of Kwamé's second album, "A Day in the Life: A Pokadelick Adventure" (1990). From an artists marketing standpoint as well as fashion statement, polka dots

Kwamé. (© Ernie Paniccioli. Used by permission.)

indeed made Kwamé stand out and immediately branded him as an artist at the same time. To some degree, it would also pigeonhole him as he attempted to break the polka dot image in years to follow.

As the need for the hip hop music video grew, so did the need to have professional stylists on the set. "Now there's a stylist and he or she is getting clothes from different designers who want to put their brand on a particular artist's back," says McDaniels. Hip hop helped made stylist superstars out of people like Sybil Pennix, June Ambrose, Misa Hylton-Brim, and Derek Khan (who ended up getting deported to his homeland of Trinidad after stealing more than $1 million in jewels from Harry Winston and Paiget in 2002. He has since made a comeback and today lives in Abu Dubai.), Andrea Lieberman, Michelle Ten, Groovey Lew Jones, Mike B., and Crystal Streets, among others. In recent times, the life of a celebrity became the basis for a reality TV show on Oxygen called *House of Glam* show, which launched in 2010. A number of the stylists featured on the show specialized in hip hop and were represented by the image agency The B. Lynn Group.

Hip hop music videos created a major product placement outlet for those looking to reach the urban target market. The early days of music videos provided a free medium to promote fashion labels very much like the editorial pages of a magazine. Brands like Cross Colours, Karl Kani, and Walker Wear capitalized on this from their inception while later labels, such as FUBU and Tommy Hilfiger, heavily placed clothes on artists as a way of gaining quick brand recognition in the 1990s. Similar to hip hop music, urban fashion labels became experts in guerrilla marketing. "We know how to get exposure with little or no money," says G. Shabazz Fuller, co-founder of the now defunct Shabazz Brothers Urbanwear (SBU), a hip hop brand launched in 1991. Urban designers like Fuller would find out about a movie set, look up the stylists, and start working their convincing gift of gab in order to place their clothes in the next video. Traditional U.S. designers had budgets such as Tommy Hilfiger, Ralph Lauren, and Calvin Klein. In the world of hip hop fashion, it became about the street promotion campaign. "The celebrities made the trend," says former stylist Roger McKenzie. "What they wore was what the people wanted to wear. We were the ones behind it, we, the stylists, were the ones doing it. If we liked it, we pulled it and placed it on [the artist.] If the artist wore it then it became major."

Once MTV realized that everything they had on its channel was sellable, including what was being seen on a music video, there went the blurring of fashion logos as they were deemed brand advertisements. "Any brand that was being seen on their screen was sellable and because hip hop was very brand-oriented, they were one of the biggest to get hit by that," says McDaniels. Some designers got creative and developed clever brand identifiers. FUBU, for example, began using the numbers "05." While the blurring of the labels occurred, the censoring of rap lyrics did not and so the promotion of brands was still powerful through this medium. Short-lived MTV hip hop video show *Station Zero* (1999) managed to briefly escape the blurring of its brands, including apparel. As hip hop's first animated video show, *Station Zero* placed products of all kinds to create a modern-day set for this hip hop Beavis and Butt-Head type of animated series.

Existing music television shows like *American Bandstand* also caught on to the hip hop phenomenon. On August 3, 1985, Run-D. M.C. performed on *American Bandstand*—the first rap act to do so.[1] *Soul Train*, which aired from 1970–2006, became a powerful medium to promote hip hop acts like R&B. Other dance shows like *Solid Gold* and *Dance Fever* would also spotlight hip hop dance and therefore, showcase the style that came with it. MTV would eventually be on the same page with hip hop when it decided to launch *Yo! MTV Raps* in 1988, hosted by Fab 5 Freddy Braithwaite and later Ed Lover and Dr. Dre. "With *Yo! MTV Raps*, Iowa, Nebraska, Washington, and other places that were far removed from a lot of the urban cultural centers got to see how exciting the music was," says Bryan Adams, founder of entertainment publicity firm Fab Communications, whose past work experience includes *Billboard* magazine and Tommy Boy Records. White teens in the suburbs started to buy the music. It sounds very cliché, but it is a very basic tale; once the other side got to see what this particular brand of music was about, it was exciting to them. It was like rock and roll back in the 1950s; teens were not supposed to like it but they did. Adams recalled when Tommy Boy got really good rotation on MTV, reaching platinum status was always next. "You'd see getting 30 spins a week on MTV then something good was about to happen. Coolio's 'Fantastic Voyage,' 60 spins, you knew that something great was about to happen. And forget about 'Gangster's Paradise.' When that video played, MTV kept that on."

As black television shows became more predominant in the mainstream media so did the fashions. Shows like *Fresh Prince of Bel-Air* and *In Living Color* became a soundboard for brands like Cross Colours.[2] Black television shows and films were on the rise during the Cross Colours' glory days and this worked to the brand's advantage. Using reject samples of the line (product removed from the collection or at times defective), some of Cross Colours' best product placement opportunities were with Will Smith's *Fresh Prince of Bel-Air.* This opened doors for other product placement opportunities on television shows with a predominately African American cast or viewership. Other shows that subscribed to the Cross Colours' push included *The Arsenio Hall Show* and *Soul Train.*[3] Product placement for Cross Colours went beyond television as local theater companies, rap music videos, and record label parties also partook. "Word got around and everybody that was doing videos called [us]. We would ship those clothes or they would show up at the office and we would give them the clothes," says Cross Colours' founder Carl Jones. The company gave lots of free products to entertainers from Special Ed to MC Hammer.[4]

The Cosby Show, A Different World, and *Martin* had a similar affect for other brands. Who could forget Bill Cosby and his Coogi sweaters in the family sitcom *The Cosby Show* or the various Historically Black Colleges and Universities (HBCU) and African American College Alliance (AACA) sweatshirts seen on its spin-off *A Different World* or comedian Martin Lawrence's much-loved *Martin. The Arsenio Hall Show* brought hip hop fashions to late night as did *The Chris Rock Show.* Queen Latifah provided an outlet on daytime talk show circuit as would supermodel Tyra Banks and talk diva Wendy Williams years later. Even mainstream television shows like *Saturday Night Live* helped bring visibility to hip hop. Tommy Hilfiger sealed his affiliation to hip hop when Snoop Dogg wore a red, white, and blue rugby shirt on *Saturday Night Live* in March 1994.

Tommy Hilfiger and his younger brother Andy, were at the Natural Museum of History for an Atlantic Records' party when they first met Snoop Doggy Dogg. Andy Hilfiger immediately invited Snoop to come up to the Tommy Hilfiger showroom to get some free clothes. Upon their arrival, Snoop Doggy Dogg and his Dogg Pound were laced with gear. "Snoop wanted the pinstripe banker suits—they were pimp suits to him, so I hooked him up but I also gave him a bunch of [other] clothes," says Andy. About a week later on a Friday about 5:00 P.M., Andy recalls getting a personal call from Snoop and being told he is going to appear on *Saturday Night Live.* Andy told him to just come to the showroom and pick out what he wanted. Unfortunately, Snoop was in rehearsals and could not come to the showroom, so Andy met up with him at Hotel Macklowe that evening. He remembers staying in the office until 9:00 P.M. and walking over to Hotel Macklowe with his assistant in the pouring rain. Upon arriving at the hotel's penthouse suite, the Dogg Pound also inquired about their gear. Andy ended up going back to his office and undressing the mannequins in order to bring them back clothes.

Andy hung out with Snoop and his crew until about midnight and left clothes for both. "When I was walking out the door, I will never forget. Snoop was sitting there and said, 'Yo, I'm gonna wear your stuff tomorrow.' To me, it was like that's cool if he does and if he doesn't," remembers Andy. The next night, while Andy was having dinner with his then girlfriend, now wife, Kim, he got a call from his brother Tommy who had seen the rapper on *Saturday Night Live.* That Monday, Andy started getting calls from his salespeople asking about the rugby shirt Snoop had worn days before. "That thing sold out that day," he recalls.

The television show *New York Undercover*, a police drama based around the lives and crimes of New Yorkers, provided endless product placement opportunities for hip hop brands and mainstream designers alike. The show, which aired from 1994 until 1998, revolved around two lead characters—J.C. Williams (played by Malik Yoba) and Eddie Torres (played by Michael DeLorenzo). Both central characters, in addition to the other characters, including Nina Moreno (played by Lauren Velez), donned the urban styles of the time as did the hip hop and R&B acts that performed at Natalie's, the show's fictional café. There were no blurring of the brands and so everyone from Tommy Hilfiger, DKNY, bebe, to Mecca USA benefited from the exposure. In fact, the showing of the logos only helped grow the show's popularity among its hip hop demographics.

Television was not the only medium to promote hip hop. As the popularity of the music grew, so did the films and directors that would attempt to portray the music and supposed lifestyle onto the silver screen. Wardrobe became essential in early films like *Flashdance*, which provided a small glimpse into the look of hip hop dance while films like *Beat Street, Breakin', House Party* (and its sequels), *Style Wars, Wild Style, Crush Groove, Do the Right Thing,* and *School Daze* (Spike Lee), *Boyz in the Hood* (John Singleton), and *New Jack*

City portrayed various aspects of hip hop life and culture with clothes being vital to character development. Director Lee, for example, tapped the late Willi Smith of WilliWear to design clothes for *School Daze*.

Trade fashion publications like consumer magazines and newspapers covered hip hop trends sporadically as initially most deemed it a passing fad. It was not until the mid-1990s when the explosion of hip hop fashion occurred at the department store level that business-to-business publications like the now defunct *DNR*, *MR*, and *Sportswear International* took notice. *DNR* took the lead in providing in-depth urban fashion coverage while others through the 2000s would follow. Therefore, hip hop magazines became the only print outlet where hip hop fashion could be spotlighted on a regular basis. *Vibe* magazine became one of the first hip hop magazines to really show urban sportswear alongside high-end fashion for which Emil Wilbekin can be given credit. Wilbekin started at *Vibe*, which was founded by music producer Quincy Jones in partnership with Time Inc. in 1993, as associate editor and was promoted two years later to style editor. He would eventually move up to fashion director and ultimately as editor in chief. Today, Wilbekin serves as managing editor of essence.com.

According to Wilbekin, the idea behind *Vibe*'s fashion pages was to create fashion stories that were about urban sportswear, athletic apparel, and celebrities. "No one wanted to shoot those types of clothing in the magazine," he recalls. Wilbekin saw a real niche in fashion styling. He strategically began pairing traditional urban sportswear labels with non-urban labels like snowboard brands. He shot acts like Das EFX, A Tribe Called Quest, and Junior M.A.F.I.A. purposely in snowboard gear. "I made urban sportswear cool by selling it in a way that was alive and worn in the culture," says Wilbekin, who has styled videos for Mary J. Blige, Joi, and Kenny Lattimore, as well as advertising campaigns and fashion shows for Sean John, Banana Republic, Rockport, Maurice Malone, and 2B! "Back then, urban sportswear was so new. People thought of it as cheap, knock-off stuff. They didn't really consider it fashion," he says.

Wilbekin saw high-end fashion more inspired by urban fashion than the other way around. He saw urban sportswear really as the driving force of fashion because it connected to the lifestyle and the youth. He viewed high-fashion more about ideas and taking expensive fabrics and doing "expensive" things to them. High-end fashion designers saw an opportunity to take cues from urban sportswear. "Instead of doing cargo pants, they would do leather cargo pants," points out Wilbekin. As hip hop music became more popular, more people began buying urban sportswear. The more black and Latino teens bought urban sportswear, the more white teens in the suburbs who saw the hip hop videos on MTV and BET followed this trend. Wilbekin's idea was always to shoot urban sportswear the way high-end fashion was photographed. "It made people look at urban sportswear in a different way and it gave it a lot of credibility," he says. This strategy might have proven effective to also lure in fashion advertising from Gucci, Prada, Versace, and Dolce & Gabbana in the same issues where FUBU, Sean John, Mecca USA, Enyce, and Phat Farm would be regularly seen. Wilbekin says, "We really brought those worlds together the same way in the early days of hip hop, it was all about the downtown models and Andy Warhol with Rakim and Whodini at the Red Parrot."

The Source became the *Rolling Stone* of the hip hop generation. Carl Jones, co-founder of Cross Colours, remembers approaching David Mays, founder of *The Source*, to begin advertising. Although Mays seemed reluctant at first, allowed fashion ads like Cross Colours took urban brands to the next level. "When people saw us in that, it established us as the hip hop line to wear, the cool line to wear, the line that relates to the music and people," says Jones, who saw a direct link to his spike in sales. Former *Source* Editor in Chief Carlito Rodriguez saw fashion being important at the magazine for two reasons. *The Source* had to do double duty—show what was coming and also predict trends. Brands like FUBU, Karl Kani, Pure Playaz, Mecca USA, and Akademiks understood the value of *The Source*, but corporate brands like Gucci and Louis Vuitton were not so open to the idea of advertising at first. "Even though we rocked that stuff they didn't see a need to advertise," says Rodriguez. Former *Source* fashion manager Roger McKenzie, today founder of Roger Mac Management (which represents actors), saw firsthand the power of his work. Whatever he had shot, the audience bought. *The Source* became the go-to resource guide for hip hop.

McKenzie shot urban brands regularly such as Mecca USA and Cybertek and eventually infused brands such as Tommy Hilfiger, Ralph Lauren, and Calvin Klein. In 1995, McKenzie joined June

Ambrose's styling agency, appropriately named the Mod Squad. "Mod Squad defined style and polished it off," says McKenzie. "We came from head to toe. The style began from underneath. You couldn't put on a Versace top and Hanes underwear. Everything had to be cohesive. We delivered it, we owned it." Under Ambrose, McKenzie worked with all the major hip hop artists including Jay-Z, Sean "P. Diddy" Combs, Mariah Carey, Trick Daddy, Foxy Brown, Lil' Kim, Busta Rhymes, and Biggie Smalls, to name a few. "By then, hip hop fashion had matured and all designers wanted to be a part of us," says McKenzie. "I remember us getting Paul Smith for R. Kelly." According to McKenzie, artists and their personal styles varied. For example, he classified Sean Combs' look as more flamboyant and trendsetting while Jay-Z was more relaxed, hip hop Brooklyn and eventually changed his look to be more sophisticated. McKenzie credits Combs for pushing the fashion envelope. "He was not afraid. He had the [musical] crew and biggest artists in the '90s."

McKenzie recalled a time when he could not get his hands on designer labels for hip hop videos, so he had the custom apparel made. "When we couldn't get it, we knocked it off. We would get fabulous magazines from around the world. We would spend thousands of dollars. We would get the fabrics and get people like Francis Hendy and 5001 Flavors to make it. Eventually, [designers] saw what we could do. We started getting 30 percent discount to get anything we wanted." According to McKenzie, hip hop video wardrobe budgets in the mid-1990s averaged between $25,000 and $30,000. Many times, stylists went over budget and by the time they were done it was more like $40,000. "When we did 'Satisfy You' with R. Kelly featuring Puffy, our wardrobe budget was $88,000 when we were done," he says.

Back in the "good old days," hip hop stylists were given five to six days to prepare or prep for a shoot. Additional days could be negotiated if necessary. There were also return clothes days on top of that. The actual video might have been shot over the course of three days. "When the music stopped selling, everything went down," says McKenzie. "People [in hip hop music] are not making the money like they were." Today, he says wardrobe budgets have been drastically reduced due to the sluggish economy and music downloading. "Now, if you get a budget of $8,000, you're lucky," he notes.

CHAPTER 4
Solidarity in Cross Colours

We changed the whole spec of the young men's industry. The Ralph
Lauren's, the Calvin Klein's, everything was snug and we didn't think
that was a street look. It was important to us that everything be
oversized.

—Carl Jones, co-founder, Cross Colours

The idea of fashion brands evolving from hip hop was never far-
fetched. Hip hop aficionados have always been style innovators from
creasing designer jeans (some pressed jeans with extra starch while
others opted for a permanent crease stitched by a local tailor) to boxing
fat shoelaces. (Shoelaces worn by urban teens in the 1980s were
almost one-half inch wide where the tongue of the sneaker actually disappeared. Many times, teens would create a checkerbox pattern with
their shoelaces in multiple or solid color waves.) So in essence, it
would only be a matter of time before urban teens could have fashion
brands of their own.

These soon-to-be brands would fall under the apparel category of
young men's, a classification used by specialty and department stores
to label male shoppers between the ages of 15 and 21. Prior to hip
hop, there was not much to putting a young men's section together.
As retail and apparel veteran Carmine Petruzello noted, it was simply
a cheaper version of men's product.[1] There was very little fashion
direction that could be spotted in this section of a department store.
Young men's was pretty much a watered-down version of what was
being offered on the men's floor; if you found khakis in men's, there
would be khakis on the young men's floor. The difference from
the men's department to the young men's department was just price;
the young men's category generally sold at a lower price point, about
$5 cheaper on average.

Interesting enough, the earliest cues of what in the late 1980s would be labeled hip hop, then ethnic, and much later urban, did not stem from the existing young men's or even men's apparel categories. The earliest cues came from a fashion designer who was well ahead of his time, the late Willi Donnell Smith. Born in Philadelphia, Smith was among a group of African American designers—including Patrick Kelly and Stephen Burrows—who gained notoriety in the late 1960s during the Black Arts Movement. Former Smith fit model and long-time friend Bethann Hardison considered him to be the godson of streetwear. "Willi was known as the king of putting clothes on the street," she says.[2]

An extremely gifted and versatile designer, Smith could spin casual or eveningwear, men's or women's designs at any given moment of time. He was among the first commercial African American designers who could easily go head-to-head with designers like Calvin Klein or Perry Ellis. What made his work so special was the fact that his designs transcended culture. Smith presented interesting patterns and colors into one garment, preferred using natural fabrics and offered unconstructed clothes as he made clothes with the everyday person in mind. Coining the term "streetwear," Smith introduced the oversized casual silhouettes in the 1970s that would later become synonymous with hip hop. Smith's fashions sold across broad demographics. He designed affordable couture creations well before H&M and Forever 21 jumped on the trend. Smith's designs could be found from Michigan to Seattle to Fulton Street, Brooklyn. "Willi spent a lot of time in the streets and his product was inspired by New York City," recalls apparel veteran Jeffrey C. Tweedy.[3] "His stuff had a lot of ethnic feeling to it and b-boy feeling to it. It was playful clothes." His sister, actress and model Toukie Smith, who frequently donned her brother's wares, could have easily been named Ms. Downtown as she was one of the most talked about models of her time.[4] Toukie Smith was the "it" fashionista of the 1970s and modeled for many top fashion houses including Chanel and Norma Kamali. She was so popular and widely admired that Bloomingdale's created a mannequin in her likeness in 1978.

Willi Smith was among the youngest designers at Digits, the sportswear company where he met his eventual business partner Laurie Mallet. The two launched WilliWear Ltd. in 1976 which was his

March 30, 1987: Willi Smith and model in miniskirt. (© Bettmann/ Corbis)

second attempt at having his own company. Smith's first try was with his sister Toukie in 1973. "He just had a natural sense of taking good constructed items and put them into a price point that worked for a lot of people," recalls Hardison. His women's collection jumpstarted the company and his men's collection followed in 1978. Smith's designs bridged casual and eveningwear at prices everyone could afford. He garnered a number of awards including the Coty American Fashion Critics' Award for Women's Fashion in 1983 and a Cutty Sark Menswear Award in 1985. His many career highlights included designing suits for the groom and groomsmen of Caroline Kennedy, the daughter of the late President John F. Kennedy, to crafting clothes for Spike Lee's 1987 film *School Daze*. Unfortunately, the fashion industry suffered a great loss at the untimely death of Smith at age 39 in 1987. He died from pneumonia, complicated by shingella, a parasitic disease, contracted on one of his trips to India. According to his estate attorney, Smith also tested positive for AIDS right before his death, but he never showed symptoms.

At the time of his death, Smith had built WilliWear into a $25 million business. His company survived a few years after his death, but without his creative vision and leadership, it would be a hard act to follow. The company managed to open a store on Fifth Avenue after his death, but its ladies division shut down in 1990 and men's shortly followed. Former New York Mayor David Dinkins in 1988, then Manhattan borough president, declared February 23 "Willi Smith Day" in honor of his accomplishments. Almost 15 years later, the Fashion Walk of Fame, the only permanent landmark paying tribute to U.S. fashion located on New York's Seventh Avenue, inducted Smith in 2002.

As the fashion world was recovering from the loss of Smith, two West Coast-based African Americans were about to embark on an apparel journey that would kickstart a fashion phenomenon and cultural movement. Los Angeles-based Carl Jones and T.J. Walker introduced the world to Cross Colours in 1989 and urban fashion has not been the same since.

The Cross Colours tale is not your ordinary rags-to-riches tale by any means. Originally from Tennessee, but raised in the Watts section of South Central Los Angeles, Jones attended Otis-Parsons, an art and design college for two years and later, Los Angeles Trade-Technical College.[5] Entrepreneurialism was in his blood as his family owned an auto-wrecking business in Gardena, California. Interested in graphic printing after college, Jones decided to go into business for himself and opened a small graphic design studio called Designers Screen Printing in 1982 in downtown Los Angeles. With it, Jones began his firsthand training in owning and running a business which he did at first with graphic arts and T-shirt designs. An ad placed in the *Los Angeles Times* soliciting a graphic designer for Jones' Designers Screen Printing. The ad would have Jones meet graphic designer T.J. Walker, his eventual business partner and right hand.

Born and raised in Meredian, Mississippi, Walker decided to move to Los Angeles after an unsuccessful stay in Europe. Walker was well-trained for the job with his A.A. in art from Meredian Junior College, a B.F.A. in commercial design from Delta State University, and his M.F.A. in graphic design, fashion illustration, and printing from Louisiana Technical University. A risk taker, Walker drove his red Datsun F10 to Los Angeles with $300 in his pocket. [6] He was 23 years old at the time and would soon be hired by Jones to develop design work for well-known clients such as Guess, ID Number, and Z. Cavaricci. Designers Screen Printing developed a healthy business and was later sold in 1985 when Jones decided he wanted to start his own surf brand after seeing how lucrative that business was. Keeping Walker aboard, Jones decided to venture into the beachwear business and founded the beach surfwear brand Surf Fetish.

On his honeymoon trip to Huatulco, Mexico, Jones would meet his future marketing person, Jamaican-born Davide Stennett. Born in Kingston, Stennett moved to the United States in 1972 and grew up in Bethel, Connecticut. Stennett, who had a degree in marketing, traveled the world as an exchange student and later as a *Gentil Organisateur* [G.O.] at Club Med where he met Jones and his Latina wife, Audrey. "They were just this youthful couple out of L.A. and I just really dug the way they dressed," remembers Stennett. He struck up a conversation with them and ironically, they were about to leave Club Med after being there only a couple of days. He and the couple exchanged information; Stennett says, "They were like 'if you ever make it to California just look us up.'" About a month later, Stennett left Club Med and relocated to San Diego. The next day, he called Jones and the rest became history. Jones picked him up in San Diego and brought Stennett to Los Angeles where he would reside for the next 20 years. Jones offered him a job at Surf Fetish as its marketing coordinator. The job became an exciting change of pace for Stennett, who had to quickly figure out the industry's ins and outs. He became responsible for coordinating all of the company's fashion shows as well as its participation in trade shows including the Super Show, NAMSB Surf Expo, and MAGIC International, which was held then at the Los Angeles Convention Center. [7]

The job had Stennett traveling all over the country and he caught on quickly to what he had to do. Attending MAGIC, an international business-to-business show, Stennett became aware of the "rumbling" in the industry which was the early recognition of the urban consumer. He noticed that the harem-like MC Hammer/Bobby Brown pants that Walker had been designing for Surf Fetish were flying off the racks. Thinking there was something to it, Stennett decided to do more research on his intuition. With Jones' permission, he decided to contact select Surf Fetish buyers to learn about the demographics of those individuals buying the pants. It turned out that it was predominately African American, young, and urban. "I shared that information with Carl but it did not go over well with his partners," says Stennett, who subsequently left the company.

Jones would later meet a fabric salesman who would alter his career and life forever and thrust him into his next apparel venture. The salesman showed Jones some African prints from Senegal. "I'm like, what am I going to do with these?" vividly recalls Jones. The fabric salesman told him, "'You know, I think you're the only guy that could probably make something creative with these. Why don't you think about it?'" Jones' initial reaction was not too surprising. Up until then, African textiles like Kente cloth were symbolic reminders of afrocentrism and the cultural explosion of the 1960s. In Western culture, the garb has historically been deemed both appropriate and oppositional depending on whom we are referring to in terms of assimilation. In general, Kente cloth is not viewed a mass market fashion, but the fabric, however, gave Jones an idea. From an authentic garment that represented Africa, this was the only thing that was available at the time. "There are maybe 10 to 15 prints done in Senegal," says Jones. He began thinking of ways he could make the fabric more commercial and appeal to a mass audience; this was the beginning of Cross Colours. While Jones did not know where to go with this concept, how to take it or how to style it, the concept became an evolutionary process from there.

Concurrently, Stennett also pushed Jones and Walker to "do their own thing" and go after the emerging "ethnic" market. Jones began researching the existing urban market as if he was going to launch another brand, but he would need a crash course in targeting this consumer. After all, Jones' expertise was in the surfwear business and not in urban fashion. Having done business with Merry-Go-Round over the years, Jones became good friends with its buyers.[8] According to Jones, the folks at Merry-Go-Round taught him in the ins and outs of retail and the urban business. The spotlight had not shone on African American culture since the 1960s and the Black Power Movement. Prior to that, recognition of the African American culture could be traced to the Harlem Renaissance days of the 1920s and 1930s. Little by little, Jones began connecting the dots and this ultimately, led him to develop a clothing brand that paid homage to African American culture.

Jones was extremely conscious of the complexities that came with marketing directly to his own people. "That meant a lot of different things—from a fit point of view, style point of view, and street point of view and from a pure advertising point of view," he says. "I thought that there was a huge void and not just a void, but a necessity and something someone needed to do." That void translated into a tremendous business opportunity. Jones was aware of what was going on within the New York street life scene; he frequently traveled to New York City and rode the subways just to get a taste of what street life was like. Traveling with Walker, both men shopped the market (by visiting trend spots and specialty stores) and frequently rode the subway into Brooklyn to check out Spike Lee's Spike's Joint on DeKalb Avenue and South Elliot Place. They would later head uptown to Harlem as they researched the concept that would be Cross Colours.

Both men understood that hip hop was not just a musical fad, but a cultural movement. Out on the West Coast, acts like N.W.A. and Ice Cube were becoming popular. But according to Jones, this so-called movement was not yet seen in the streets, but just on television. They noticed that black and Latino kids in New York were wearing their pants two times their clothing size and hanging off their butts. This was a very different look then what was being seen in Los Angeles. On the West Coast, black and Latino teens were still wearing apparel true-to-size. "These kids [in New York] were like a size 28 or 30 [waist] and wearing a size 36 pants," Jones says. Walker took notes as the two came up with ways to incorporate what they discovered in

New York and integrated it into their apparel concept. Walker sketched some of the teens he had seen on the bus and subway, paying particular attention to how they wore their pants. He brought the sketches back to Los Angeles and came up with the idea of keeping the silhouette baggy, but keeping the waist tapered; this became *THE* signature look of Cross Colours.

"We changed the whole spec of the young men's industry," says Jones. "The Ralph Lauren's, the Calvin Klein's, everything was snug and we didn't think that was a street look. It was important to us that everything be oversized." This silhouette worked for both men and women. For men, it solved the problem of comfort and fit. As for women, the tapered waist line accommodated their smaller figures. On purpose, Jones and Walker made their size medium tops actually fit like a large and their large tops fit like an extra large. Cross Colours' pants were made with the same idea in mind. A Cross Colours 32-waist jean was actually cut with the body of a 34 or 36 specification. The waist on the jean was fitted, but the body was larger mimicking the silhouette of someone with a more strapping frame. This became especially appealing to the heavier-set consumer as well, a customer poorly addressed by the fashion industry. No longer would they have to shop at the "husky" section of a store, which was just a nice way of labeling fashions for overweight boys (and even girls) having trouble fitting their pants especially at the waist and hips.

Initially, Jones went to his Surf Fetish partners to secure financial backing for his new commercial venture. But after failing to come to terms, Jones decided to resign, sell his shares in the company, and move on. Walker stayed on for a while and eventually left and joined Jones on his quest. Jones' success at Surf Fetish allowed him the ability to come up with a substantial amount of capital to start another company. As reported in *Black Enterprise*, Jones mortgaged his Beverly Hills home, sold his red Ferrari and 17 Harley-Davidson motorcycles, along with his Surf Fetish shares and took a bank loan to raise the $1 million to fund what became Cross Colours. Jones made Walker his partner and vice president and Stennett was made head of marketing. The three men became inseparable. "When we were all together in this nucleus things really exploded," says Stennett. "We were free to do whatever we wanted to do. And the fact that we were three black men had a lot to do with our conviction in what we were doing. It had a lot to do with the passion we felt."

Selecting the right name was key. In fact, Cross Colours was not the original name intended for the brand; the company's first choice was actually Cross Culture. "We didn't want it to come off as a racist thing or a black thing or a product for African Americans only," says Jones, who contradicted himself. In fact, the brand was made by African Americans, owned by African Americans, and directly marketed to African Americans. Afraid to alienate the white teen consumer, Jones intentionally played off the unification and diversity of hip hop to appeal to a broader audience with key phrases around his logo like "Post Hip Hop Nation" and "Academic Hard Wear." Promoting or advocating hip hop would allow him to target a diverse customer base while speaking directly to African American youth. "It was hip hop and from the street but we thought it was something everyone could relate to. So, let's mix cultures and put it all together," he says.

After contacting a trademark attorney, it became apparent that the desired name was already in use. Brainstorming led to the company's actual name and it worked for several reasons. To not waste time, energy, and designs already created prior to learning about the name dilemma, Jones and Walker decided to modify the existing company branding logos originally developed. Walker had already designed a logo which made both of them very happy. It consisted of a "C" with an "X" in the middle and a "C." Being Jamaican and from the West Indies, Stennett suggested using the British spelling of Colors, that is Colours, to put a different spin on the name. By this time, Jones and Walker had done prints with these letters so they decided to go with the British spelling. For one, the change of spelling gave the company a more European flair. Cross Colours also wanted to distinguish the brand from the 1988 gang film, *Colors* as gang violence became prevalent throughout the Los Angeles area in the 1980s and early 1990s. Gangs like the Bloods (red) and Crips (blue) fought over turf and identifiers of distinct gangs became the colors they chose to wear. Wearing the wrong color in a particular neighborhood could get one killed. Understanding that color affiliation was a predominant indicator of gang alliance, Cross Colours strategically chose to twist the play on colors into something positive.

Cross Colours' primary palette became inspired by both Africa and Jamaica. "We combined the two," says Walker. "Each color stood for something. The black was for the people. The red was for the blood of the people, green was for the Earth, and yellow for the Sun." Popular colors found in the Cross Colours palette consisted of bright purple, orange, yellow, blue, red, and green. The message behind the brand was so powerful that it transcended the African American community and ventured into other communities of color. "What Cross Colors represented in the early days was kind of a representation of how music sounded. It was loud. It was flavorful like if you think of Jazzy Jeff and Fresh Prince. It represented that time period and what people were wearing [then] and how they looked," says fashion expert Emil Wilbekin. "The clothes were fuller and larger cut, so that kind of offered a different [fashion] perspective."

Wanting to unite teens through peace and unity, Cross Colours focused on positive messages through Ebonics. "Love Sees No Colors," "Stop D Violence," "Educate 2 Elevate," and "Clothing Without Prejudice" were just a handful of sayings utilized on T-shirts. "Instead of fighting about all these colors, why not wear all the colors?" says Stennett. "Therefore, that was the whole premise and the platform for everything." British singer George Michael's second album, *Listen without Prejudice* (1990), would inspire the company's slogan, which was determined by Audrey, Jones's wife. Its tagline, "Clothing without Prejudice," became an integral part of the company's overall mission. However, the obstacles surrounding the company's name went beyond the change of the name; it also received a threat of a potential trademark lawsuit by designer Alexander Julian, who had an existing apparel brand called Colours. "I remember specifically being on the phone with his legal team and trying to explain to them we are doing something urban and that it was spelled completely differently. It's Cross Colours and not just Colours," recalls Stennett. "We never heard back from them so we were good to go."

With a name and concept in place, it became Stennett's role to identify the target market and successful marketing strategies of the new company. He strategically chose to go after what was being called at the time the "ethnic" market which translated to the African American population. An unknown African actor/model named Djimon Hounsou, who later went on to model for Thierry Mugler and Calvin Klein, was hired to be the Cross Colours spokesmodel.[9] "He was a doorman at a club in L.A.," says Stennett, of the Benin-born, two-time Academy Award nominee, and husband of supermodel Kimora Lee Simmons. "For me, it was important that we use the blackest guy I could find. He's a very dark man from Africa and we were not apologetic for that." The symbolic representation of the brand became more powerful than the clothes themselves. While the founders set out to launch apparel, what they in fact created was a movement. As a conscious clothing line, it focused on advocating peace, promoting unity, and put a call to action to stop violence.

Cross Colours also put the West Coast on the map as it showed people that fashion direction did not only derive from the fashion capital of New York. The West Coast, which up until then was known for surf, skate, and laid-back bohemian styles, had hip hop change that view. Cross Colours' unifying message brought the brand unconditional support from just about every black community leader, politician, entertainer, athlete, and hip hop celebrity. A list of Cross Colours' fans could read like a who's who celebrity guide—from Los Angeles Mayor Tom Bradley, musical groups like TLC, SWV and Shai, Snoop Dogg, LL Cool J, actor Cuba Gooding, Jr., boxing legend Muhammad Ali, and rapper Queen Latifah to singer/dancer Paula Abdul. It seemed that everyone bought into the company's motto and message like President Obama's "Blueprint for Change." While designer brands have always been aspirational, the lifestyle seemed unattainable for those of a certain class or economic status. Cross Colours spoke volumes among all classes leading potential consumers to believe that anything is possible. "[Celebrities] would come and give their support without asking for anything in return," says Walker. "People had a sense of ownership with our company. That was a big part of how we promoted the brand and the name of the company."

From a business point of view, Cross Colours took a multi-level approach to building its brand. On the retail front, the company went after the big retail goliaths or national specialty chains of the time rather than put a lot of effort into the mom-and-pop local stores in the hood. It made sense since Jones had strong sales connections to national specialty stores dating back to his Surf Fetish days. Department stores were a stretch back then. This would later prove to be a poor choice. On the marketing side, Stennett's plan was to aggressively promote the brand through several tactics including product placement, advertising, and trade show participation. Jones admitted the distribution of free clothes got out of control and they eventually established a product placement budget and procedures because

TLC's debut look is synonymous with the brand Cross Colours.
(© Ernie Paniccioli. Used by permission.)

product placement inventory would at times cut into inventory that was
needed to ship to stores. Black publications such as *Jet*, *Ebony*, and
Word Up! were utilized to spread the word to the black community
about Cross Colours and its antigang violence stance. "I thought it

was the best way to go because we did not start off with a ton of money," says Stennett.

Jones and Walker rented a loft studio at 810 Traction Avenue, next to Little Tokyo in downtown Los Angeles. It was there that Jones and Walker figured out what they needed to do. They developed designs and patterns, figured out how to sell the product, and get the sales and production team together. Among the brand's first salesmen were Peter Mintz and African American Erich Walker (no relation to T.J.). Mintz, who was Jewish and from Long island, had previous experience working the New York nightlife scene in the early 1980s, He had attended the Fashion Institute of Technology (FIT) and gone through Federated's executive training program before opening his own sales showroom, located at 1466 Broadway in Manhattan with his friend Richie Smith. At Cross Colours, Mintz was hired as a sales associate for the Northeast and mid-Atlantic states. Erich Walker, on the other hand, did not get into fashion by traditional channels. While his mother owned a retail store, and Erich Walker attended *Ebony* fashion shows with her, his dream was to be a professional baseball player. The idea became short-lived and he would eventually relocate to California. That is where Erich Walker began his fashion career as a sales rep selling missy wear. A referral by a friend landed him an interview with Jones and he ultimately became one of Jones' first black sales representatives and later became Cross Colours' regional sales manager for the Midwest.

Cross Colours would soon be shown at a variety of trade shows including the Black Expo USA and the NAMSB (National Association of Men's Sportswear Buyers) Show at the Javits Convention Center in New York.[10] "NAMSB was our first domestic U.S. show," recalled Mintz. "We proceeded to book $10 million at this small trade show. There began the journey. We hit a road and toured like a band as soon as we hit our first trade show."

Buyers, up until this point, had never seen anything like Cross Colours. Before the appearance of Cross Colours, the inner city business was predominately made up of Levi's, Wrangler, Troop, Fila, Kangol, British Knights, Puma, and Champion. Hip hop stores just did not exist. Consumer expos like the Black Expo USA proved to be vital way to reach the end consumer. "We knew without a doubt that [the Black Expo USA] was the vehicle to hit the masses directly," says

Stennett. "The moment we left you could almost see and track sales by market according to [what city] we had been at a Black Expo. [You could also tell] how well we were selling on the retail level." The formula was simple; once at a Black Expo, they made appointments to see local retailers and to secure radio and magazine interviews. After Cross Colours would leave a particular city, a local buzz would follow it in each market. The company also participated in the SEHM[11] show in Paris, twice. This was unheard of for a young men's brand, let alone an African American-owned company. Jones' vision was responsible for this success as he wanted to test the European market. "That was brilliant," says Walker. "He made us look beyond our imagination."

National retailer Merry-Go-Round ended up giving Cross Colours its first $200,000 order and Jones played that to his advantage in order to get its next big order from national retailer Edison Bros.[12] Derek Tucker was the president of St. Louis-based Oaktree, which was owned and operated by Edison Bros. While he did not like the samples, he placed a test order. Among Cross Colours' first boutique specialty store orders came from the trendsetting boutique Fred Segal in Santa Monica, California and from Stuart "Izzy" Ezrailson, the grandfather of the specialty store business, who owned a mid-Atlantic chain of stores at the time called Up Against The Wall (UATW). He flew to Los Angeles to meet Jones and Walker personally. This was a coup for the duo, who was preparing to show their line at an upcoming MAGIC International trade show in Las Vegas.

Cross Colours featured its line at the March 1990 MAGIC show held at the Las Vegas Convention Center. By this time, Jones had spent at least a quarter of a million dollars in sampling, his studio, screen prints, and graphics. With little time to promote themselves, Cross Colours rented two booths and began to show its goods to potential buyers. "There were no black faces," recalls Jones. "At the time, [what is now considered] streetwear consisted of one to two aisles. I can say for sure we were the only black-owned [company] at the show doing streetwear. People were really curious as to what we were doing." Mintz and Walker were among the Cross Colours salesmen who attended the first MAGIC show. Cross Colours was located next to a company called Jam World, a contemporary casual lifestyle brand. Cross Colours stuck out like a sore thumb. The 20-foot by 10-foot booth was built like a wood crate and hip hop music was played in the background. "What made us stand out so prevalently was not only the music that was coming out of our booth, but that we had a closed booth by appointment only," recalled Walker. "You just felt the buzz from the outside because they were so many people waiting by a velvet rope." Buyers who came into the booth were given the VIP nightclub-like treatment. "We had this doorman. He became this iconic figure creating this supply and demand," Mintz says.

"The next thing you know, there were at least 50 buyers waiting [to see the line]," added Jones. Among those buyers was Tucker, who became the first retailer to give Cross Colours a $2 million order. At the time, Tucker was running close to 400 stores across the United States as well as Puerto Rico, Alaska, and Hawaii. Practically all private label-driven, this meant its doors were housed with in-house labels.[13] Oaktree had found success with the urban customer when it developed its own brand called U Men Clothing, which T.J. Walker had actually freelanced for as a designer. Tucker felt Cross Colours would just be an evolution of U Men. "The order was so big, Jones couldn't finance it. I went to Edison Bros. [parent of Oaktree] and told them this is the greatest thing we are going to have in our stores. I want to give a $2 million letter of credit. I believe in it that much," says Tucker.

However, Jones was able to produce all the merchandise without drawing from the line of credit. Curious to see how Cross Colours was doing in the local Las Vegas area, Tucker opted to visit one of his Las Vegas mall-based stores to get a gauge on sales. "The manager said 'I've never seen anything like it,'" says Tucker. His reaction gave Tucker the incentive the next day to up his order. Another obvious motivator was the fact that its direct competitor Merry-Go-Round had also placed a large order. In fact, it was a $4 million order and this began a feuding war between the two retailers. "I said Stuart Lucas is buying $4 million, I'll give you $10 million," says Tucker. "That's how they did so much business so fast."

In the MAGIC show's four-day run, Jones received $25 million worth of orders. This type of paper trail was unheard of for an upcoming brand, let alone one with an urban customer base. Cross Colours had received so many orders that Jones ended up purchasing a five-piece luggage set to transport them back home. But if Jones was stressed going into the show, he was even more stressed coming out of it. With such large orders to fill, Jones would need $10 million to produce his line and successfully ship it to retailers. Jones talked to his bank, the factory, and retailers like Edison Bros. and Merry-Go-Round who were all willing to help. Cross Colours starting producing the easiest things to turn around—T-shirts and hats. It would take the company several months to get its jeans ready between obtaining the fabric and getting the silhouette right. Soon after shipping hats and T-shirts, Cross Colours received calls from retailers that the product was selling out in a day. "We had 100 percent sell-throughs," says Jones. "The moment the product was shipped, it was gone. This was unheard of."

According to Jones, Cross Colours wrote a total of $30 million its first year in business and shipped $15 million its first year. The second year, it had $68 million in sales and shipped about $25 to $30 million. Retail and apparel veteran Petruzello, today president of Buffalo David Bitton, U.S. Division, was among the retailers who witnessed the phenomenon firsthand. At the time, Petruzello was a buyer with Chess King.[14] Petruzello wanted to carry Cross Colours in his store, but he could not get it because the company had a "great deal" with Merry-Go-Round. When he eventually went to Merry-Go-Round, he saw the kind of business that was done with Cross Colours. He called it a "phenomenon just from the sell-throughs." Not all retailers were sold on the idea of putting Cross Colours in their stores, but many did end up riding the wave. Skeptics, like Miller's Outpost, eventually tried the line. According to Jones, Miller's Outpost eventually became a $4 million dollar account.

Among the things that contributed to Cross Colours' growing popularity was also its charitable component. The company became an active financial contributor to the community by providing donations to a local Los Angeles community organizer, who was a former gang member. Cross Colours donated proceeds to the organization on a monthly basis. "We supported him in his neighborhood and what he was doing," Jones says. "He helped kids get out of drugs and was against gang violence. He brought kids in and we gave them jobs at the warehouse. We felt we had to do our part with the local community."

Jones and T.J. Walker had big plans that went beyond Cross Colours. Their dream was also to build a conglomerate of African American brands under one roof. After all, Cross Colours had the setup—the distribution, the manufacturing, the credit lines with vendors, and the overall established relationships in the business. In 1992, it renamed its corporation, Threads 4 Life. Karl Kani became the first and only brand to actually complete a deal with Threads 4 Life, the parent of Cross Colours. "I thought his ideas were different than ours, but related to same market," Jones says. According to T.J. Walker, Kani sales shot up overnight. He attributed it not only to piggybacking off of Cross Colours' distribution channels, but to also having a harder urban appeal.

Cross Colours hired Tweedy, whose urban experience included working for Spike Lee's Spike's Joint store. On a trip to Los Angeles, he met with Jones and Walker. A casual conversation turned into Tweedy moving to the West Coast and becoming the president of Karl Kani. "We made $94 million in a matter of three years and had new licensing deals in footwear and women's," recalled Tweedy. As hip hop music kept growing, the music itself started to splinter into different directions as did the fashion that followed it. While Cross Colours offered a softer side of hip hop style, Kani offered metal hardware on baggy jeans, which appealed to the hard-edge street consumer. From Tupac Shakur, Sean "Puffy" Combs to Poor Righteous Teachers (PRT), Kani kept acquiring loyal celebrity fans. "Karl had a sophisticated eye," says Tweedy. "His inspiration at the time was Nautica, Timberland, and Armani. He understood fabric and how to put together a collection."

By Cross Colours' third year in business (1993), the company had written $80 million in sales and shipped about $35 to $40 million. According to Walker, Kani did anywhere from $10 to $20 million his first year under the Threads 4 Life umbrella. "It eroded a lot of the Cross Colours business," Walker admitted. "It became so popular so fast that the consumer that was wearing Cross Colours didn't want to wear bright yellow, green, and red. They now had something a little more street."

While other designers such as April Walker, founder of Walker Wear, attempted to follow in Kani's footsteps, Cross Colours never made it past year five. The year 1994 marked the end of Cross Colours when its biggest account, Merry-Go-Round went into Chapter 11 bankruptcy. "We let one store control us to a certain extent," regretted Jones. But it was not just one store as it seemed that many of the national chains that

Cross Colours was in business with were filing for bankruptcy around the same time due to the popularity of off-price and discount chains as well as increased competition from department stores. While Cross Colours grew faster than Calvin Klein and Guess in its early days, the company was unable to keep its foothold in the marketplace. It was ahead of its time and had no model to follow. It had experienced unprecedented sales from $0 to close to $100 million in just four years. But with this phenomenal growth came a lot of problems. Unfortunately, Cross Colours had placed all its "eggs in one basket" instead of building a strong distribution foundation. "Cross Colours sort of imploded," says Petruzello. "That was a huge piece of [Merry-Go-Round's] volume, percentage-wise. So, all of a sudden [MGRE's] business dropped off and they had this huge debt from purchase."

Poor financial management also plagued Cross Colours, from overspending to mismanagement. "We were very good with marketing and knew how to make clothing but the business sort of, the tail wagged the dog, sort of speak," admits Jones. "The business grew way too fast and I didn't control the growth. I was thinking that I'm the next Levi's for African Americans, that's where my head was and nothing is going to stop me." Moving to an extremely large facility on Tube Way gave the company huge overhead expenses. When stores started experiencing financial difficulties, so did Cross Colours. Banks were not extending lines of credit or providing cash advances. The company began experiencing outstanding production bills and employees were not able to get paid. Once creditors came knocking and the company was unable to draw them money from the banks, it was time to close shop. Cross Colours' financial advisor gave the founders a clear indication of what was going on; the company had no choice but to end it all. "It was painful," Walker recalls sadly. "It was a disappointing situation as well because we had such high hopes for the company. We were becoming a household name and were on our way to being that."

While Cross Colours took pride in the fact that its product was "Made in the USA" (specifically in Los Angeles), having considered doing production overseas would have provided better pricing and eventually, margins. However, that idea came much too late. Having had enough assets and inventory, Cross Colours was able to pay the bank, the factory, and "walked away from it clean" though rumors spread that the company had gone bankrupt. Both Jones and Walker believed they would make a return to the garment business after a much-needed break. Multiple attempts to relaunch Cross Colours failed. Jones did try to launch two other lines—Jones Juke Joint and Carl Jones in the late 1990s—but neither lived up to his Cross Colours' expectations. Walker went on to launch the short-lived Modisch, a contemporary lifestyle brand with Stennett and Tucker.[15]

There is no question that Cross Colours was a training ground for talent very much like Ralph Lauren has been for many individuals. As for many of the former Cross Colours' employees, they stayed on the urban fashion trail. April Walker continued to push Walker Wear and eventually shifted her energies to working at other brands including Phat Farm and being a successful entrepreneur. Tony Shellman, who had worked briefly for Walker Wear during Cross Colours' involvement, founded Mecca USA, Enyce, and Parish Nation. Peter Mintz went on to sales at Mecca USA while Erich Walker followed Shellman to Mecca USA and Enyce. Today, Mintz and Erich Walker conduct sales for Akademiks. Kani found a new backer and went on his own and is the sole survivor of the original pioneering urban brands. June Ambrose, who did marketing at Cross Colours, went on to becoming one of the top celebrity fashion stylists in the business. Tweedy, who headed Kani, led several successful urban brands including Sean "Puffy" Combs' Sean John.

As for Jones and T.J. Walker, both have remained in Southern California and in the garment business. Jones has moved from the men's business to women while Walker teaches at Fashion Institute of Design and Merchandising (FIDM) and continues to focus on his artwork. Stennett is currently living in Atlanta and is the owner and creative director of Davide & Co., a multidimensional lifestyle-driven, business development and marketing firm. Tucker is the owner of a consulting and licensing company. More than a decade later, Cross Colours did in fact make its return. Relaunched as a multicultural streetwear brand, it has been produced by Urban Trends since 2007. Sold primary in Europe and online, the line resembles nothing like the afrocentric Cross Colours we grew to love. As the first major urban fashion powerhouse, Cross Colours set a precedent for large volume sales for other urban brands to follow and supercede. Representing Brooklyn, New York, Kani would pick up where Cross Colours left off. Fellow Brooklynite April Walker would attempt to do the same.

CHAPTER 5
Brooklyn's Finest

I remember going to Fresh Fest, seeing Run-D.M.C. in leather pants,
shell toes and pimp hats on stage and LL with a boom box at Madison
Square Garden. I knew this was my love. Hip hop was our rock and roll.
It defied everything I'd been taught. It grabbed my creative senses and
latched on to my rebellious teenage spirit.

—Designer April Walker

Hip hop might have started in the South Bronx, but urban fashion has
its concrete roots in the borough of Brooklyn. Three early black fashion pioneers call the BK home—Karl Kani, April Walker, and filmmaker Spike Lee.

While Lee (born in Atlanta and raised in Brooklyn) will always be
known for his acting, directing, and filmmaking abilities, fashion is
also something with which he is familiar. It started with as a promotional vehicle for his production company, 40 Acres and a Mule, which
he founded in 1986. Lee began producing T-shirts as film memorabilia
much the way the music industry promotes artists through merchandise
sold at concerts and catalogs. He sold T-shirts from his Fort Greene
offices, which were located at 124 Dekalb Avenue in a converted fire-
house, until the demand for products called for a larger facility and
operation. In 1990, Lee opened Spike's Joint as a 40 Acres and a
Mule memorabilia haven that quickly built a reputation for also finding
cool clothes. Spike's Joint was located at 75 S. Elliot Place at the corner of Lafayette in the Fort Greene section of Brooklyn and gave fans
and customers the opportunity to purchase authentic Lee memorabilia
such as "Do the Right Thing" and "Mo' Better Blues" T-shirts to
Malcolm X baseball caps and leather jackets.

The success of the Brooklyn store would have Lee open a second
store in 1992 in Los Angeles called Spike's Joint West. Located at

May, 1992: Spike Lee in Spike's Joint in Ft. Greene, Brooklyn. (© John Van Hasselt/Sygma/Corbis)

7265 Melrose Place, the 1,800-square-foot shop was in the perfect location of "fashion meets Hollywood." An Atlanta shop would be added to the Lee franchise as well as a 400-square-foot shop called Spike's Joint Kids, which carried a miniature version of his unisex lines called Spike's Joint and Joints by Spike Lee. Jeffrey C. Tweedy was executive vice president of 40 Acres and a Mule's clothing and retail operation for three years. Previously the vice president of sales at Ralph Lauren, he recalls meeting Lee through a referral. "It was a casual conversation of what he wanted to do," says Tweedy, who would later go on to work for Cross Colours, Karl Kani, Shaquille O'Neal's TWIsM, Mecca USA, Beyoncé's House of Dereon, and Sean "P. Diddy" Combs' Sean John. Tweedy says, "I left Ralph Lauren and people couldn't believe it. One thing I like to do is build new brands, new companies. The knack for doing that is exciting."

According to Tweedy, about 20 percent of Spike Lee's store was clothing. While the fashions carried in the store were initially film-specific merchandise, it expanded to also include apparel products unrelated to Lee films. Lee's apparel products became known for their colors and lingo like "Peace, you dig?" and "All that and a bag of chips." Lee built a loyal following that included Michael Jordan, Denzel Washington, and Tom Cruise, who were seen wearing the popular Malcolm X hats at the time. "Spike's Joint was taking movie memorabilia and really having one place where you could be all his movie memorabilia," says Tweedy. "It was the Disney store and MTV store before they did, before they even thought of it." Lee's retail vision went beyond his stores as his merchandise was featured in 125 in-store shops at Macy's.

Fellow filmmaker and Brooklynite Matty Rich attempted to follow Lee's fashion footsteps. Raised in the Red Hook Housing Project, the *Straight out of Brooklyn* director opened his own store called Matty Rich Red Hook in 1991 in the Park Slope section of Brooklyn. Like Lee, Rich sold his own clothing line under the name Matty Rich Wear. Fellow actor, Christopher Martin, also known as Play of the rap duo Kid 'n Play, carried his line in his store called IV Plai in Elmhurst, Queens. Unfortunately, Rich found little success in the apparel business and was forced to close shop in 1992. Lee stayed in the fashion business until 1997 when he was forced to close his shops down due to sluggish sales. He remained connected to fashion over the years while continuing to promote his brand through select ventures and other fashion-related events. Lee produced a short film and several runway shows for Marc Ecko (7th on Sixth and Council of Fashion Designers Association) in addition to having Ecko produce a 40 Acres and a Mule collection under Ecko's Cut and Sew label for fall 2006. Lee also launched a New Era "Spike Lee Joint" Collection of hats during the 2008 Major League Baseball (MLB) All-Star Game. Lee's no stranger to New Era as their relationship stems back to his Spike's Joint store days when he carried the brand in his shop. Lastly, Lee collaborated with Nike to create the Air Jordan Spizikes in 2009. The idea was not so far-fetched since Lee was crucial to the rise of the Air Jordan. (Remember the funny 1991 commercials featuring Lee as the character Mars Blackmon from *She's Gotta Have It?*)

Although not born in Brooklyn, Carl Williams, known as fashion designer Karl Kani, represents the borough to the fullest. His story is a classic rags-to-riches tale—Brooklyn guy with no college education, fashion background, money, or blueprint to succeed becomes a multi-millionaire. Out of the original pioneering designers, his brand is the only one left standing. Born in San José, Costa Rica to a Costa Rican mother and a Panamanian father, a nurse and entrepreneur, respectively, Kani lived in Panama until age three before his family pursued the American dream. The Williams family settled in Bedford-Stuyvesant and Kani's father started his own printing company named after Kani and his sister—the Carl Ronnie Composition service. Located at 225 Canal Street in New York City, the company did typeset and letterhead for banks and various companies.

Kani, who was raised in Bedford-Stuyvesant (Bed-Stuy) from ages 3 to 11, traces his fashion aesthetics to his father who had a unique style of fashion he brought from his native Panama. According to Kani, his father always had his clothes tailor made. Kani shopped with his father on Delancey Street for fabrics and later brought them to a Haitian tailor on Flatbush Avenue. Kani's father would then instruct the tailor as to what he wanted to get made and the tailor got it done. This showed Kani that one really did not need to know how to sew to create clothing. "If you get an idea, you can always brand your idea and have someone else sew the clothes for you," Kani says. By age 11, Kani and his family had moved to East New York and lived in the housing projects of Starrett City.[1] Hip hop was becoming popular and Kani recalls "It was about getting money and getting fly." Kani and some friends started a little crew (immediate circle of friends). Kani, a five percenter, spinned and went by the deejay name of Jazzy Na, short for his street name Naquan.[2] Changing one's name on the street was common back then as all of Kani's friends seemed to have done it. Kani notes that "It was funny because, people used to call my house and asking for Naquan. And my mother was not having it. She'd say 'there ain't no Naquan living here.'"

Kani gravitated to deejaying as he could never get rapping down pack. He quickly discovered that rapping was not easy so he left it to the guys who could rap; he became more of a behind-the-scenes dude. The fact that Kani could not rap well led him to do clothing. Hip hop was just exploding and Kani wanted to be part of it in a big way. Having a father with an impeccable sense of style gave Kani the idea to start making clothes for some of the MC's. Fashion would now take Kani from behind the scenes to the forefront. Kani relied on his father's tailor to craft his initial clothing designs. Back then, Lee jean suits and campers' shirts were popular in the hood, so Kani took his

Lee suit (denim jeans and matching jacket), bought five yards of linen and told the tailor to make him his first design, a linen jean suit. The rest is history. Kani recalls, "When I wore that, everybody was like 'man, that was so fresh, where did you get that? Where did you get that from?' I was getting so much attention from it." Kani purposely did not tell how he got the outfit made as that would be breaking the fashion code of the streets. He says that "I wasn't going to give up the spot. That's what made me."

Kani started making clothes for people in his crew and dudes in the neighborhood. At that time, Kani would take his customers' jean suits and replicate them, creating a pattern in their size and making outfits in different fabrics. Kani was hardly turning a profit; if he was making $10 to $20 an outfit, that was a lot. He would have his customers cover the cost of the fabric, then take it to the tailor, and he would add anywhere from $10 to $20 to the final price tag to allow him to buy more fabric to make more clothing. At the time, Kani says that he was not really trying to be a designer; he was just trying to make clothes. "I didn't even put my name on the clothes," Kani admits. That came later as a result of seeing someone in Ditmas Park rockin' his suit and having his designs questioned. "I told these girls, I made that outfit there," remembers Kani. "They were like, 'no, you didn't.' They were like, 'if you made it, why's your name not on it?' That's when it hit me."

Kani suddenly realized that he needed to start putting his name on the clothes so people could identify his designs. He researched where to get labels for his clothes. Kani found a company in California that printed labels and began ordering and placing them in his clothes. At this point, he knew that his hustle could be a full-fledged business. From that point on, Kani, now 16 and attending Canarsie High School, realized that making clothing had to be taken a little more seriously. He stopped deejaying and started focusing more on dressing artists so he could really stand out from the crowd. At the time, Kani designs were called Seasons. The concept behind the name was simple; "I thought my clothes were good for all seasons," he says. Kani would keep his clothes in trunk of his car and he and AZ, a friend from Starrett City, would go out hustling with them. That was the hustle game—hustling Kani's clothes to anyone they saw who was fly (stylish). "People were buying them because people couldn't find them anywhere and because they were hot (stylish)," Kani remembers.

Kani and AZ found customers in front of nightclubs and specialty shops like the Village Hut and Love People. "We used to be out there when the club was out with the trunk open with the clothes," Kani says. He would do this for about five hours a day. Customers would also hit Kani and AZ up on their beepers, as this was the primary mode of communication back then. At this point, Kani had expanded his designs to include velour sweatsuits with leather trimming and his tailor was cranking out anywhere from 20 to 30 outfits a week. When the velours started to hit, that is when Kani knew he needed more help as he had a lot of potential customers and he could not handle the growing incoming volume. Around this time, in 1987, AZ caught a case in New York and he moved to California to live with his brother. Kani's business slowed down without AZ, his right hand so AZ suggested that Kani relocate to California. Kani turned down the idea at first but as he gave it more thought, he realized that California might be the best place for him since many clothing manufacturers were based there. In 1989, Kani, now 19, decided to get into making better clothing and mass producing to sell to stores. He moved to California on June 23, 1989 and stayed with AZ, who was renting a room in Orange County. That situation did not last long as AZ's landlord caught wind that the room had multiple occupants.

Not having enough money to rent an apartment, the two friends decided to find a storefront in which to work and live. "AZ's not from L.A., so he finds a store on Crenshaw and 43rd Street, right in the middle of the hood," remembered Kani. "Being from New York, you come to California, you see all these palm trees and beautiful weather, you don't know you're in a bad neighborhood. 'Cause in New York, you know when you are in a bad neighborhood. In California, everything is dressed up." The 1,000-square-foot shop was located at 4312 Crenshaw Boulevard. It had a sauna with a wood seating area and Kani and AZ used its platform for a bed by putting fabric on the platform and sleeping on top of it.

By relocating to California, Kani thought he could "get paid" by bringing a new sense of fashion to guys in California. However, Kani said that "They weren't trying to hear that. They wanted no part of it. No velour suits, no linens, nothing. N.W.A. was really popular and just coming out the box. We had a hard time." Kani was living by the seat of his pants, figuratively and literally. He had paid the first and last month for the storefront, but could not afford the monthly rent of $900. After the third month, the landlord told Kani to leave. Kani recalls that the landlord, who was from the streets, had some brothers that were gangbangers. "They were not too happy with the fact that we were out there not paying rent in their sister's spot," Kani says. "So I went back to New York to try to hustle some money together, so we could put an ad out and pay the rent."

While in New York, random guys at gunpoint robbed the store on Crenshaw Boulevard and left Kani without his sewing machine and fabrics. Kani's mother, who had received a telephone call from AZ, asked Kani not to return. "Something inside told me to go back and figure this thing out. So we went back, got the money together, moved out of the store," he says. Kani was able to borrow $3,000 from past customers, which gave him enough to move out the store, get an apartment in Hollywood, place an ad in *Right On!* Magazine, and have a little pocket money. The ad cost Kani $1,250 and it featured Kani and his friend AZ posing in their jean suits. Kani listed a 1-800-221-KANI number in this ad which produced excellent results by putting Kani's clothing into stores. Teens started calling up from all over requesting the jeans. "We used to ask each kid when they called where they shopped in their area. They used to tell us the name of the store. We used to write down the name of the stores and eventually got the phone numbers for the stores and started having the kids call the stores requesting the jeans," says Kani.

Kani's first account was Simon's in the Brownsville section of Brooklyn. "Mike Tyson bought my clothes [there]," says Kani. "It was a hot spot back in the days." Big accounts included the popular specialty chain Up Against the Wall in Washington, D.C., owned at the time by the founder of the specialty store business, Stuart "Izzy" Ezrailson. In the early days, Kani struggled with manufacturing his apparel. As the business started to grow, it became more difficult for him to fulfill the brand's growing demand. The problem was not getting orders, but having the money to produce the items. Kani took on a "whatever it took, by any means necessary" attitude and paying rent was last thing he considered. He had an apartment-hopping technique that worked for close to two years; he would pay first and last month's rent, then stay three or four months before getting evicted.

Making jeans soon became Kani's meal ticket. Not knowing anything about the process, Kani decided to stake out the Guess factory in Los Angeles. The plan was to wait for the workers to get off work and talk to every Hispanic man that came out of the building. Kani, in his broken and ungrammatically correct Spanish, would ask "*¿Usted trabajo (sic) máquina, más dinero?*" which translated to "You work machine, more money?" Kani's idea was to find a worker interested in a side hustle to teach him the denim business and sew some jeans. Finally, one Hispanic man answered his awkward question, in English, "Look, are you going to pay me more money?" Kani was happy to have finally found someone who spoke English. Juan Carlos, a pattern maker and sewer at the Guess factory, agreed to take on the job. From that moment, Kani learned where to get fabrics and employed Juan Carlos to make patterns and sew clothes. Juan Carlos soon educated Kani on denim and got him where he needed to be in the business.

At this point, Kani wanted to do away with the Seasons name. "I wanted to do something that identified more with who I was as a designer because I felt like that's where I wanted to go," Kani says. His actual surname was Williams, but he did not feel that Carl Williams Jeans had the right ring. Having a lot of doubts about himself, especially about making it California, Kani started giving much thought to his clothing line's new name. He started doodling on a piece of paper. When the paper filled up, the words "Carl" and "Can I" were on the paper. This is how the brand name Karl Kani came about. Spelling Karl and Kani with K's instead of C's, Kani utilized his own name without a legal trademark to save money.

In 1991, Kani reluctantly decided to attend a Cross Colours' fashion show. His attendance paid off as Kani is invited by Cross Colours' founder Carl Jones to the company's headquarters the next day. "Our conversation lasted 15 minutes," says Kani, who ended up striking a deal with the Threads 4 Life division of Cross Colours. With the money he received from the deal, Kani was able to trademark his company name and its assets. "I thought his ideas were different than ours, but related to same market," says Jones. "It worked with Karl. We had the channels, the distribution, the manufacturing, credit with vendors, the fabric and we had the relationships. His look was a little more street, hardcore than ours." Within two weeks, Kani had both his own office and access to a 50,000-square-foot warehouse.

Kani moved to the Cross Colours' offices in Santa Fe on 25th Street. At that time, he hired a sales staff which consisted of his friends.

Karl Kani women's fashion show model. (© Ronnie Wright. Used by permission.)

"I wanted them to make money. These were my friends from Brooklyn and they had no experience in sales. I taught them the game and how to making things happen," said Kani. Jones also put his relationships to work. "At the time, we owned 60 percent of it, we financed it," says Jones. He called up Merry-Go-Round, one of his major accounts, and soon after an order was given for Karl Kani Jeans. "We ran through production and did T-shirts and shipped it to Merry-Go-Round. I will never forget it did not sell," admits Jones. Asking for another chance, a reluctant Merry-Go-Round complied. "I got a call in a couple of weeks and they said 'I want to return everything.' We started pulling stuff out of the store and all of a sudden, I get a call. 'That stuff we shipped you back, it started to sell.'" Jones had the garments shipped back and that was the beginning of the success of the Karl Kani brand. Merry-Go-Round would soon become a $3 million account for Kani. Retailer Antonio Gray attributed Kani's success to trend-right product and strategic marketing. "Karl Kani had that hang tag on his garment where you can see. It was Karl dressed in his clothes," he recalls. "So there was this image of a young black man with his name on the back pocket of his jeans. That was really revolutionary at the time." By the time of the Cross Colours demise, Kani had earned in about $80 million in sales.

Kani was able to go to his footwear licensee, Skechers, who had grown the Kani footwear business to $43 million, to get out the company out of the Cross Colours' deal in 1993. At the time, Kani had a lien on the trademark and owed money to the banks. Once with Skechers, Kani hired Derek Tucker, formerly of Cross Colours and Oaktree, to serve as president. "Karl Kani was refined [compared to Cross Colours]. It had big logos, but in a tasteful way," says Tucker, who stayed on as president for three years. Tucker eventually held the Karl Kani Endurance license, which developed active apparel. "Karl has a high taste level. He is like the Ralph Lauren of the urban business. Kani was classic, not real flashy but had a strong message that it was urban," notes Tucker. At the time, Tweedy, who had left Spike's Joint to work for Cross Colours, was now sales manager for Kani. "He was inspired by Nautica, Timberland, and Armani," says Tweedy, who would eventually head up Kani until his departure to join Shaq's apparel line TWIsM (The World is Mine) in the late 1990s.

Kani attributes his company's success to brand exposure on music television like *Yo! MTV Raps* with Dr. Dre and Ed Lover and MTV's *Fade to Black* with Todd 1. The company also benefited from a fan base which included Tupac Shakur, Sean "P. Diddy" Combs, Snoop Dogg, Redman, Method Man, and Heavy D over the years. However, Kani has had a series of highs and lows. He has had dinner with President Bill Clinton and held a fashion show at the White House.

He was called upon by General Colin Powell, the National Urban League, and the Congress of Black Churches to take part in a ceremony inducting the first group of 25 young students nationwide into the Thurgood Marshall Achievers Society. Los Angeles Mayor Richard Riordan recruited Kani as an advisor to "LA's Best," an afterschool project providing education, recreation, and enrichment activities to over 5,000 children in economically and socially disadvantaged neighborhoods. Unfortunately, being a pioneer does not mean you can always stay on top of the industry. Once urban fashion became mainstream by the year 2000, Kani felt the retail push towards new brands and his label became overshadowed in the United States. Survival has meant looking towards the international market in places like Japan, Germany, Amsterdam, Russia, and Switzerland. Kani said, "I had to make a decision—fight this movement or go elsewhere. I said let the American market come to us."

Hip hop designer April Walker, unlike Kani and Lee, actually stumbled into the apparel business. A communications and business student at SUNY-New Paltz in the 1980s, this Brooklynite of Mexican and African American descent would frequently head uptown to catch Amateur Night at the Apollo Theater and hang out at Dapper Dan's shop. "From Dapper Dan, a light bulb went off," says Walker, who was born in Los Angeles and raised in the Bedford-Stuyvesant and Clinton Hill areas of New York. Walker attended Brooklyn Technical High School and later transferred to Bishop Loughlin, where she went to her prom with her high school sweetheart, Houston Rockets' point guard Mark Jackson. "In school, I was always that fashion person. But the light bulb never went off until I went to Dap's and I saw his hustle and saw what he was doing. It was so unconventional and hip hop was so big then," remembers Walker. Hip hop was part of Walker from the very beginning. "I felt it, breathed it," she says. "I remember going to Fresh Fest, seeing Run-D.M.C. in leather pants, shell toes, and pimp hats on stage and LL with a boom box at Madison Square Garden. I knew this was my love," says Walker. "Hip hop was our rock and roll. It defied everything I'd been taught. It grabbed my creative senses and latched on to my rebellious teenage spirit."

Looking to become the Brooklyn Dapper Dan, Walker opened her own tailor shop called Fashion in Effect in 1988. She had saved for a year to open her shop on a shoestring budget that came from her savings accumulated from her American Express job as well as small business loan. Located on Greene Avenue, between Grand and Cambridge in Brooklyn, Walker hired a few tailors stolen from Dapper Dan to produce her version of designer knock-offs as well as ready-to-wear and flamboyant original designs. She wanted to make money and that was her whole objective. Walker says, "The main difference was that in Harlem during that period they spent a lot more money than Brooklyn people." At the time, sequins was really popular so she would produce everything from sequined gowns to sequined tuxedo jackets and prom dresses. "If you had it, we would make it," says Walker. Her shop made everything from knock-off Nike velour sweatsuits and Gucci outfits to even providing seat covers for a Chicago detail shop.

Walker wanted to be like Dapper Dan until he started getting in trouble with manufacturers like MCM for counterfeiting merchandise. It was then that Walker realized that her shop—in the direction it was going—would be short-lived. "I knew that I couldn't do that forever so I leaned more towards original designs that I was making and simultaneously I started getting a different clientele," she says. Hip hop

From left-right: Wrecks-N-Effect (A-Plus and Markell Riley) Carl Banks, April Walker, Jaz-O, and Jay-Z. (© Ernie Paniccioli. Used by permission.)

celebrities like Biggie started shopping at Walker's store as well as MC Lyte, Shinehead, Shaggie, and Audio Two. "Those were my core customers and they opened the doors for me to start styling," says Walker. Styling became a whole new business from her custom tailor shop. She did both simultaneously until her store was robbed on Christmas eve in 1990. Walker remembers that "It was horrible and totally spontaneous. It was a very ugly experience and I remember saying this is not cool." Since Walker had already established a clientele, she decided to close shop and operate her fashion business out of her loft. She began seeing clients by appointment only. Her clientele grew to include Run-D.M.C., EPMD, Queen Latifah, and LL Cool J as well as Flava Unit and Def Jam. Customers gravitated to her denim suits. "This was before I launched Walker Wear," says Walker. "They looked like the rough and rugged suits that were in the Walker Wear line. It would just always come back to everyone asking me for those suits." Walker attributes the late Jam Master Jay of Run-D.M.C. for sparking her interest to launch her own clothing line.

In 1992, Walker Wear was launched to specifically "create fashion that wasn't out there." The company addressed men's need for style and comfort. Walker utilized her experience making custom clothes and applied it for a larger audience. "Whether it was for a blue collar worker or entertainer, they'd ask me to make big pockets. I wanted to define fashion in definite way," she says. Walker did so with her contrast stitching, by offering bigger cuts, a longer crotch area, and stash pockets. She stayed true to earth tones and muted colors that could be coordinated back to Timberlands. With limited marketing dollars, Walker was strategic about her marketing strategies. She would find out Nike's forecasting in order to compete and learned several tricks from records companies. Walker remembers, "I'd pick five stores in five cities and we made sure before [the product] got there we had kids calling every day before the delivery." Walker Wear sold to local stores like Dr. Jay's, national chains like Merry-Go-Round, and even department stores such as Macy's. Walker's first trade show was at an off-site location during the NAMSB exhibition. Taking up a suite inside the Flat Hotel located at 135 West 52nd Street in New York, Walker made her line available to 10 buyers. The invited stores included Simon's, Merry-Go-Round, Dr. Jay's, and CODA. "Everybody bought," says Walker as she raked in about $300,000 in orders at her first trade show.

Walker took a similar approach with the MAGIC Show in Las Vegas. She rented a suite at Bally's Las Vegas Hotel and Casino on Las Vegas Boulevard. Walker Wear outdid her previous trade show in sales. The next summer, Walker got a call from Cross Colours and eventually met with Cross Colours' Jeffrey C. Tweedy at the Royalton at 44 West 44th Street in New York. She notes that "I went, met with Cross Colours, and we struck a deal in theory." Her lawyer at the time, Londell Mcmillian, a prominent entertainment attorney who has represented many entertainers from Prince to Michael Jackson before his death, started the negotiations process. Walker remembers that "We went out to L.A. and put together a sample line. They didn't want to sign until basically we showed and proved."

"We worked with her," confirmed Cross Colours' founder TJ Walker. "She was definitely considered. We wanted to support and actually did take her to the MAGIC show." Walker joined Cross Colours and Karl Kani at the MAGIC show in Las Vegas. "Urban fashion was not a category," she recalled of the trade show's convention layout. "There was no name for it." Walker was given a convention meeting room to present to buyers. "We made our room like a big jail cell and did about $2 million at that show." Unfortunately Cross Colours and Walker could not agree on terms and so a deal was never struck. "We didn't see eye to eye and we decided to part ways," says Walker. "We walked from that deal and decided to stay independent." Her decision might have been a blessing in disguise as shortly thereafter, Cross Colours stopped doing business.

Walker would eventually try striking several deals over the lifespan of her brand. "USA Classics went declared bankruptcy the day after I signed with them," says Walker. "I had to purchase my goods from bankruptcy in order to ship and make sure my accounts received their goods. I did and shipped to Merry-Go-Round, Dr. Jay's, and Macy's." Walker ended up working with her team to independently manufacture domestically in Los Angeles. Her company had a styling division and styled countless videos, album covers, and also did many custom designed outfits. Later Mike Tyson became a brief partner with Walker Wear, but because the boxing world and apparel business are vastly different, this partnership did not last. "Apparel operates on timelines and boxing is much the same; unfortunately the timelines weren't in sync," Walker says.

Walker's final try at striking a deal with another company was with AND1, originally to partner with her for Walker Wear, but the two decided to collaborate on a women's line instead. Unfortunately, the new line called Dimes (named after her Shar Pei) had tremendous potential, but became short-lived. "They actually decided after we started working on it together that they didn't want to dive into the women's biz because they didn't understand it," Walker says. "We parted was amicably and I own the marks." Walker's fashion career in between her brands included consulting for various sportswear firms and working for Phat Farm as vice president of licensing. She gave up launching Walker Wear once she started to dislike the industry she grew to love. "I felt that there was little trace of creativity left and it became purely a paper chase at the time," admitted Walker. "Being an independent company for so many years, and being the only woman in a male dominated industry took a toll on me and I just needed a break."

Walker then took time out to travel and to do some self-introspection. She wanted to start other creative projects and looked towards the pet business for inspiration. She had seen her Fort Greene neighborhood gentrifying with many dog owners moving into the neighborhood and thought that it would be a good time to start a pet boutique. In 2003, Walker switched gears and moved into the pet retail business, opening the Walker Wear Pet Shop in the Fort Greene area of Brooklyn. Located at 759 Fulton Street, the store doubled as a pet store and pet photography studio. It also provided pet-sitting services, carried premium all-natural and organic pet food, treats, and offered an assortment of pet accessories from fashionable pet coats and booties to kitty tiaras. The shop would spark Walker's next business venture—organic dog food. Papa Jack's, named after Walker's father, was started in his kitchen. Walker says that "[a]s a father and daughter team, we were skeptical about many of the choices out there, so we were cooking for our dog every night, and we knew there had to be others out there like us."

The Walkers found that there were many pet owners that felt the same way so they decided to package their recipe of dog food and treats. "Pet owners could not always get what they wanted and needed, so we began working on creating our own all natural pet food, treats, and products to fulfill this need," says Walker, who tested product on her dog Dimes and eventually conducted doggie focus groups. The cooking experiment became a full-fledged business that took four years in the making. The Brooklyn-based Papa Jack's is now produced from a commercial kitchen and the gourmet line of dog food includes Papa Here's The Beef Dinner, Papa Jack's Gobble Gobble Dinner (Turkey), Papa Jack's Yum Chow Dinner (Chicken), Papa Jack's Neat Treats, Peanut Pup Scout Treats, Papa Jack's Neat Treat Apple Flax Treats, and Papa Jack's Banana Dana Treats. The all-natural pet food sells directly online and to select retailers. Despite being in the pet business, Walker continues to stay involved in the fashion industry. She runs a consulting business called A. Walker Group where she works with creative designers and brands in different stages of their brand development. Based on firsthand account interviews with pioneering and legendary hip hop fashion brands, Walker is currently producing a documentary film entitled *Labeled*. The film is the compelling and personal story of the creation of hip hop fashion told through Walker's eyes. Acting as her own muse, Walker, along with key hip hop fashionistas, tells the unapologetic tale of how a multi-billion dollar apparel industry came to fruition. The film takes the audience through the roller coaster of emotions felt by these fashion entrepreneurs and designers: the very same feelings of resentment, success, humility, and contentment that shaped Walker's career history. This spirit of entrepreneurialism has always followed Walker, who credits breaking into fashion after watching Harlem tailor Dapper Dan at his craft. Custom apparel and accessories has always played an important role in ethnic cultures. This is especially true for the hip hop generation that made household names of custom specialists like The Might Shirt Kings (graffiti artists known for their custom shirts and jean jackets), Jacob the Jeweler (known for his diamond-encrusted jewelry), and 5001 Flavors (the predominant custom company for development of apparel for hip hop videos as well as athletes).

CHAPTER 6
Tailor-Made

Custom enabled people in hip hop to have their own identity. They were able to express who they were or what they wanted and the ability to create things that weren't really there.
　　　—Edwin Sacasa aka Shirt King Phade, The Mighty Shirt Kings

Custom apparel has always had a special place in the hearts of hip hop loyalists. It is no surprise that part of the infatuation developed as a means of standing out for the ladies, in the crowd, at the club, in a battle, or on the streets.

The need to dress uniquely produced a handful of legendary custom designers within select boroughs of New York during the early days of hip hop. The tradition is still alive today. In Queens, the graffiti-inspired The Mighty Shirt Kings drew hundreds to the Colosseum Mall on 165th Street and a block north from Jamaica Avenue. The Mighty Shirt Kings were known for their name sweatshirts and one-of-a-kind character designs worn by LL Cool J, the late Jam Master Jay, and Salt-N-Pepa. For a more sophisticated look, the go-to guy was none other than Harlem tailor Dapper Dan on 125th Street and Lenox Avenue. Every hustler and rapper looking for the luxurious touch of custom design would head to Dap for his one-of-a-kind wares. In the 1990s, 5001 Flavors cornered the market by creating music video wardrobes for camps like Bad Boy Entertainment while Jacob Arabo, aka Jacob the Jeweler, brought new meaning to the term "bling-bling" as the "it" jeweler in hip hop. Also in the 1990s, the up-and-coming custom tailor Miguel Navarro was extremely popular. Unfortunately, his life was cut short in early December 1996 when he was murdered at his shop at 341 West 38th Street. At age 29, Navarro had an impressive track record with Miguel Navarro Inc., which drew business from celebrities like Sean (P. Diddy) Combs.

While designers embrace all celebrities today, many in the hip hop community did not feel the love early on and turned to custom designers for one-of-a-kind pieces. "Traditionally, the fashion industry didn't necessarily cater to the hip hop community," remembered Vinnie Brown of the rap group Naughty by Nature. Brown continues, "That left a huge void there. You had the Louis Vuitton's and Gucci's that would never cater to the audience, but we had Dapper Dan. You have nothing for us, so we'll print your patterns on leather with a custom swag. The kids were putting it on the music, making up their own product and that definitely made the higher end brands take notice."

THE MIGHTY SHIRT KINGS

The Mighty Shirt Kings were the first "unofficial stylists" of hip hop. The trio, made up of Ed Sacasa aka Shirt King Phade, Mighty Nike, and King Kasheme, became famous for their colorful hand-painted clothes throughout the mid-1980s and 1990s. Sacasa, who is Honduran and Guatemalan, fell in love with fashion at young age, becoming a "mini me" of his older brother. "Whatever he would buy, he would by for me," recalled Sacasa, who was born in East New York, Brooklyn. Having moved to the Bronx in 1972, Sacasa was able to witness firsthand the beginning of the hip hop phenomenon. While clothes became his first love, Sacasa also quickly grew an affinity for graffiti. He remembers that "There were two guys in my building, two deejays—one was Jerry Dunlap, aka Deejay One Time. The other was Doc La Roc, Amar, aka Doc La Roc. They both were artists and used to paint on their pants and jackets. They noticed my artwork and my love for graffiti. They told me I need to go to enroll for art and design."

Sacasa attended the High School of Art and Design in 1977, the same year in which he did his first graffiti piece. It was at Art and Design where Sacasa was able to meet top graffiti artists including Daze, Lady Pink, and Jay-5. In the ninth grade, he met his soon-to-be business partner Mighty Nike, a Belgian whose nickname stuck because of the many pairs of Nike sneakers he rocked in all different flavors. Around the same time, Sacasa met his other soon-to-be business partner King Kasheme, an African American who was doing graffiti under the name Quartz-2. Kasheme was from South Jamaica,

Queens while Nike was from Brooklyn's Marcy Projects, in the same building as Jay-Z. All three were into clothes at the time. "We used to go to 42nd Street and watch karate movies, be dressed up and take our 42nd Street pictures, and then go home and draw our clothes," recalled Sacasa. "We would draw exactly what we had on that day."

Sacasa graduated from high school in 1981. Intimidated by "top writers and so many artists" at Art and Design, he opted to major in photography. Sacasa moved back to Brooklyn (Brownsville) while attending New York City College of Technology in downtown Brooklyn for two years. He later transferred to Savannah College of Art and Design in 1984, where he took up video production. At home on a break in December 1984, it was George aka Sound 7 that put Sacasa on his destined career track. Sacasa recalls, "He called me up one day and says, 'I want to teach you something. I want to teach you how to airbrush.' I'm watching him and I'm like, I don't want to do that. He put [the airbrush] in my hand, he told me what to do and I went crazy. He was like 'use the force, young Luke.'"

Having been given a compressor and airbrush, Sacasa created his first airbrushed shirt—Ernie and Bert from *Sesame Street*. Sacasa had quit painting on the trains in 1981 when he decided to go to college. He says, "I loved graffiti but I didn't want to be illegal anymore. I didn't want deface or damage property cause I was getting older and I wouldn't want someone to write on my car or on the side of my house that I own. Then I'm going to have to pay to clean. So, [I said to myself,] you know what, I'm gonna have to grow up in my mentality." Airbrushing became the next big thing for Sacasa after painting trains. While he always seemed to work a regular job, Pathmark being one of them, soon airbrushing would almost quadruple his take-home pay. But it was not until Sacasa's mother paid him for a shirt design that he thought of incorporating his business. "She took the shirt to work and came back with orders," he recalled. Charging from $5 to $15 at the time, Sacasa began growing his list of clientele from his mother's co-workers to local friends from the hood. He started itemizing and seeing exactly what each person wanted in terms of color scheme and design. A former stickup kid and drug dealer friend of Sacasa's (today a pastor) commissioned him to do a shirt. Although reluctant at first to do shirts for drug dealers, that is where the money was to be found. During the time when crack cocaine was popular, Sacasa recalls being in Harlem and seeing long lines of people around the block. "I was seeing professional people," he says. "I guess that's why it fooled people."

Sacasa ended up making 15 shirts for one particular crack dealer for $25 each. Sacasa remembers, "He dug into a pile of money and handed it to me upfront. I told myself I'd never work for anybody again in my life." From that point on, Sacasa began maneuvering his way to drug dealers because they were spending. "They got introduced in their mind to custom," he says. Most of Sacasa's early work was personalizing shirts with people's names, an idea came from his tagging train days. "If I was going to do wild style, it was going to be complicated. If I did a bubble style, it was cool. I took that same mentality to the shirt," he says. Larry Love from Grandmaster Flash was his first hip hop celebrity client. But it was his second celebrity client, the late Jam Master Jay, who helped fuel the reputation of The Mighty Shirt Kings. Kasheme, who had a background in construction, had worked on the late Jam Master Jay's basement studio in Hollis, Queens. Sacasa was introduced to Jam Master Jay through King Kasheme. Sacasa vividly recalled showing Jay a black sweatshirt with a hand-painted gold chain around the neck. And Jam Master Jay's reaction? "'I want that and put the JMJ here and then I want one that says Little Jason for my son,'" remembers Sacasa.

Customers soon became regular for The Mighty Shirt Kings so Sacasa and his high school buddies Mighty Nike and King Kasheme began renting a booth inside the Jamaica Colosseum Mall in June 1986. They went from a regular-sized booth to a larger booth to a triple booth to eventually taking over the entire downstairs level of the mall. On average, art work was priced at $50. Customized gear varied from jeans, sweatshirts, and T-shirts to caps. Surprisingly, The Mighty Shirt Kings opened to no customers on their first day. "I told them [Nike and Kasheme] word of mouth, it's going to work," recalls Sacasa. Over time, The Mighty Shirt Kings gained loyal fans from LL Cool J, Run-D.M.C., Bell Biv DeVoe, Salt-N-Pepa, Heavy D, Eric B. and Rakim, Jay-Z, De La Soul, Bill Cosby, Audio 2, MC Lyte, and Luke Campbell. It became a meeting place after a while and even representatives from record companies started coming to hang out. Soon The Mighty Shirt Kings were expanding their business to include designing album covers and producing product for videos. "We provided them their steez. We fanned their egos for them with our clothes," Sacasa says.

MC Shan wearing a Shirt Kings custom T-shirt. (© Ernie Paniccioli. Used by permission.)

Over the course of about seven years, The Mighty Shirt Kings built their reputation and the number of stores, with Miami being their second location. It was there that The Mighty Shirt Kings became contracted to paint a club. Campbell, of the infamous 2 Live Crew, owned a teen club/skating rink called Pac-Jam. He commissioned a paint job from The Mighty Shirt Kings and the gig brought them $7,000. "It was our first couple of gees ever," Sacasa says. While Sacasa and Kasheme worked and managed the Miami store location, Mighty Nike ran the Colosseum location with the help of Sacasa's cousin Sike from East New York, Derek, Tyson (the cousin of FUBU's Keith Perrin), and Nate. By the end of 1988, Sacasa and King Kasheme had moved back to New York and opened a store location in Roosevelt, Long Island. King Kasheme eventually moved to Virginia and set up shop there. By 1989, The Mighty Shirt Kings had closed their shop inside the Jamaica Colosseum and relocated the shop to Harlem and later to Baltimore.

Sacasa opened a booth at the 125th Street Mart in Harlem. He only stayed for a few months because Harlem tailor Dapper Dan asked him to relocate to his store. Sacasa recalls, "He loved my stuff so much that he said 'just come work with me.' We have been together ever since in '89. That's been my mentor." While Sacasa worked out of Harlem, Mighty Nike was at the Colosseum and Kasheme was over-seeing the Virginia location. It was around this time that Sacasa began incorporating rhinestones into his designs after being influenced by Mike Tyson and Don King. He also met Michael Bivins of the teen heartthrob group New Edition and later the adult Bell Biv Devoe. A year later, Sacasa found himself creating clothes for Bivins and going on tour with him. What started as designing a pair of custom overalls, turned into nine custom outfits per show on average. Sacasa had previ-ously toured with Eric B. and Rakim while later tours included LL Cool J, Big Daddy Kane, and Slick Rick.

The fun unfortunately came to an end for Sacasa in 1991when he went to jail. "I was a business man whose mind was still in the streets. It was fear of being legit, acting grown up, and doing grown up things," he says. The Mighty Shirt Kings business lasted for another two years and later dissolved as the employees went their separate ways. Sacasa came out of jail in 1997 and he was able to go back into the industry. He designed some product for Universal while teaching himself how to use a Mac. Sacasa stayed in the industry for two years and then went back into church. He later worked as a union painter in Staten Island for Donald Trump for two years until the events of 9/11. Then, he started working in a soup kitchen and later provided children's art classes through the Jewish Board of Family Children's Services. In May 2006, Sacasa moved to Los Angeles to pursue a movie adaptation of his autobiography. He continues to do custom design and primarily focuses on shows. His work has been on display at Con Art, the Norman Maxwell Gallery, and the Crewest Gallery all in Los Angeles; the Bakery Gallery in the Bronx, the Museum of Phoenix, as well as the Museum of the City of New York. Sacasa's ultimate goal is to finance his own airbrush school so he can teach children how to airbrush and develop their own clothing lines.

THE HARLEM LEGEND: THE ONE AND ONLY DAPPER DAN

Drug dealers, hustlers, rap stars, entertainers, and athletes would rely on one man—the legendary Dapper Dan for their custom wares from the early to late 1980s. Taking the logos of luxury designers like Louis Vuitton, Gucci, Chanel, and MCM, Dapper Dan was the A-list designer for the streets. "He took the logo designer expensive handbags that women were wearing and got fabric that was made like that and copied them," says Emil Wilbekin, managing editor of essence.com.

Well before athletic maker Nike had apparel, Dapper Dan had been making fake Nike fashion in addition to his signature counterfeit Gucci outfits made famous by Eric B. and Rakim. A 24-hour custom boutique located on 125th Street between Fifth and Madison Avenues, his shop catered to the lifestyle of the rich—legally and illegally—and famous. While hustlers from Harlem made it their top shop, hustlers from all over the country made sure to get outfits made by the counterfeit king. "It was totally not what you would expect," remembers designer April Walker, who when she opened her own custom shop, stole a few designers from Dap. Walker says, "It was a 24/7 custom tailor shop that on fire any given day you could see Mike Tyson or some Japanese tourist in his shop. The cheapest item it carried had a $300 price tag for a plain velour suit. That was in the early '80s. You were like this is what I want to do and trying to figure out how. He [Dapper Dan] inspired me."

Naughty by Nature's Vinnie Brown recalls there was "no authentic" luxury brand available to hip hop entertainers back in the day, so if one was a hip hop fan when Big Daddy Kane and the Juice Crew were out,

Rakim donning a custom Dapper Dan outfit. (© Ernie Paniccioli. Used by permission.)

than you loved Dapper Dan's stuff. Brown, like so many other entertainers, visited Dan's tailor shop. Naughty by Nature's Treach and Kay Gee purchased Dapper Dan's famous "Gucci" suits. Although Brown never did buy a suit, he recalled the custom wares being expensive; outfits averaged from $375 to $3000, depending on what it was.

Dapper Dan could make anything from casual streetwear and tailored suits to car interiors. As a designer ahead of his time, Dap could pimp anybody's ride with custom interiors, tire covers, and special covers; that work came out of a Spanish Harlem-based garage on 118th Street. The who's who in hip hop shopped there from Salt-N- Pepa, Biz Markie, LL Cool J, Big Daddy Kane, Doug E. Fresh, Heavy D., Slick Rick, and boxing champ Mike Tyson.

Haussan, who ran production for Dapper Dan in the 1980s and later worked for Shabazz Brothers Urbanwear (SBU), commonly refers to Dapper Dan as his uncle, although they are not blood-related. He was a close friend of his son, Chuckie. According to Haussan, Dapper Dan took him under his wing in 1981 at the age of 17. "Dap was always into staying fly," says Haussan. "We used to get Ferre and Boss, different things—whatever we could get our hands on we used to take around the neighborhood. Then we actually started selling garments trimmed in Louis Vuitton and Gucci we cut from bags. We would get the big bags, cut them and used them for trimming on denim and what not. That was like the first custom garments we were doing. After that, it evolved into entire garments in Louis, Fendi, and MCM." According to Haussan, there was a demand for this type of clothing and Dapper Dan just happened to be the person to meet it. "There was money in the street and that's what it was about," he says. "[Hustlers] had [designer] bags and they didn't have the clothes to go with it. The designers were not doing any all-over print jackets and shirts like what we were doing. That was just an idea that Dap had and we ran with it."

Located next to the Celebrity Club, a popular Harlem nightclub, Dapper Dan Boutique's business grew by word of mouth. Since the store never closed, it was operated in two shifts; 12 Africans from Senegal sewed at a time and rotated. "We were doing butter-soft stuff. Leather was big and customers wanted to match their Timbs," says Haussan. "In the summer, silk and linen were popular. We even did velour trimmed in leather with leather cuffs and collars. Leather was always top choice." Competition existed but for the most part, each competitor had its own niche. B & E Fashions in Queens, for example, was known for the counterfeit Nike velour suits designed by Barry White, who later co-founded Shabazz Brothers Urbanwear (SBU). Haussan says, "We used to make them but I used to send people to Queens to get them 'cause that was our cheapest item and that was like $370. We had so many leather orders that I wouldn't take many orders for those Nike suits." What made Dapper Dan unique from other tailors was his ability to mass-produce his own fabrics donning the trademarks of high-end and luxury designers. "That was like printing money," says Haussan. "The Africans from Senegal are master leather sewers." The turn-around time for a garment depended on several factors: who paid the most and how bad a customer wanted it. An outfit could be made in a few days if a customer paid a premium; otherwise, it took five to seven days to deliver a finished garment. Dapper Dan kept impeccable files of his clients. Stored in thick ledger books, the measurements of custom-ers and their past designs were recorded for future reference.

Over the years, Dapper Dan went from local legend to receiving mainstream notoriety, due in part to MTV coverage, mentions on *Monday Night Football*, and photo shoots in magazines like *Rolling Stone*. The attention was not always favorable, however. Television news cameras put Dapper Dan's store in the spotlight on August 23, 1988.[1] News broke that Tyson and Mitch "Blood" Green had had a street fight in front of the shop around 4:30 A.M. The media began to question why Tyson would be at a tailor shop at that hour, exposing the shop's unusual business practices to the public. Even the *Daily News Record*, the men's fashion bible and trade publication of record at the time, covered the incident two days later with a story titled, "Shoppers treated like champs at Harlem boutique." Tyson, who had visited the Dapper Dan's Boutique that summer morning to obtain a custom $850 leather jacket with the words "Don't Believe the Hype," inadvertently brought attention to the local haberdashery.

Conflicting reports came out from Tyson sucker-punching Green to Green actually provoking the fight. "[Mitch] instigated it cause some-body from the neighborhood must have told him that Mike was there cause Mike had the yellow Bentley parked out front," says Haussan. "Mitch came around on his bike cause the door was locked. He was curs-ing and calling Mike a faggot. Mike was about to leave and Mitch was just waiting up there and got in his face. Mike told him to get out my face and Mike just snuffed him." Green got a broken nose, five stitches, and collected $45,000 in a civil lawsuit for his pain and suffering. The verdict came just three months after Tyson was banned from boxing for the infamous 1997 "bite fight" match when Evander Holyfield lost a piece of his right ear due to Tyson's bizarre biting frenzy.

Associate justice of the U.S. Supreme Court Sonia Sotomayor, then attorney for the private firm Pavia & Harcourt LLP, was no fan of Dapper Dan's Boutique either. In her personal data questionnaire form submitted during her Supreme Court nomination hearings in 2009, she described working for Pavia & Harcourt, which represented Fendi and its national anticounterfeiting program. In 1989, Sotomayor was the attorney representing Fendi, which sued Dapper Dan's Boutique (Fendi S.a.s. Di Paola Fendi e Sorelle v. Dapper Dan's Boutique, 89 Civ. 0477) and the case was presided over by the Hon. Miriam G. Cedarbaum. Dapper Dan never went to court and Sotomayor won on default. As a result, the Fendi merchandise was destroyed. Lawsuits such as this one would eventually drive Dapper Dan to close shop and go underground. The "Black Style Now" fashion exhibit at the Museum of the City of New York, which ran from September 9, 2006 to February 19, 2007, paid homage to Dapper Dan and displayed some of his craftsmanship including a "LV" logo calfskin topcoat and a velour "Nike" team jacket. Dapper Dan, who is close to 70 today, still designs and has been under the radar since his legal woes in the late 1980s. No longer as easily accessible, Dapper Dan's exclusive clients track him down through the code of the streets. As someone who knows him well said, "Those who know, know how to find him. Those who don't, won't."

5001 FLAVORS

Before Guy Wood knew there was such a thing as a stylist, he was doing it. "I used to dress the drug dealers in my neighborhood," recalls Wood, vice president and head designer of 5001 Flavors. "They'd pay me to go downtown and pick out their shoes and outfit for a party. That was 1991, but I had already been dressing people in the community since 1980." Wood would go to 147th Street and Seventh Avenue in Manhattan to get paid by the young hustlers on the corner. "They would ask me to help them put their outfit together," remembers Wood, who was born in the Bronx and raised in Harlem. The clientele also liked the way Wood dressed as he never dressed his age; at 17, Wood was dressing like a number man or dope dealer. He would wear suede-front cardigans and "stuff that our fathers" were wearing. Wood's fashionable sense of style came as early as age 11. His mother, who was a seamstress, would make her son's fashion requests.

"I started telling my mother I want this vest that this guy has on this album cover or I want these pants with the extension. I used to watch the older kids in my neighborhood that were very much into fashion. I would just pick the pieces from what they were doing. My crew was a little younger and I would be the leader and say we have to go get this sweater. We'd have to go to Delancey Street and to Jew Land [in the Bronx] and get these cardigans," Wood remembers.

Shopping for hustlers became Wood's daily grind. "They would take care of me," says Wood, referring to the $200 he would get paid for just going shopping for clothes. At that time, that was considered "big" money. He would also earn himself an outfit. "I would be able to get an outfit and be at the party with them that night, too," Wood says. His outfit—a silk shirt, silk pants, and alligator shoes—would cost him an average of $120. Wood recalls, "I didn't want to stand on the corner and take the risk that these gentlemen were taking, but I liked the stuff they liked, I liked the women they liked, I liked the cars that they had, and I liked the clothes they wore." Seeing the potential of fashion skills, Wood decided to take it to the next level. "A lot of people were approaching me when I'd go to these industry parties," he says. "They liked what I was wearing and asked me where I was getting it from. I would tell them I designed it."

In 1991, Wood enlisted his tailor, Rafael Rosario, who worked out of a tailor shop in the Lower East Side to design clothes for him on the side. On his days off and after work hours, Ralfie, as he was called, made blazers, linen outfits, silk shirts, silk vests, very Versace-ish for Wood. "I convinced him that we could make this a business," Wood says. Becoming friends, he persuaded Ralfie to leave his job to work full-time with him. The two have now been working together for more than 20 years. With a reliable tailor in place, Wood went after customers. Wood, and his then girlfriend of two years and now wife Sharene (Barnett) Wood, formulated the company as they saw a need for custom tailors. "The tastemakers that were coming up like Sean Combs realized that you have to have an image, a story to what are you selling," says Sharene, who met Wood at a Bronx dinner in 1989. "We came into the industry when there was a need for someone to help tell that story."

Wood always knew he wanted to work for himself. "Sharene was just a person that always had my back. I couldn't do it without her and she couldn't do it without me." Wood pitched Sharene his idea while sitting in her Columbia University dorm room; it became a "lightbulb moment." At the time, she was working at a health care management consulting firm full-time and going to school full-time studying sociology. "This was something that kind of came up and I didn't realize how big it could be," Sharene says. Guy Wood could not have launched 5001 Flavors without friend Troy Johnson as well. "He had the gift of gab, he loved the night life, and he would befriend all this artists and sell them the clothes," says Guy. Johnson was given the task of handling sales and became the company's pitchman from inception until 2000, while Guy and Sharene Wood were behind the scenes. Guy focused on design while Sharene handled all the administrative tasks. The company faced obstacles early on. "When we came in to the game, we were going into the record label and they are saying 'why should we hire you guys when Karl Kani and Cross Colours send us boxes of free clothes?' I would say 'well, they send everybody the same box. Your artist is special. When he hits the stage do you want him to have the same outfit that the people in the crowd have?'" Wood remembers that his answer would usually end that discussion.

The company became headquartered in Wood's family-owned Harlem brownstone where the company is still based today. "The room might've been the size of a closet," says Wood, who has since expanded his operation to six tailors and taken a larger space in the house. By 1992, Wood officially incorporated his company after building a healthy clientele of primarily music labels and artists. Among them was Epic artist Eric Gable, who pitched Wood to be his stylist. "I am like 'what's a stylist?' He said 'a guy that shops and is given a budget.' I had been doing that for years. I called it shorty! And that's how it all came to fruition," Wood recalls.

Once Wood landed Gable as a client, he quit his job as an off-track betting teller the same day he collected a check. Gable's outfits consisted of a leather motorcycle vest, jacket, a western shirt in leather, and jeans with leather on the back pockets as well as a few suits. As a thank-you gesture, Gable referred 5001 Flavors to Sony, his first record label client. Uptown Records became another 5001 Flavors coup. "Andre Harrell [founder of Uptown Records] opened the flood gate and it was ridiculous," says Wood. He recalled meeting with Uptown Records' A&R (artists and repertoire) person Jeff Redd and head stylist Sybil Pennix. "I sat down with them and I showed them what I could do," he says. In time, Wood started designing for Uptown artists like Guy and Mary J. Blige. Wood gives lots of credit to Sean "P. Diddy" Combs. "When Puff came in the game, he changed the image of his groups. That was his forte," says Wood. "He tailor-made their music and clothes, and gave each person an image. That's why Uptown [Records] was winning. He was a genius on that aspect. He took Jodeci and gave them their swagger. He gave Mary J. Blige her swagger and Heavy D. He gave everybody their own swagger."

Once Combs was fired from Uptown Records and formed Bad Boy Records in 1993, 5001 Flavors was right along his side for the ride. Wood says, "When Puff got his shot, we were right on with Puff. We did everything for Biggie. We were part of the creative process and part of designing his look." 5001 Flavors designed garments for Biggie (The Notorious B.I.G.) for videos like "Juicy" to "Hypnotized." Wood considered The Notorious B.I.G. a great friend. "He was more than just a client; he was like my partner because I watched him rise from this little guy in personality to become this big mega star. Puff said 'I want to make him not the guy of the corner, the guy that all the guys on the corner work for,'" recalls Wood. Customers for 5001 Flavors then and now come primarily by word of mouth. "It is like a never-ending flow of possible opportunities, so when you do a great job you get great referrals," Sharene Wood says, who also runs the Wood Agency, which represents and manages the careers of stylists. "You are making mini movies so, the visuals are very important and the treatment and you are kind of trying to tell the story."

On a given day, 5001 Flavors could be juggling four to five different projects because they all have different due dates. "You might have one that is due on Friday and it's Wednesday, so then something comes in for today so you got to stop the Friday project and jump on this Wednesday, so there is a lot of jumping around," Sharene says. 5001 Flavors used a variety of fabrics from denim to cashmere silk, leather, and furs. There have been many artists that the company has worked with to include: Prince Markie Dee (formerly of The Fat Boys), Horace Brown, Father MC, Jodeci, Aretha Franklin, Mariah Carey, Jennifer Lopez, Queen Latifah, Nas, Shaquille O'Neal, Will Smith, Timbaland, Usher, Jadakiss, and Fat Joe. Its notable designs include a leather one-piece gas station suit that Biggie wore in a 112 video and on the cover of *The Source*; it was also replicated for the *Notorious* biopic film.

Other designs include a leather baseball shirt for Biggie in the "Juicy" video and the yellow double-breasted suit in "Hypnotized" video, a leather one-piece mechanic suit worn by Sean Combs that said "King of New York" for his "Been Around the World" video, a varsity jacket for Chris Brown and a Boy Scout-inspired shirt for the cover of *Vibe*, a snake-skin jacket and zebra print pants for R. Kelly's "I Believe I Can Fly" video. "I don't charge for their status, I don't charge for their size the jacket is the jacket," noted Guy Wood. "I don't charge if this guy

The Notorious B.I.G. wearing 5001 Flavors. (Chi Modu)

has forty thousand records sold or this guy has four records sold." Clothing budgets vary widely and can range from $300 to $150,000.

The company has also had the opportunity to design a sweatsuit with rhinestones for the Victoria's Secret catalogue. Today, 5001 Flavors' clients have expanded to include comedians, television and radio personalities, athletes, pastors, and people in the Harlem community.

JACOB THE JEWELER

Custom jewelry has always played a role in the hip hop culture. In the early days of hip hop, it was all about yellow-gold name finger rings, bamboo name earrings, name-plate chains, and gold caps like those donned by

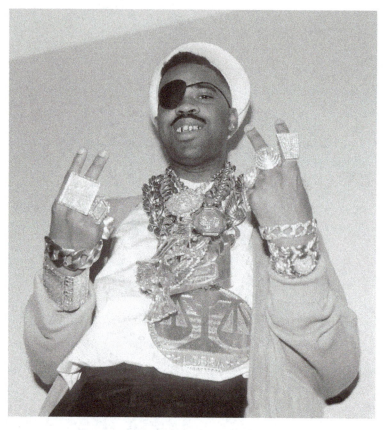

Slick Rick, one of the original kings of custom bling. (© Ernie Paniccioli. Used by permission.)

Jacob Arabo and Pharrell. (Djamilla Rosa Cochran/WireImage /Getty Images)

Slick Rick. Before Jacob "the Jeweler" Arabov, there was the Ecuadorian Tito Caicedo, known as "Tito the Jeweler" or "Manny" who serviced the drug world with his custom pieces in the 1970s and early 1980s.

In the mid-1990s, when we saw a shift to platinum jewelry and a "Girl's Best Friend" as Jay-Z referred to diamonds, it was Arabov who became the go-to guy. His first hip hop client was Biggie by way of his then-girlfriend and later wife, R&B singer Faith Evans. From then on, his couture jewelry house became a staple for any hip hop artist looking for customized bling. Best of all, Arabov became a favorite for those who preferred to buy jewelry with large sums of cash with no questions asked. Separating himself from his competition in Manhattan's Diamond District, the Uzbekistan-born Arabov strategically focused on the music and entertainment field for clientele after rappers bragged about his lavish diamond-encrusted "Five Time Zone" watches, crosses, and Jesus pendants in a variety of colored diamonds. His hip hop clientele reads like a who's who list of the hip hop elite: Jay-Z, Pharrell, Lil' Kim, Busta Rhymes, Nelly, Wyclef Jean, Nas, Tyrese, 50 Cent, Tyson Beckford, Jennifer Lopez, and Beyoncé Knowles, to name a few. NBA athletes from Michael Jordan to LeBron James have also been fans to the NBA itself which signed a licensing deal with Arabov in 2004 to create his famous "Five Time Zone" watches for all 29 NBA teams.

Unfortunately, Arabov tainted his image in 2006 when he was arrested at his Jacob & Co. flagship at 48 East 57th Street, and initially charged with conspiracy to launder money in connection with the Detroit Black Mafia Family drug ring. A 2007 plea deal resulted in the money laundering charges being dropped; however, Arabov plead guilty to falsifying records and lying to federal investigators. He was sentenced to 30 months and was released from federal prison in September 2010. Arabov has kept a low profile since then, but this surely has not deterred hip hop stars or any celebrity from desiring his exquisite jewels.

Like Arabov's jewels, hip hop aficionados will continue to seek styles that are rare, hard to find, or one-of-a-kind. In essence, this is what hip hop is all about. Celebrity clothing lines, which became a subcategory of urban fashion in the late 1990s, attempted to have a similar caché. Once considered a novelty, now they have become a necessity for every rapper and celebrity to have in order to get the most of their brand equity.

CHAPTER 7
Hip Hopreneurs

The fashion designers that were coming up in the early '90s reminded me of the hip hop artists coming up in the early '80s. It was the same feeling I got. I was whipped. I couldn't wait to see what the next design was gonna be.

—Veejay Ralph McDaniels

Hip hop created the most effective movement for the business advancement of black and Latino men and women in the history of the music industry. And the fashion industry would see a parallel advancement in terms of the ownership of our cultural expression called hip hop. Thanks to individuals like Clarence Avant (the Godfather of black music), Russell Simmons and others were put in ownership positions of our music. In fashion, we had mentors like Dapper Dan on the creative side, but there was no established black and Latino power or financial base, so we came to blaze a new trail. It happened somewhat organically and our fashion grew to become the multibillion dollar urbanwear industry. There were predominately three distinct types of fashion urban entrepreneurs. First, there were the people who grew up in hip hop culture, who, with no formal fashion training and no financial backing, founded brands. This type of entrepreneur was common in the late 1980s. Second, there were those who grew up around hip hop culture, had some fashion training, and had the ability to find financial backers. We saw more of this type of entrepreneur in the mid-1990s.

Third, there were those people who were inspired and influenced by hip hop who wanted to jump on the trend and had the infrastructure and resources in place. It was simply a matter of building the proper team to promote a credible urban brand. In this case, the idea for the hip hop brand or attaining an urban demographic came from a manufacturer rather than vice versa. "Even the companies that weren't by us had to put one of us in front of the [trade show] booth, employ us," says Ralph Reynolds, vice president and creative director of the Rp55 Group. "We needed to wear the uniform of hip hop. A lot of first stuff designed was crazy—oversized, weird designs, and really out there. We didn't know how to do this beyond T-shirts. The customer was so ready and thirsty that they wore the brands. Then the flood gates open. The black guy got in front of booth and began doing business."

The early 1990s marked the explosion of hip hop apparel brands and a push towards department store distribution, which targeted a predominately male audience. It also became the decade of the African American urban fashion designer and entrepreneur.[1] The fashion industry had not seen such a wave since the days of Patrick Kelly, Willi Smith, and Stephen Burrows. The West Coast, predominately Seattle and parts of California, had that market on lock with surf, skate, and casual sportswear looks in the 1980s. Designing for the category of young men's, as the market was known, brought the youth fashion pendulum back to the East Coast. Maurice Malone and Pelle Pelle hailed from Detroit while Mecca USA, FUBU, Triple 5 Soul, PNB Nation, School of Hard Knocks, and Shabazz Brothers Urbanwear (SBU) had roots in the "Big Apple." Ecko Unlimited came out of New Jersey and Rp55 represented Virginia. These brands would differ from the more "established guard" of Tommy Hilfiger, Nautica, and Ralph Lauren Polo, in that these new brands marketed themselves with a direct association to hip hop as opposed to being influenced by the predominant music genre of the times. Some consumers of color would hold these hip hop brands in higher regard because of the connotation of being black-owned and operated. These new brands provided youth consumers with an alternative to the status quo and made the choice to give their dollars to the brands that represented them. "The fashion designers that were coming up in the early '90s reminded me of the hip hop artists coming up in the early '80s," remembers Veejay Ralph McDaniels and former owner of the Brooklyn-based specialty store Uncle Ralph's Urban Gear. "It was the same feeling I got. I was whipped. I couldn't wait to see what the next design was gonna be."

MAURICE MALONE

Originally, Maurice Malone wanted to be a special effects artist. "I did a claymation movie before Celebrity Death Match for friends for entertainment," remembers Malone, who moved from his hometown of Detroit to Los Angeles to attend community college. Homesick on holiday break, Malone visited his mother back in Detroit and never returned to Los Angeles. "I had asked my mother to get me a car. She promised me if I came home on holiday break, she'd get me a car. I didn't get a car so I didn't go back," Malone says. Out of boredom in 1984, he designed and made a hat that he had seen on MTV. From that point, Malone started making patterns and experimenting with different fabrics, including leather. Discovering that he had to be a registered company to purchase expensive fabrics, Malone decided to become a registered business in order to be able to buy his goods. "It was only $1 to get a license for a state business license," he says. This was the beginning of Malone's fashion entrepreneurial endeavors. For the next five years, he sold hats under the name Hardwear by Maurice Malone.

Malone started making hats for friends and eventually had a steady clientele who would buy hats from his basement. At 19 years old, he was making more than $100 a week. "It was better than working at Burger King," he admits. From designing hats, Malone expanded into designing long shirts that looked more like lab gowns. "I didn't know how to sew so I went to the library," he says, in order to teach himself the skill. He later launched Label X by Maurice Malone, which lasted for about a year. By this time, he had relocated to New York to be closer to the clothing industry. "I couldn't find people who could sew and make clothes in Detroit, they were really messing up my production," Malone says. "My friend from high school, his sister knew a guy who was in the fabric business. She introduced him to me and wanted to go into business." They did and this is how Malone expanded his designs to include denim. "I had this idea from going to nightclubs," Malone recalls. "My roommates were a deejay and bartender at nightclubs. I would see Kid Capri deejaying at Powerhouse, and KRS-1 and Public Enemy walking around. I would only see them on TV when I was in Detroit. I told my partner if I can get some extra clothes made, I can give it to these guys and they will wear it."

However, Malone's partner was not into giving anything away for free. Two weeks later, Malone received a telephone call from a friend who owned a store in Detroit. "She called me and said 'Have you ever heard of this brand called Cross Colours? They are starting to get a pretty good buzz and it reminds me of you.' That was the first time I heard the name," says Malone. He then noticed the brand on the television show, *Fresh Prince of Bel-Air.* A few months later, Malone wanted to call his jean line, Maurice Malone—Blue Jeans for Your Ass. "He [the partner] shot that down. It was at that point I was like I am never going to get anywhere with this guy. I decided to move back to Detroit," remembers Malone. He then started sewing clothes and found a little retail store that allowed him to rent their sewing machines in their basement. Malone would pay the store everyday to use the machines by the hour. He would then sell his clothes at a table, and at his own parties. "I got inspired by the New York hip hop parties," Malone says. "I was emulating the parties were like what I saw at Powerhouse. We started doing these parties that inspired the *8 Mile* movie."

Malone called his parties "The Rhythm Kitchen" and he used them as a vehicle to promote and sell his clothes. He also started doing his Blue Jeans for Your Ass label on his own. From the proceeds from the parties and clothing sales, Malone saved enough to open a store in 1993 called The Hip Hop Shop. The store was on Seven Mile between Southfield and Greenfield Roads in Detroit. Malone hosted freestyle battles just like the ones featured in the Eminem film, *8 Mile.* Every Saturday evening, The Hip Hop Shop would push the clothes to the side and host an open mike night from 5:00 to 7:00 P.M. Malone remembers, "We never had to worry about stealing because it was a community spot." Among the attendees would be members of the rap group D12, Eminem, and his original deejay, Proof who was one of the store managers. The store would stay open until 1997.

Malone met Ertis Pratt, a shoe salesman who would become his company president, at a concert held in Orchestra Hall in downtown Detroit in 1989. Pratt had seen people in Detroit wearing "Blue Jeans for Your Ass" T-shirts. "I looked in the room and at least 10 percent of the kids were wearing Maurice Malone. I wanted to know who this Maurice Malone was," Pratt remembers. He would eventually meet Malone and work with him for the next 10 years. The two worked out of a bedroom in the house of Malone's mother, located on the west side of Detroit on Hawthorne Street and Joy Road. "We ended up growing the business to over $2 million by the time we ended up moving from the bedroom of his mother's house," recalls Pratt. Over the years, Malone would find several investors and financial backers. "My best way to describe the investors in the early stages of hip hop clothing was like the music industry," says Pratt. "Aspiring musicians like designers were told by investors they'll be taught everything they need to know in the business, yet many were stealing them blind." So Malone went through stages of bad investments, got ripped off by the investors and later sued them, but eventually grew a very successful business. While Malone considered himself a high-end designer, where he saw the most success came from his urban designs. He admits, "That's what I got to be known for. It was a lot easier to communicate and get respect." MTV became a supportive force for hip hop designers like Malone who remembers that "It [MTV] was also the biggest hindrance for someone who likes to design. I didn't want to rely on celebrities to make me or break me. Before MTV was blowing logos, if you had a shirt on that was the hottest thing, you would be sure that everyone was going to order it. If you could get something on an artist it would get to the point where that would drive sales."

Malone became known for his signature designs such as his logo-cuff jeans, stash-pocket jeans, his "come equipped" underwear that stashed condoms, and hockey jerseys which had sayings such as New York Ballers, Team Nubian, and Newark Bricks. He says that "we just took people's areas or areas that people were from to give them pride for their area." Malone was also among the first urban brands to do the 7th on Sixth fashion shows in New York City; "It was something I always dreamed of doing," he says. This runway show became a showcase for Malone's urban sportswear, but also served as a platform to show women and his suits, of which he was most proud because he owned it 100 percent of his suit company. Unfortunately, Malone became directly affected by the aftermath of the events of 9/11. "Everyone canceled their orders after 9/11 because everyone got nervous. I got stuck with this entire inventory. I was on loan from the bank because I ran a lot of advertisements in magazines. I spent all this money and I went in using my own money instead of using the banks. I didn't anticipate for a loss my first season," he remembers of this sad time.

Malone and his company struggled for the next few years; he remained in business, but did not have the earlier financing. Simultaneously, he started a record label called Hostile Takeover, similar to what other hip hop apparel labels like FUBU did at the time. He ran the record label from 1994 until 2004, but that venture also proved unsuccessful. Malone admits, "I know why all the people in the music business go into the clothing business because the music business is tricky. It's hard to make money there." By 2006, Malone stopped running his own companies and began freelance design and production for various brands including 50 Cent's G-Unit, Division E, Lord and Legends, FUBU, and Master P. when he was trying to come out with an apparel line. He continues to freelance and consult in the apparel industry while working on a new suit collection of his own. "It's a cross between G-star and Diesel, but take away graphics and logos," Malone says.

SHABAZZ BROTHERS URBANWEAR (SBU)

In 1978, G. Shabazz Fuller worked with his homeboy's uncle's record store called Sikulu's Record Shack on 125th Street in Harlem, across from AJ Lester, Floresheim Shoes, and the Apollo Theater (which was closed at the time). It gave Fuller access to all the latest beats and being the first around his way to wear the freshest fashion pieces. Fuller considered himself to be a music and fashion addict growing up in Westchester County; any jam he heard about, he had to be there. The same applied to fashion; "I had to be the first with it around my way," Fuller says. In the tradition of talented artists before like Langston Hughes, Zora Neal Hurston, and even Frank Lucas, Fuller became drawn to Harlem to pursue his fortune. "I decided to capitalize on my discriminating eye by identifying what's hot, sourcing it, and selling it to the community," he says, "That meant hooking up with Delancey Street sheepskin dealers and also linking with the exclusive North American importers of Cazal frames, selling to the community around the boroughs and D.C."

After being introduced to "wholesaling" (hustling) items from the Garment District in the early 1980s on 125th Street in Harlem, Fordham Road in the Bronx, Jamaica Avenue in Queens, and Fulton Street in Brooklyn and being influenced by the Five-Percent Nation (of Islam) to "do for self and kind" (black, Native American, Latino) for economic growth and advancement, Fuller launched his own apparel brand. He began selling and later, designing furs around 1984 and later worked with Melquan Entertainment as co-manager for hip hop talent from 1986 to 1991, launching and managing the careers of RZA and GZA of the Wu-Tang Clan. Fuller knew Melquan from attending Howard University and he had started the label with his father. "We learned in music—furs give you entrée to lot of people," Fuller says. For example, Shabazz Furs' celebrity clientele included Quincy Jones, Big Daddy Kane, and Charles Oakley.

Fuller first met his eventual business partner Barry White (no relation to the singer) selling furs in 1984. White had designed the velour warm-up with the leather Nike swoosh worn by the rappers Rob Base and Rakim. Under the influence of Dapper Dan, White created knock-offs like the velour warm-up suits with a leather Nike swoosh. As hip hop videos travelled nationwide, the fashions became immediately in demand as much as the music, if not more. "It's because those bags Gucci, MCM, were all the rage. That's why when he made the outfits out of [the fabrics], it became a panic. I would open my trunk and could stop traffic," Fuller remembers. He was selling the knockoff goods at about $250 to primarily a male customer base that included street fast-money dudes and rappers. "RZA and I sold the suits to the fast money cats on Staten Island who would later become the Clan," says Fuller. "From traveling with music, I knew these looks were in strong demand nationwide by the late 1980s."

Fuller convinced White to collaborate and launch Shabazz Brothers Urbanwear in 1991, particularly after he showed White how Cross Colors was doing well with some of his "urbanwear" looks. White was the perfect partner for Fuller because he had connections and experience He had owned a store called B & E Fashions (Barry White and Eric Kelly) located inside the Jamaica Colosseum Mall in Queens in the 1980s. B & E produced custom T-shirts and velour warm-up suits upstairs from the Mighty Shirt Kings, the graffiti artists who were known for their caricatures and Eddie Gold Cap, who did all of the custom gold teeth for celebrities. Fuller met White while he worked with RZA from the Wu-Tang Clan. "He would sell wholesale to me and RZA," says Fuller. "Barry also knew how to manufacture materials like Louis Vuitton and Gucci. He would supply April [Walker]." After closing B & E, White was left with his store in New Haven. Haussan, a mutual friend who worked for Dapper Dan, had two stores in Baltimore. At the end of 1991, Fuller, White, and Haussan all decided to come together to launch SBU.

At first, they wanted to formulate a line with the legendary Dapper Dan. "Dap was the man," says Fuller. "The idea was to get Dap out there and help Dap start a line. We talked to Dap, he was like 'yeah.' From about '90 to '91, Dap kept bullshitting us so we were like let's not wait for Dap and we decided to do our own thing." The three came up with the name Shabazz Brothers Urbanwear (SBU). "'Shabazz' means 'original' and we are brothers, although not biological brothers, in originality," says Fuller. "That's where the concept came from. Barry had coined that word 'urbanwear' like way back in like '86. So from that Barry's word 'urbanwear,' we came up with the concept of Shabazz Brothers Urbanwear." Fuller and White added Haussan to their team because he had worked for Dapper Dan and became the "glue that held everything together." Haussan was never given one specific task, but handled everything from sourcing, merchandising, sales, promotions, and events.

Fuller and White tested the market for the potential viability of their brand. They did a small run of outerwear in a quilted field jacket design and labelled half of the run "Timberland" and the other half "Shabazz Brothers." When they put them both out on a table on 125th Street in Harlem, customers snapped up the Shabazz Brothers' jacket and left the identical Timberland design. "That's when we knew it was time to go hard with our new brand," says Fuller.

Fuller and White started with 10-dozen T-shirts; they later expanded to include Mad Flava Hats and sold their goods primarily on 125th Street, between Seventh and Eighth Avenues in front of a Woolworth's that is now Champs. "We had our table set up until [Mayor Rudolph W.] Giuliani ran us off in '94," remembered Fuller. "We had own area, our own spot. We had organization and protocol of our own. Everybody recognized who was who and you had to get your neighbor's permission." Fuller and White predominately sold airbrushed and printed T-shirts, both retail and wholesale to other street vendors and to mom-and-pop retailers. "From sourcing unique items, you get a feel for what the market is missing and potential opportunities," says Fuller. One day, Sharon Pattishaw and Damaris Vega-Bennett, then buyers from New York's specialty chain Dr. Jay's, hunted them down and found them. Soon, Shabazz Brothers Urbanwear landed a $12,000 account and Dr. Jay's became SBU's first retail account.

The rest, as they say, is history. Little by little the brand of Shabazz Brothers Urbanwear began to grow. In 1993 and 1994, Fuller booked talent for the Black Expo USA and in exchange, was given a promotional booth to promote and sell Shabazz Brothers Urbanwear. Between 1993 and 1994, with the Expo alone, Fuller and White promoted in the black communities of most major markets nationwide, including New York, Philadelphia, Baltimore, Washington, D.C., Atlanta, Houston, Chicago, Detroit, Los Angeles, and Miami. Utilizing his street promotions team from Melquan Entertainment, and relationships at radio and retail around the country, Fuller marketed his brand like a hip hop recording act—with stickers, snipes (guerilla marketing campaigns), posters, radio interviews, and giveaways. "There were no street teams in the fashion industry before this," says Fuller. Shabazz Brothers Urbanwear got the attention of the brand management team of Sprite and Coca-Cola USA in 1997. Sprite brand managers felt SBU's "commitment to originality, as expressed in the '4 LIFE' logo, most closely reflected Sprite's message to 'Obey Your Thirst,' " and selected SBU to partner in its 1997–1998 multimillion dollar "Under The Cap" promotion. This promotion was a win-win situation for both brands, increasing Sprite sales 31 percent during the promotion and giving SBU tremendous exposure via radio and TV commercials, giveaways, and appearances.[2]

Shabazz Brothers Urbanwear never received any backing until 1999 and Fuller admits he made mistakes along the way with his brand. While the brand did $10 million in sales, it really had no real operating money. "We weren't in position to compete and needed capital to grow the business," Fuller says. In 1999, SBU was engaged by a licensee of Shaquille O'Neal's TWIsM brand to oversee the brand management responsibilities, while partnering in the expansion of the SBU brand. This partnership, though showing great potential, was structurally flawed and SBU did not match its prior brand-building success. After dissolving the TWIsM partnership, SBU created Shabazz Design Lab to consult apparel companies looking to compete in the young men's and/or women's contemporary streetwear arena. In 2000, the company was approached by Cullen, a cashmere resource for the better goods market, to oversee the launch and brand management of its new venture, "Xctasy Patrick Clark." This brand, built around couture designer Patrick Robinson (who later served from 2007 to 2011 as executive vice president of Gap Global Design for Adult and Body), was a directional denim collection that consisted of young men's and women's product targeted at the better goods market.[3] Shabazz Design Lab team developed all brand identity elements, brand presentation book, media kits, and promotional materials. While the collection was initially well received and placed in Saks, Bergdorf Goodman, and Nordstrom, as well as better specialty stores including Atrium, Lisa Kline, and Fred Segal, the brand never hit in the urban market. Fuller and White ended up sitting on their brand trademark from 2000 on and moved into the private sector. Presently, they supply stores with private label and urban novelty T-shirts and closeout goods.

PNB NATION CLOTHING CO.

PNB Nation Clothing Co. made a name for themselves as the socially conscious brand famous for T-shirt sayings like "People Never Believe," "Please No Bacon," "Police Need Backup," "Proud Nubian Brothers," "Puerto Ricans 'N Blacks," and "Post No Bills." Ahead of its time, PNB not only set the blueprint for statement T-shirts, but embraced multiculturalism and educating their customers. "PNB was really unique because no one knew what PNB meant," says fashion expert Emil Wilbekin. "They tied cultural history to their clothing line. You would buy a T-shirt that would say '1935' and they would have a hang-tag that would tell you some important fact, so it was a history lesson and art lesson all in one."

The idea was originally conceived by graffiti artists Roger "Brue" McHayle and James "Bluster" Alicea at their high school lunch table in 1987 as a vehicle for self-expression. They turned to clothing and selected the name PNB from seeing construction sites all over New York City and reinterpreted its meaning. McHayle, who is Chinese and Jamaican from Brooklyn, and Alicea, who is Puerto Rican from the Lower East Side, both attended the High School of Art and Design. The duo would practice bombing trains and painting walls throughout Brooklyn and Manhattan. Upon graduating high school, McHayle attended Cooper Union where he studied fine arts and minored in photography. It was at Cooper Union where McHayle met Kahlil "Zulu"

Williams who is Japanese and black from Harlem. Williams eventually joined PNB and brought in his good friend Isaac "West" Rubenstein who is Jewish from the Upper West Side of Manhattan. McHayle would add his friend Sung Choi, who is Korean, as the last founding member. "The commonality there was that they were all graffiti artists. They took that art form and applied to garments," says Shara McHayle, who joined the company as partner in 1995 and headed sales and marketing. Pooling $100 from each partner, PNB then purchased blanks and screen-printed T-shirts at Cooper Union, where McHayle and Williams were students.

McHayle's experience as an intern while in college landed him free office space at Woo Art, a video production studio. He brought the concept of PNB to the owners in hopes of renting out space. It was literally the size of a cubicle at 133 West 19th Street, on the third floor. From 1991 to 1994, PNB produced T-shirts and a few pieces of garments. They put them in a garbage bag and sold it to Cooper Union, becoming PNB's first retail account. In 1995, as sales reached $150,000, McHayle had his 24-year-old sister Shara join the company. Initially working for free, Shara would eventually be named partner for her contribution to the growing company (Alicea and Choi were no longer with the company at this point). PNB secured its trademark and relocated to bigger space on the second floor of 133 West 19th Street. Working as an automobile insurance adjuster and going to school at the Fashion Institute of Technology (FIT), Shara decided to quit her job to work to join PNB. "I was pursuing my career goals and taking care of my family," she recalled, now owner of a marketing and management company, Bounce Media and who also has a lifestyle brand in development. "Early on, I had a mid-life crisis since I had decided to have kids really young. I believed in the social commentary aspect of the brand and believed in it that much that I came on board to work for free." With limited marketing dollars, she turned to pushing public relations tactics as a way to build the brand. Shara strategically did product placement and publicity in consumer and trade publications such as *Rap Pages*, *The Source*, *Stress*, *Vibe*, *MR*, *DNR*, and *Sportswear International*.

PNB also struck a chord with hip hop artists like Wu-Tang Clan's Method Man, Snoop Dogg, Eminem, and Lauryn Hill, as well as the underground hip hop scene. The company also found success with product placement in films such as *Friday* and Spike Lee's *Bamboozled* and *Clockers* as well as television shows such as *Martin, The Wayan*

Brothers, Living Single, The Jamie Foxx Show, New York Undercover, The Dave Chappelle Show, and *90210*. "We were rooted in hip hop and had a social point of view," says McHayle. PNB also never forgot about the importance of giving back to the community; it held sample sales in Harlem, for example. "Social awareness played into our marketing efforts even if it was not profitable," says McHayle. "We would sell samples in communities that didn't have money."

While PNB did a great job developing its brand awareness, it struggled without an infusion of capital. Remaining independent presented the company with challenges fulfilling orders by not having backroom support, that is being able to open letters of credit with factories. In 1998, PNB began conversations with Dr. Jay's, a young men's specialty chain based in New York as a potential investor. The buyer for Dr. Jay's, Damaris Vega-Bennett, introduced PNB to George Feldenkreis, CEO of the Miami-based Supreme International. "We had brand awareness and orders. While we had those things, we struggled to fulfill to deliver on time," notes McHayle. PNB had reported sales of $2.9 million when it signed a three-year licensing deal with Supreme International to source and sell PNB. Unfortunately, while the brand grew to $14 million in sales, the relationship did not work. "We were arrogant and didn't know the business," admitted McHayle. "We had to educate them (Supreme International) and they had to educate us." PNB then went on to sign a licensing deal with International News in 2001. At the end of the agreement in 2004, PNB was sold to American Dream Team Network (ADTN) 9. At that point, the remaining members of the original team parted ways. Brue McHayle relocated to Portland to work for Nike; Rubenstein headed to Supreme International; Williams became the design director at American Rag for Macy's; Alicea went on to design for Rocawear; and Choi founded CLAE footwear.

AKADEMIKS

Brothers Donwan and Emmett Harrell are not your typical fashion entrepreneurs. From Robert Stock, Joseph Abboud, Donna Karan, and Nike, Donwan Harrell has always been at the forefront of fashion design. The same can be said for his brother Emmett, whose past design experience included head designer and creative director of

Mecca USA and creative director of Phat Farm before launching Akademiks in 1999.

During his five-year tenure at Nike working out of its Hong Kong offices, Donwan would eventually become homesick, so he began to explore his options back in the United States. He eventually moved to the New York as design director at Mecca USA. In March 1999, both brothers left Mecca USA to join its competitor, Phat Farm. However, they really were destined for their own brand. The Virginia natives had identified a loop in the urban streetwear category; both wanted to develop a bridge brand that would bring together the skate and urban markets. A meeting in 1999 with Elliot Betesh, owner of the famous New York specialty chain Dr. Jay's, would prove successful. In one day, a deal was signed and the brothers struck a partnership with Betesh and Oved Apparel forming Kemistre 8, the parent company to Akademiks. After looking at over 200 possible names, Akademiks was chosen as the idea was to educate the consumer about fashion.

The new brand focused on what the brothers did best—quality design and fabrications. Over the years, Akademiks has utilized clever marketing campaigns that, at times, have been socially conscious and at other times, controversial. In March 2000, Akademiks developed an ad in response to the "not guilty" verdict handed down on February 25, 2000 to the four plainclothes New York City police officers who shot 41 times and killed Amadou Diallo, the 23-year-old unarmed Guinean immigrant in the vestibule of his Soundview apartment building in the Bronx. The ad displayed the words "41 shots" and displayed 19 bullet holes as a reminder of the tragedy that occurred on February 4, 1999. The tagline read "In pursuit of truth, no matter how bitter it may be. Rest in peace."

Three months later, Akademiks debuted five key philosophies in its consumer ads: wisdom, courage, knowledge, strength, and leadership. In March 2001, the company launched a celebrity crossmarketing campaign with DJ Clue and the rapper Fabulous. Four years later, Akademiks found itself in controversy as its sexy model posed in its "Read Books, Get Brain (slang for oral sex)" ads that were banned from New York MTA buses. In the fall of 2010, the company launched the Ultimate 10 Tour to celebrate its 10-year anniversary with a number of high profile personalities from sports, music, and entertainment.

Today, as a multimillion company, Akademiks produces several brand spin-offs including Prps in 2004 and Stash House in 2006.

THE STORY OF MECCA USA

"I was that urban kid that lived outside of the mecca," says Tony Shellman, one of the founders of Mecca USA. "I was watching the mecca on TV—on *Video Music Box* with Ralph McDaniels, and whatever video station I could get on my little cable box in Seattle, Washington in 1981," he recalls. At the time, Shellman could not get any further away from the mecca than he was, but he eventually moved to the mecca of New York City via the young men's clothing business. He was exposed to the fashion industry through retail and living in Seattle, where the young men's business prospered. His first job was working at Nordstrom's in the children's clothing department at age 16. Shellman then switched his high-class job at Nordstrom's for a chic gig at Zebra Club, a trendy specialty store that carried all the popular brands at that time like Generra, Gotcha, Sha Safari, Inc., Code Blue, and B.U.M. Equipment. It was there that he met the late Michael Alesko, owner of Zebra Club and International News (with Amit and Raj Shah), all of whom would back the Mecca brand. Shellman moved to New York in 1989 to study marketing at the Parsons School of Design and worked simultaneously for International News. He would eventually work briefly for Cross Colours and Walker Wear until one day in July 1994, when he pitched his idea for an urban clothing label to his boss Evan Davis in Pronto Pizza at the corner of 42nd and Sixth Avenues to discuss what became Mecca USA.

Shellman enlisted his dear friend and college roommate Lando Felix to develop presentation boards for the original Mecca concept. Felix, a Filipino American, was raised in central Seattle, a multicultural neighborhood made up of black, white, and Asian families. Felix's family resided on the black side of the city. "The music that we listened to at that time was kind of segregated. You either listened to the rock radio station or soul and R&B. There wasn't a rap radio station at that time," says Felix, who, as one of seven children, naturally listened to his brothers' record collections. Coming from a small town, Felix experienced hip hop through media. "The first time we heard Rappers

Delight was on the radio waves and there was a pioneering Filipino deejay Nastiness and he teamed up with a local deejay named Anthony Ray, whose rapping name was Sir Mix-a-Lot. They used to deejay parties at The Boys Club. That was our version of 'doing it in the park' like the New Yorkers," Felix remembers.

The hip hop phenomenon influenced Felix on the artistic side. Admittedly, he was not a great b-boy dancer and as it was too expensive to buy deejay equipment, Felix leaned towards graffiti. "It was easier to do the art thing," says Felix, who at an early age knew he wanted to relocate to New York. To master his craft, he studied at Parsons School of Design and took on various apparel jobs including working as a buyer for Canal Jean Co. and designing for D-Lo. "Tony [Shellman] had a meeting on Thursday and I helped him put together illustration boards," recalled Felix. "I called in sick Monday and Tuesday to help put those boards together. Tony got on a plane [to Seattle] on Wednesday, presented on Thursday, and told me they wanted to hire me Friday and send me to Hong Kong to start making samples." Felix was the middle of designing the spring collection for D-Lo, he worked all weekend, but that Thursday he turned in his resignation. Felix says, "[My boss] felt betrayed. He told me to take the day off and think about it. That Friday and Saturday I worked all day and put together a spring collection for him. I slid the keys and all the tech packs for spring collection under their office doors."

Later that week, Felix hopped on a plane to Hong Kong to start the Mecca project. "We worked on our initial handshake deal with International News," says Felix. "It was easy because Mike [Alesko] knew us personally and practically raised us in the industry. He completely felt this and he was looking for something. He knew this grunge look was dying and people were not just going to buy plaid shirts for ever. He wanted to get his finger on the pulse and he put us on." Not able to get samples ready on time for the August MAGIC show, Shellman and Felix flipped it around and made it an opportunity. They called exclusive buyers straight to their apartment at 242 West 30th Street; apartment 2B became the first offices of Mecca USA. The line broke in October 1994. "We made it a cool thing and it came off as more organic. Two guys launching a brand out of their apartment, but little did they know that we had a multimillion dollar brand behind us. Internally, we were running like IBM, but externally we looked otherwise. We knew we could play a public relations story about making it in New York," Felix says.

Key product placement in places like *The Source* magazine helped the brand gain notoriety such as Mecca's soccer jerseys in an editorial featuring the Alcoholics and in a Biggie's (The Notorious B.I.G.) Big Poppa video. Felix says, "We had one sample line and I was told go to go to Nell's and only give out clothes to Puff [P. Diddy] or Groovey Lew. I was given a big bag of samples. I remember getting yelled at cause there was a cigarette burn in one of the samples. It was fine once the video hit because now buyers were calling us." Felix's design instincts drew him to develop the jerseys.

> We were just looking how can we twist what was going on in the streets. At that time, people were rocking hockey jerseys. We saw basically cats Timbs, baggy jeans but then they were throwing on some kind of athletic-type jersey. Cats don't play soccer in the hood so let's start soccer jerseys cause they are bright and then having the opportunity to travel to Europe where we saw stores dedicated to soccer. Sports and colors just make sense.

Mecca got its inspiration from the Nigerian soccer team. "We came up with all kind of names," says Shellman, who had an industrious and creative mind and the late Alesko's full support. The Seattle-based International News was under the helm of Alesko until his untimely death in 1998. "Mecca kept sticking because New York is the mecca of fashion," notes Shellman.

Mecca USA (United Sports Apparel) was launched in spring 1994. Shellman wanted to break away from the confining labels of urban and hip hop by focusing on quality production, the use of innovative fabrics and washes, and attention to detail. He was influenced by everything from footwear to international cultures, lifestyles, and trends. Mecca targeted 15- to 35-year-old male and female urban professionals by focusing on exclusive specialty stores throughout the country, including Fred Segal, Zebra Club, Lark Stores, The Buckle, Transit/Active Wearhouse, Up Against the Wall, and Dr. Jay's. In addition, the brand was sold to department stores such as Bloomingdales, Macy's East & West, and Filene's. Internationally, it had product in Toronto, London, Paris, Milan, Amsterdam, Berlin, Tokyo, and Hong

Kong. Mecca became known for Mecca DNM which is its denim-based line of clothing. In fall 1997, it introduced The New Frontier ad campaign, based on Nat Love, the first black cowboy. Focusing heavily on denim product, the brand continues to offer a wide assortment of casual sportswear.

RP55 GROUP

Entrepreneur Ralph Reynolds was a graffiti artist and oil painter before trying his hand at making clothes. In his early twenties, Reynolds decided that he needed to learn how to do T-shirts. "I made $850," he recalled. "I pretty quickly stopped painting in 1983 and began hustling T-shirts in the streets." Reynolds sold T-shirts for a few years. At first, he put his art on T-shirts but that did not sell. Figuring out what the demand was on the street, Reynolds turned to developing T-shirts about hip hop culture. He created b-boy shirts and New York T-shirts and sold them in Greenwich Village by Washington Square Park.

Born and raised in Uptown Manhattan, Reynolds went from hustling to doing drugs and ended up in Virginia Beach with 47 cents to his name in 1989. He hustled his way back up and started doing T-shirts again and eventually, working at a store called Deuce in Norfolk, Virginia. Reynolds took the job on the condition that the owners would help finance his T-shirt company. Two years later and no backing had been received, so Reynolds decided to look elsewhere. Ron Perry, his eventual partner, sold T-shirts from Washington, D.C. Reynolds recalls, "We started Bigs World—born in a ghetto store. They were hip hop street shirts. There was a T-shirts' fashion war in D.C. Everybody was doing shirts of all kind. We started two brands—Rmark—that's me Ralph Mark Gilbert Reynolds and then RP55. His name is Ron Perry and he was born in 1955. I did one T-shirt, RP55 go hard and it exploded. We kept doing more RP55 shirts until it became all we did."

Reynolds left the store Deuce and became partners with Perry in 1993. At the time, Reynolds was happy if he could make $500 weekly. As the demand for his product grew, Reynolds realized that he needed backing. He met his partners in 1994 at a NAMSB trade show in New York and has been with them (George Metzger and Mike Shckot) ever since. In

1996, Perry left the company. The business that started out of a 4,500-square-foot warehouse is now located in a 116,000-square-foot facility in Virginia Beach. Reynolds stopped making RP55 in 1999 and was behind the Azzure brand for nine years before that partnership ended with Rueben Campos in 2007. Reynolds has launched Indigo Red and Shmack, a fusion of skate and activewear with urban clothing. Most recently, Reynolds launched rapper TI's Akoo Clothing Line in 2008. "I saw TI as a type of iconic celebrity to be that iconic brand," he says.

Time is all the urban market needed as brands evolved from both coasts and made major department store retailers take notice. Cross Colours' contribution to fashion paved the way for urban brands to launch and do what Cross Colours could not. Although its success was short-lived, Cross Colours gave up-and-coming brands something to aspire to in terms of volume sales and overall ground-breaking success. Brands like Maurice Malone, Mecca USA, PNB Nation, and Akademiks helped build an urban marketplace that was taking marketshare from the big players of fashion. No bigger player would there be in the late 1990s than FUBU, a company that more than triple the sales volume of Cross Colours at its peak. What simply began as a means of making "easy money" in the basement of Daymond John's home in Hollis, Queens, turned him into the CEO of an incredibly successful multimedia (clothing, music, movies, television, and Internet) company.

CHAPTER 8
How FUBU Changed the World

Our numbers [$350 million] inspired designers, entrepreneurs, and music personas to jump into the [apparel] business. Some people thought it was very easy. With little money they'd go and sell their mom's and grandma's house because they had their eye on the prize and no love for the business. For the few of us that made it, many lost a lot.

—"The Shark" Daymond John

Flat-screen televisions and a black leather sofa set the mood in FUBU's black marble reception area on the 66th floor of the Empire State Building in New York City. Mahogany wood doors with metal trim lead to the main conference room and scattered executive offices accent the space's casual but business-like environment. Each day starts off differently for "The Shark" Daymond John, Keith Perrin, J. Alexander Martin, and Carl Brown, the founders of FUBU which was relaunched as FB Legacy in 2010.

The FUBU team were just a few years out of high school when they came up with the idea of a clothing line. John and Brown knew each other from the time they were children and lived just one house away in Hollis, Queens. They both met Martin and Perrin in high school and have since become inseparable. Before FUBU, John worked as a waiter at Red Lobster, Brown did odd jobs, Martin had joined the military to fight in Desert Storm, and Perrin managed apartment buildings in Harlem. In 1992, while shopping for a hat with Brown, John realized that there were no neighborhood retail shops that carried what he was looking for. "I wanted to buy a certain type of hat and me and Carl went all over the city looking for it," recalls John. "So when we saw the hat, I said, you know, 'I can make this hat. This is pretty simple.'" The idea to make tie-top hats was not as far-fetched as it might have initially sounded as John had learned sewing skills from his mom,

FUBU Founders. (© Ernie Paniccioli. Used by permission.)

Margot. "I had to stand over her and watch," he proudly remembered. Eventually, all of those years observing and taking note of his mother's work paid off for John.

Martin, the most stylish of the group, first acted as a consultant, assisting in sourcing fabric, while Brown took on the task of cutting the fabric. John sewed it together and Perrin sold the finish product as did the others on Jamaica Avenue and anywhere they felt they could get customers. "We made a couple of hats and [started selling them] on Friday or Saturday before Easter Sunday," John recalled. "We went out in front of the Jamaica Colosseum Mall and sold $800 worth of hats." They would do it for about three or four hours as the hats became an easy way to make some extra cash. It was Martin, upon returning from fighting in Desert Storm and winning a scholarship to attend the prestigious Fashion Institute of Technology (FIT), who would entertain the apparel conversation. Martin had already been gaining the business knowledge needed as a part-time salesperson (aspiring to be a buyer) at Macy's in the Roosevelt Field Mall, Long Island. He gave the group the incentive to develop a name. Realizing that they needed to separate themselves from the competition that was peddling similar products on the streets, the group collectively began to strategize on the company's concept and moniker. Wanting to select a name with importance, they finally agreed to FUBU, an acronym meaning "For Us, By Us."

The name chosen could take on a number of interpretations and meanings. "Our brand was not named after a person, but rather a conscience movement," says John. "We had been frustrated by the fashion companies like Timberlands who had voiced at one point that their product was not made with us, the urban customer in mind. We created a brand for us, by us, but we didn't want to be guilty of the same form of racism or prejudice that they insinuated. So the FUBU acronym took on different meanings to different people. For us, FUBU was about a generation claiming and recognizing our place in the marketplace."

FUBU was launched with a few T-shirts and hats and later expanded to include sweatshirts, sweatpants, and polyester-fleece tops. "We had no idea how to make jeans," John remembered. "But before then, we took the T-shirt and we had the name FUBU put on it." Using their street smarts and their "hood connections," the group reached out to everyone they knew from around the way. Music directors such as Queens' native Hype Williams and Long Island's Ralph McDaniels became immediate pillars of support while longtime high-school friend LL Cool J would provide the international exposure the brand needed to cross over into mainstream. It started with a *Source* magazine advertisement photo-op and evolved into a spokesperson relationship with all the fringe benefits—product worn during all of LL Cool J's public appearances and music videos. "That was a good 10 to 20 T-shirts [we placed] at that point," John says. "We started to put them on other guys [like Brand Nubian] and before you knew it, people started recognizing the logo." This was, of course, the era of pre-banning clothing logos on major networks such as *MTV* and *Black Entertainment Television* (*BET*). The product placement in videos and constant television airplay gave team FUBU the street credibility they needed and the illusion to fans that they were bigger than they actually were. Three years into the clothing hustle, team FUBU made their way to Las Vegas to showcase their goods not too far from the famous MAGIC International convention. John, Brown, and Perrin found out about the show through Martin, who had learned of the three-day event while a student at FIT.

"There were just a few of us [black designers]," John says. "It was like six of us and we would stay in an area." Unable to afford the expensive exhibition costs of a trade show, FUBU joined other black designers in a hotel suite set up as an alternate route to showcasing product. Like their urban predecessors, team FUBU rented out a suite in the Mirage Hotel & Casino, conveniently located on the Las Vegas Strip and just a few miles away from the main convention area. Every day, the men would head out to the MAGIC convention to hand out flyers with the hope of luring retailers to preview their limited line of T-shirts, sweatshirts, and polyester-fleece tops. Their direct marketing tactic proved successful as seasoned buyers from reputable urban stores such as The Lark in Chicago and Up Against the Wall in Washington, D.C. were among the first to visit, preview, and buy. At the end of the trip, FUBU successfully wrote $300,000 worth of orders.[1] There was just one problem—how to fulfill them.

The FUBU team had limited manpower and had not set up their infrastructure to produce large quantities of products. Getting their hands fast on some cash was the only way the team could actually complete the large orders. John immediately turned to his mother, an American Airlines airline attendant, and managed to convince her to take out a second mortgage on her home for $100,000. Martin also contributed $5,000 to the FUBU cash pot from monies he received from an accident settlement. With money no longer a main obstacle, the team developed a game plan that would launch their business. Realizing that her house would no longer be a home, John's mother, Margot, moved out to allow the transformation of her son's company to take place. One half of the house, which consisted of a basement and two other floors, would be kept as sleeping quarters, while the other half would be converted into an office and an assembly line fully-equipped with multiple sewing machines, sample room, and space for the needed help. With the temporary cash flow in place and equipment to manufacture thousands of pieced goods, Martin took the responsibility of finding the additional help. He researched fabric houses and learned the basics to production, while also taking the responsibilities of finding freelancers. Through a friend of a friend, Martin met Kianga "Kiki" Peterson in 1993. Peterson, 19 years old at the time, was studying women's design and was intrigued by this new brand.

Martin liked her portfolio and sketching abilities, so Peterson began working for FUBU for free three to four times a week out at the FUBU factory, which was John's converted house. The brand was mainly T-shirts made from blanks, given a FUBU twist, and then sold. Peterson would sit on John's couch to watch videos for inspiration and draw for hours at a time. Martin and John would explain the company's direction and she would deliver it to them to the best of her ability. Newly arrived in New York, designing for a start-up company owned by African Americans seemed to be the most important thing in Peterson's world. "They got me hype. Anything that I could do was fun anyway. I felt like I was really doing something," she says. Others in her immediate circle, however, were not as enthusiastic about her nonpaying experience. Peterson's response to them would always be, "I know, but they're [FUBU] gonna be big one day."

Peterson's gut feelings (the kind that push your instincts to the highest level and make you do things that seem illogical and at times, irrational) were correct. While she learned fashion fundamentals at FIT, FUBU taught her the business of fashion—how to address the needs of consumers and make what they want. She stuck by the FUBU team through good and bad times for the next two years. All along, Peterson attended school full-time and worked at FUBU full-time for no money or time for herself. "I could only really keep a job in the summer time because I was a full-time student," she remembers. Peterson's jobs varied from working on doing window displays at the now defunct Herman's Sporting Goods and pattern making at the lingerie company Val Mode to interning at Uptown Records and working under music stylist Sybil Pennix. "I tried getting [FUBU] stuff in the videos," Peterson says. "They were in so much already. Almost any video I told them about, they knew about."

The breakthrough year for FUBU was 1995. John's mother placed FUBU's destiny into her own hands. With key buzzwords such as "$300,000 worth of orders" and "seeking backing," she planted the seed for additional financing in a classified ad that ran in *The New York Times* and *Daily News*. Calls from potential capital investors came pouring in, about 20 in all, responding to the ad. But in the end, it was Samsung International, the tenth largest corporation in the world that would make the "right" offer. Samsung executives were interested in the brand from the beginning. They had heard about FUBU at MAGIC and had even spotted FUBU product on the red-hot television series *New York Undercover* during the early stages of negotiations; Rapper turned actor Fredro Starr of the rap group Onyx was in an episode wearing a FUBU hockey jersey. Neither FUBU nor Samsung have ever disclosed the specifics of their deal. According to John, Samsung assists in the "production and distribution of orders." Over the years, the FUBU founders have disputed allegations of being "sell-outs" and rumors that not all founders have actual ownership of the company. What no one can dispute is the fact that teens fell for FUBU fashion.

THE LL FACTOR—SOMETHING LIKE A PHENOMENON

Fubu's success was truly something like a phenomenon, thanks in part to superstar LL Cool J. There has never been a doubt on the part of the FUBU founders, its investors, or the fashion community that without LL Cool J, the FUBU rags-to-riches story might have played out somewhat differently. The brand did have potential from the start as the apparel catered to its audience and had a strong message. But LL Cool J, as its spokesperson, unofficially at first and later officially, absolutely accelerated its growth.

It started in 1994, two years after the inception of the clothing company. Daymond John, the CEO of FUBU, asked his high-school friend LL Cool J, the Def Jam multiplatinum rap artist turned actor, to model FUBU for an upcoming *Source* magazine ad shoot. LL Cool J, born James Todd Smith, agreed and over the next eight years, he would become FUBU's strongest and most consistent supporter. At first, it was done straight "out of love" for John, his product, and what FUBU stood for. LL Cool J could appreciate the fact that these four brothers were just trying to "make it happen" so money was not a necessity. Like many other entertainers including Brand Nubians, LL Cool J was naturally fond of the product's style, colors, and fit. In turn, team FUBU considered LL's support of their fashion as a big I.O.U. Patience is definitely a virtue, as LL Cool J had no doubt that the FUBU brothers would let him down and soon give he the props he so

LL Cool J in the mid-nineties served as a spokesman for FUBU. (© Ernie Paniccioli. Used by permission.)

rightfully deserved. Once additional financing came through by way of Samsung America, LL Cool J would receive more than just a thank-you from his longtime friends. He was named the official FUBU spokesperson in 1996 and signed to a three-year negotiable contract for an undisclosed amount. The new title came with a lump sum payment to match his years of loyal commitment to the brand. What was once considered a favor was not part of LL Cool J's daily work ritual.

Once having some access to LL Cool J for magazine and video shoots and occasional print ads, he would now be available for all major television and public appearances. Making sure to capitalize on his visibility, FUBU took its marketing efforts to the next level with a million-dollar TV campaign featuring the Queens' native. A 30-second and one-minute national commercial aired in late July/early August 1997 on the UPN, WB, BET, MSG, and MTV networks. FUBU hired New York-based Big Dog Films, which had produced Def Jam music videos, for the assignment. The *In the House* star wrote the FUBU commercial which Big Dog's Steve Carr directed. The 30-second commercial was filmed at the Broadway Studios in Long Island City, NY, over a two-day period. In the end, FUBU spent

$120,000 on the commercial. The first two commercials focused on LL and his thoughts on the fashion industry and FUBU. LL states, "I just felt like it was time for a change. You've got all these billion-dollar clothing companies, but they don't have any style." He later concludes by saying whether you are 5 or 55 years old, "These [FUBU] clothes make statement, but you got to get your own." The commercials ran parallel to a recent Gap commercial he had completed. The message in the 30-second FUBU commercial might have contradicted what he said in the Gap TV commercial, "I know that you like your outfits stylish. Any other line but the Gap is childish."

It was apparent that the Gap was looking to target the African American audience and went after LL Cool J because he was one of the most versatile contenders to promote the Gap line of easy-fit jeans for the "How Easy is This?" ad campaign. The problem was that LL was signed to another apparel company, FUBU, which was a competitor. "He told them it was partly his, which was incorrect, but he was our Michael Jordan of Nike. He said, 'You guys have to allow me to wear the hat, just my hat,' " John recalls LL Cool J telling The Gap. Gap ad executives allowed his request; for the shoot, LL dressed in Gap clothing from his neck down, but strategically wore a FUBU hat. As if this were not strange enough, LL infused a plug for FUBU in his a cappella rhyme, "Gap is *for us, by us* on the low." John considered this one of his brand's biggest successes, "It was the tipping point—the voice of a culture sneaking up on Middle America." Consumers were baffled; was this a Gap ad or was FUBU now being sold at Gap? "The same reason we created 'for us, by us' as a culture was the same frustration he [LL Cool J] had when he had all these execs [around him]. He slipped it in there if they got it and they didn't get it," says John. Heads rolled at the Gap camp as a result of the lyrical mishap, but the Gap still came ahead. The company ended up re-airing the ad a year later, says John.

The Gap commercial only helped the exploding urban brand achieve mass notoriety sooner. FUBU cleverly piggybacked its commercial after that of the Gap to maximize its national publicity exposure. Although it is never general practice for an advertiser to promote another competitor, it was evident that both the Gap and FUBU benefited from the odd campaign. Gap was associated with a cool brand and FUBU got a free multimillion national TV campaign. This same year, 1997, also marked a critical year for FUBU at retail and LL Cool J was with the brand every step of the way. Macy's gave FUBU its windows to display merchandise and would eventually benefit from having LL appear for a personal customer meet-and-greet at the Macy's Herald Square location on 34th Street. LL even managed to promote the growing urban apparel brand in his 1998 autobiography *I Make My Own Rules* written with Karen Hunter. "Fortunately, I don't have to labor much over what I'm going to wear, because I always wear FUBU," he wrote. "So I'll put on a pair of FUBU jeans, rolling up the left leg to expose my tattoos, a FUBU shirt or sweatshirt if it's cold, and a FUBU hat."

BRAND BUILDING

Marketing and branding are what FUBU did best. Early on the company implemented creative tactics such as spray-painting their name on the security gates of local retailers in New York City, Newark, and Philadelphia. Brown, who at the time was the director of sales and distribution, had approached several stores with the clever promotional idea. Soon FUBU spray-painted gates would appear in Washington, D.C., Virginia, and Florida. With Samsung by its side, FUBU relocated its offices to the Empire State Building in 1995, where it is still based today. Sales were pegged at $7 million at the time and by the following year, sales dramatically increased to $30 million with the aid of major department store distribution.[2]

In spring 1997, Federated Department Stores (now known as Macy's) kicked off its experimental urban concept with its Macy' East, Rich's/Lazarus, Burdines, and Bon Marché divisions. FUBU, Mecca, and Wu Wear (affiliated with the multiplatinum rap group Wu-Tang Clan), were among the brands featured in their new matrix. FUBU was grossing close to $30 million a year and was being sold at major retailers such as Mercantile, The Buckle, Gadzooks, Dr. Jay's, Casual Male, Champs, and Finish Line.[3] John had projected sales to almost double to $50 million with Federated Department Stores by its side. Simultaneously, FUBU made its runway debut along with leading designers during the 7th on Sixth men's shows. "The world will be looking at me," a then 27-year-old John says. FUBU became the first urban brand to participate in the event followed by Ecko Unlimited and

Maurice Malone. "But showing at 7th on Sixth doesn't mean I've made it. Making it means longevity," noted John. Using the runway as its platform, FUBU was able to catch the attention of the most influential and powerful—the fashion press, the retail community, and ultimately, the world. It would be FUBU's first and only attempt to participate in such a high-profiled event. And it was all it needed.

FUBU became an instant success as its street credibility became widespread, making it the undisputed urban market leader. Soon other major department stores, including Nordstrom, Mercantile, and J.C. Penney, that once steered clear of urban wear began to re-evaluate their position. The MAGIC show became part of FUBU's regular trade show routine. By the summer of 1997, FUBU had built a creative exhibition space at MAGIC that included stadium bleachers, television monitors playing LL Cool J's most popular videos, 7th on Sixth fashion-show footage, while salespeople wearing microphones were busy taking orders. By the following MAGIC show, FUBU would need to create a new and bigger booth to accommodate its growing number of licensees—including backpacks, socks, and dress shirts—as well as its growing retail clientele looking to pick up the "blazin'" brand.

FUBU's rapid rise in popularity got the attention of Representative Floyd H. Flake (Dem.-N.Y.), who proclaimed October 7, 1997 to be FUBU Day in New York's Sixth Congressional District. FUBU's sales stood at $70 million and distribution was at over 2,500 stores across the country at that point.[4] Product placement on popular music videos as well as television shows such as *New York Undercover* and *The Wayans Brothers* helped boost an already popular brand, while regional trade shows such as the Southeastern Men's Market Show in Atlanta became another indicator of FUBU's growing success. But the ultimate FUBU coup was when the company's longtime supporter LL Cool J, managed to slip in a promotion for FUBU during the filming of his Gap commercial in 1997. A year later, FUBU expanded its design team and recruited Bobby Joseph an in-demand freelance designer to assist them with graphics and design. Joseph had built a solid reputation over the years for his graphic and design work for some of the most recognizable names in the business including African American College Association (AACA), 5001 Flavors, Walker Wear, Reebok, Phat Farm, And 1, Mecca, and Sean John.

Joseph had already established a working relationship with FUBU, accepting freelance gigs to design 5-to-10 piece collections over the years to items for the historic FUBU NBA line.

The FUBU NBA licensing deal was a first for both the NBA and FUBU. For FUBU, it represented the brand's first partnership with a professional sports league. For the NBA, it was an alliance with one of the hottest urban brands that could bring a new twist to the authentic licensed market and ultimately, increase ticket sales. FUBU had built a strong reputation within the apparel business and had a large following of leading sports specialty retailers because of its active fashion hits like the "05" football jersey and satin baseball jackets. But amid a groundbreaking deal, the two parties would have to endure the basketball leagues' possible lockout. The controversy had FUBU and its retailers on its toes, worried that the prebooked FUBU NBA apparel would turn into a flop if ball players were a no-go. When the NBA saved itself just 29 hours before the league's board of governors was set to vote on canceling the season, it meant salvation for players, loyal fans, and FUBU retailers looking to cash in on the NBA synergy.

FUBU had initially shipped its NBA products exclusively to the NBA store in December 1998 and a few weeks later, product hit retailers such as Foot Locker and Champs. It's intent was to make FUBU NBA a $50 million subdivision of its already $200-million apparel business.[5] To help aid this cause, it enlisted Phil Pabon, formerly the head of marketing at Mecca USA and Enyce, as its vice president of marketing of men's for FUBU and FUBU NBA. But months into his position, Pabon would make a quick exit (although he returned years later)—an early sign of "creative differences" and a bigger sign that FUBU NBA was not going to be all that was initially thought to be. FUBU would need another hit as the sour NBA deal could damper the company's reputation.

The company decided to launch a higher-priced denim collection called FUBU Platinum to compete with new rival Sean John by Sean "P. Diddy" Combs. Rumors were already circulating in the industry that FUBU was "falling off' as sales would soon plateau at $350 million ($200 million in menswear and $150 million from licensing).[6] But FUBU Platinum would prove to succeed at retail and provide the company with a lifeline. Other brand extensions would soon follow under the FUBU Platinum umbrella including Fat Albert and the Junkyard Gang, Muhammad Ali, and the Harlem Globetrotters. Over the course of its existence, FUBU received accolades from the Congressional Awards, the NAACP Awards, the Pratt Institute Award, the Christopher Wallace Award, the Online Hip Hop Award, a Citation of Honor from the Queens Borough President, the key to the city of Las Vegas, the first Essence Award ever given to a company, a Black History Month Award from then Senator Hillary Rodham Clinton, and wax replica statues were created of FUBU founders in 2003 for The Great Blacks in Wax Museum in Baltimore.

FUBU also received other merits of distinction for its active community involvement. Through its FUBU Foundation, the company gave donations to Hip Hop Cares (for victims of the World Trade Center tragedy); City Harvest during Thanksgiving; the New York City Parks & Recreation Department to refurbish basketball courts; the Allen Christian School, a division of the Cathedral of the Allen A.M.E. Church; the Christopher Wallace Memorial Foundation; ESB for Kids; the Partnership for the Homeless; and the Fresh Air Fund. And on an individual basis, the founders participated in "Principle for a Day" and other student-affiliated programs.

What started as a small line of tops and hats grew into a full lifestyle collection that included Platinum FUBU (with vignettes dedicated to Fat Albert and the Gang, Muhammad Ali, and the Harlem Globetrotters), ladies, footwear (for both men and women), activewear, swimwear, suits, dress shirts, ties, tuxedos, fragrance, handbags, socks, girls' and boys' sportswear, accessories, and a home collection before stopping U.S. distribution in 2003. At its peak, FUBU was found in more than 5,000 stores including Macy's, Foot Locker, Footaction, Rich's, Kaufman's, The Buckle, and Dr. Jay's. Other distribution channels included international freestanding stores located throughout Japan, Germany, France, England, Australia, Mexico, South Africa, Saudi Arabia, Greece, Lebanon, and Barbados.

FUBU eventually ventured into music. In December 2000, it launched FB Entertainment, at one time a separate division under the FUBU corporate umbrella. The new venture allowed the FUBU founders to lend their creative talents in areas outside of fashion. Music became FUBU's first breakthrough outside of fashion with the release of its first CD, "The Goodlife" under the FUBU Records division of FB Entertainment.

"Fatty Girl" featuring rappers LL Cool J, Ludacris, and Keith Murray, became the first single release from the company's compilation CD "The Goodlife" and was given frequent radio and video play.

FUBU also produced a small assortment of junior apparel with the same name under its FUBU's ladies division to capture the synergy between the music and the FUBU brand. Distributed by Universal Records, the compilation CD was released in September 2001 featuring original music from established and new artists such as LL Cool J, Ludacris, Nate Dogg, Nas, JS of 54th Platoon, Ludacris, and The E.N.D. Among the CD's most popular hits included "50 Playaz Deep" by Detroit native Drunken Master featuring Lola Damone in addition to "Fatty Girl." In 2002, FUBU Records signed an exclusive deal with Koch Entertainment Distribution, one of North America's largest independent distributors, with plans to release the company's sophomore album featuring FUBU's first signed group—54th Platoon. The New Orleans group made up of JS, Nu Black, Nut, and T.L., was signed in July 2002 to a $1 million record deal.

However, much has changed since then. FUBU clothing disappeared off U.S. shelves in 2003 and FB Entertainment dissolved before that time. What caused the FUBU demise is hard to exactly pinpoint; the brand was overdistributed and eventually lost its specialness with mom-and-pop specialty stores that had helped to build the brand from inception. In addition, the market went from enlisting celebrity to endorse product to actually having them own brands. Sean John and Rocawear would eventually steer customers away from existing urban brands like FUBU as they were the next best thing. "FUBU started to decline," admits John. "Black (recording) artists came in and wanted brands of their own. Our numbers inspired designers, entrepreneurs, and music personas to jump into the business. Some people thought it was very easy. With little money they'd go and sell their mom's and grandma's house because they had their eye on the prize and no love for the business. For the few of us that made it, many lost a lot and added confusion to a bubbling market."

By 2003, FUBU's U.S. apparel business had dried up so the company pulled the young men's product out of the market. "We still had suits, sneakers, and bedding," says John. "We were growing in Europe and Asia. We focused on that business then." With less emphasis on FUBU domestically, the strategy became to acquire brands and licenses. The labels varied from Willie Esco (targeting the Latino consumer), Coogi (Australian knitwear), Kappa USA (a soccer brand), Ted Baker (a British sportswear company), Heatherette (a trendy brand of former club kid Richie Rich), and Drunkn Munky (skatewear).

Daymond John has been able to transcend from his hip hop designer beginnings. He entered the world of publishing with his books, *The Brand Within: The Power of Branding from Birth to the Boardroom* (2010) and *Display of Power: How FUBU Changed a World of Fashion, Branding and Lifestyle* (2007). He has also taken on television with appearances on CNBC's *The Big Idea with Donny Deutsch* which caught the attention of British reality-TV producer Mark Burnett. Known for hit shows like *Survivor*, *The Apprentice*, and *Are You Smarter than a Fifth Grader?*, Burnett tapped John because he understood how to break down a 90-second elevator pitch. John became one of the five multimillionaires starring in ABC's entrepreneur show *Shark Tank*, which premiered in fall 2009. *Shark Tank* would be the U.S. version of *Dragons' Den*, which originated in Japan and has versions in Britain, Canada, Australia, New Zealand, Israel, The Netherlands, Finland, and the Middle East.[7] The other members of team FUBU have also pursued other career endeavors in addition to the existing FUBU brand. Brown is the president of Seraphin Cognac and CCLB Branding, which provides services to the wine and spirits industry; Perrin runs the talent firm Keith Perrin Agency and hosts the *Industry* radio show on onpoint.fm; and Marin owns a TV network called Fashion News Network. As for Peterson, who worked alongside team FUBU in its infancy stage, she made her career as a juniors sportswear designer. In 2012, she launched a women's contemporary line called K.Milele (Swahili for *Sunbeam Everlasting*). The television show *Shark Tank* has not distracted John and his partners from their first love—designing clothes. FUBU in 2010 gave itself a makeover and is on a comeback trail. "With the 80s style coming in, the kids started seeking the 90s style," says John. While presently off the U.S. radar, FUBU has kept itself busy designing custom apparel for recording artists. To commemorate its contributions to fashion, FUBU has launched FB Legacy, which takes on an Abercrombie & Fitch meets Carhartt feel. And only time will tell if FUBU can have a second coming. No matter what, FUBU has many achievements to be proud of. "We created the biggest hard goods' commodity by youth and people of color," brags John. "Through FUBU's doors, I've employed over 2,000 people in New York alone and out of those who have come through my doors, 50 percent have gone on to other careers in fashion or media." Many former employees have gone onto celebrity-driven clothing lines that have stolen the thunder of the once red-hot brand.

CHAPTER 9
Hip Hop Hooray

Fashion sells the image [of an artist or group] and it sells the message that you are trying to get across. It makes people buy into you. If people like the way you look, they like your aura, they will buy into that and they actually duplicate it too.

—Vinnie Brown, Naughty by Nature

For years, fashion houses have sought after the famous and prominent in hopes of gaining market share whether it has been giving away free clothes, inviting them to exclusive fashion shows, or signing them to six- and seven-figure endorsement deals. Early hip hop endorsement deals included Whodini and Le Coq Sportif, LL Cool J and Troop, to Run-D.M.C.'s $1.5 million deal with Adidas. In the 1990s, we saw LL Cool J sign with FUBU, the late Lisa "Left Eye" Lopes and Ja Rule sign with Calvin Klein, Tyrese with Guess, Queen Latifah with Lane Bryant, Lil Kim with Iceberg, and Mary J. Blige with Mac Cosmetics.

But in the early 1990s, a new trend occurred—the official "end of the designer" as we once knew it. Traditional clothing designer personalities became uninteresting to the public and thus, the celebrity hip hop apparel designer was born. Existing designers and apparel manufacturers took their celebrity relationships to the next level by courting celebrities with their "own" apparel lines and select joint venture opportunities. This business proposition proved to be quite profitable, especially in the youth market.

As hip hop artists and moguls discovered their power to brand, many decided to also promote their own lines. "They started to see I can rock Kani or I can be down with FUBU," says Erin Patton, who is widely regarded as one of the nation's foremost experts on branding, sports marketing, and hip hop culture. He is founder of The Mastermind

Group (TMG), a brand management and strategic marketing consulting firm that has provided counsel to an exclusive client roster of Fortune 500 brands and pop culture icons. "Then you had cats like Diddy and we can take it one step further. We can create our own brand, that's not just a brand but that becomes part of our movement. Phat Farm would be a part of the same equation," notes Patton.

New York City Breakers (through MadSoul Clothing Company), Chuck D. (Rapp Style International), Russell Simmons (Phat Farm), Wu-Tang Clan (Wu Wear), Naughty by Nature (Naughty Gear), The Notorious B.I.G. (Brooklyn Mint), Busta Rhymes (Bushi), The Fugees (Refugee Camp), Fat Joe (FJ560), Ruff Ryders (Ruff Ryders), Jay-Z and former partner Damon Dash (Rocawear), Damon Dash (CEO), Nelly (Vokal for men and Apple Bottoms for women), 50 Cent (G-Unit), Afeni Shakur (Makavelli), LL Cool J (Todd Smith), Bow Wow (Shago Clothing), Ja Rule and Irv Gotti (Erving Geoffrey), Master P (No Limit), Eminem (Shady), Outkast (Outkast), Benjamin Bixby (Andre 3000), Snoop Dogg (Snoop Dogg and K-Nine), Ice-T (Icewear), Cash Money Millionaires (Cash Money Collection), Sisqo (Dragon Collection), R. Kelly (Chiany), Fabolous (Rich Young), Sean "P. Diddy" Combs (Sean John), Pharell Williams (Billionaire Boys Club/Ice Cream), Beyoncé (House of Dereon), Jennifer Lopez (J.Lo), Eve (Fetish), Young Jeezy (8732 Clothing), and T.I. (Akoo Clothing Line), are just examples of well-known artists with their own fashion brands. "These artists recognized that they could take their fan base. We can create a brand around this movement and create distinct products that speak to it," added Patton. "It really became outside of the music itself, the first entrepreneurial opportunity for this generation, self-made individuals looking to redefine and re-create the American dream," he says. "Russell makes part of their value proposition with Phat Farm Classic American Flava, a new twist on being self-made and what the American dream looked like. That was really the first industry where these individuals could actually come in as entrepreneurs and take their brand and movement and parlay it into millions."

Artists were not the only ones jumping onto the fashion bandwagon. Prominent record labels such as Def Jam Recordings and Warner Bros. Records began promoting their companies with custom varsity jackets. "Tommy Boy [Records later called Tommy Boy Entertainment] was always very fashion forward, when I started in late 1990," recalled Bryan Adams, a former employee of Tommy Boy Records and currently the founder and chief publicist for Fab Communications. "Tommy Boy went a different direction and did a Carhartt jacket, which is known for being a rugged jacket." According to Adams, the record label brought Willie Turner (now deceased) on board in the mid-1990s to focus on developing Tommy Boy merchandise. Tommy Boy utilized the back page of *The Source* to promote its goods. Its radio promotions director, Fat Man Scoop, would model outfits featured in the ads. Turner eventually left Tommy Boy to pursue his own dreams and founded 11 Blocks, an entertainment-driven design firm based on 29th Street between Sixth and Seventh Avenues in Manhattan. His company was a novelty at the time.

Existing fashion manufacturers had not caught on to focusing solely on entertainment-driven brands. Turner designed a variety of artist-driven fashion labels including The Notorious B.I.G.'s Brooklyn Mint until his death in 1997 and The Fugees' Refugee Camp. He also came close to launching a line for TLC under the label and one of their hit songs "Crazy Sexy Cool." Unfortunately, The Notorious B.I.G's clothing line was in its infancy stage when the rapper was killed. Adams, who served as the 11 Blocks' publicist, recalls the line existing for about one season. Although Turner was talented and had good intentions, he never was able to fully launch his entertainment brands at retail due to financial issues. He finally closed shop in 1998. "I don't remember anybody doing clothing lines for rappers before him," says Adams. "He was an actual design house person with retail experience, fashion experience; experienced artists stitching people, the whole garment maker. Willie and 11 Blocks were pioneers in that."

Music mogul Russell Simmons, a master visionary who has long shaped the cutting edge of hip hop, became the first music mogul to break into fashion. Like hip hop music, he realized that fashion was an integral part of self-expression, cutting across geographic, race, and class boundaries. In 1992, he created Phat Fashions and sold Phat Farm out of a trendy boutique on Prince Street in SoHo, New York City. Phat Farm became the urban market's answer to Ralph Lauren. Simmons took classic American preppy styles like khakis pants, polo shirts, button-front shirts, and argyle sweaters and gave them an urban fit. The success of Phat Farm at both a wholesale and retail level would soon inspire others from the hip hop community to follow suit. What started with jeans, khakis, knits, and T-shirts over time grew to include eyewear, Motorola cell phones, soft drinks (Def Con3), the Rush Card (a nondebit bank card), and suits. Simmons would sell Phat Farm to Kellwood Company for $140 million in 2004. Kimora Lee Simmons,

Russell and Kimora Lee Simmons. (© Ernie Paniccioli. Used by permission.)

who founded Baby Phat with ex-husband Russell, stayed on board with Kellwood through 2010. The bittersweet departure quickly had Kimora lee Simmons disassociate herself with Baby Phat as aired on the airwaves of New York's Hot 97, the well-known hip hop radio station.

Vinnie Brown of the rap group Naughty by Nature, decided to get into the clothing business in 1993 just as the group was building its fame and notoriety. In addition to a short-lived wholesale business, Naughty Gear had a 1,200-square-foot shop in the heart of Newark, New Jersey. DJ Kay Gee, Treach, and Brown lived in a five-block radius of one another in East Orange, New Jersey and went to the same high school. When Kay Gee was a senior and Treach and Brown were juniors, the trio decided to form a group to perform during Kay Gee's senior talent show. "We didn't even have a name for the group, but we only had routines back then, performance routines," recalled Brown. The year was 1987 and the group decided to start their routine with a Beastie Boys song, "It's the New Style." The group decided to keep the name New Style and signed its first record deal a year later with Sugar Hill. Brown recalls, "We were young anxious kids and eager to get on and we jumped at the first deal that was available. Sugar Hill Records at that point was just totally defunct."

The group sought out Queen Latifah's Flava Unit after that experience. "They were from Jersey and they knew about us because we put in a lot of work around the way," says Brown. "We chased them down and invited them to a talent show, threw a party and the whole Flava Unit came out. They got to see our following and everything." Flava Unit decided to sign the trio for management. Treach came up with the name Naughty by Nature; it was the title of a song the group had as the New Style and in 1990, the group was signed to Tommy Boy. "We didn't have an identity for the group," says Brown. "As the New Style we had hi-top fades and it was more of a Heavy D and the Boyz look. As Naughty, we had no fashion gimmicks and looked liked we just came off the block."

Tommy Boy worked with developing the logo and hired Mark Weinberg as its designer it. Once it was decided that "O.P.P." was going to be the first single, stickers and promotional merchandise followed. T-shirts dropped with "Down with O.P.P." written across the chest as well as Naughty boxers. "We made boxers and a gang of

Naughty by Nature in front of their Naughty Gear Store in Newark, New Jersey. (© Ernie Paniccioli. Used by permission.)

T-shirts and just flooded everyone with them. We spent 10 to 20 thousand dollars out of our own pockets." Kay Gee's mother and sister sold them from the block, the house. "We started selling so many tees that it was ridiculous. What eventually happened as former street kids, someone alerted the Feds and they came around and stung two of our guys. [The Feds] tried to twist us up in it once that whole stuff happened," recalled Brown. The group had been touring and on the road and as a result of the sting, they were unable to sell T-shirts off the block. Naughty by Nature then developed other products for mail order. It was an idea they got from watching Eazy E. do it for N.W.A. as well as from Public Enemy. After getting advice from both camps, the group approached Tommy Boy to pursue mail order for Naughty by Nature's *Nineteen Naughty III* album which became the first time fans saw Naughty bedsheets, boxers, and hoodies. "That was the first time we were officially branding ourselves," says Brown.

As Naughty by Nature was gaining momentum, brands started approaching the group for endorsement deals. "We had an audience of two million people and they wanted to just give us free clothes and keep pimping us out and not do real business with us," says Brown. "That pissed me off." Already having a mail order business in place, Brown decided to take it to the next level and opened a clothing store that would hopefully do for Naughty what Spike's Joint did for Spike Lee's films. Brown's idea was to develop merchandise for every album the group released. Merchandise would be developed for every artist released on Kay Gee's label as well as for every movie Treach did. At least, that was the plan. "Fashion sells the image [of an artist or group] and it sells the message that you are trying to get across," says Brown. "It makes people buy into you. If people like the way you look, they like your aura, they will buy into that and they actually duplicate it too."

The store, Naughty Gear Inc., opened in 1994 at 106 Halsey Street in the heart of downtown Newark, New Jersey. Brown wanted to replicate the sense of community which Lee's Spike's Joint had in Brooklyn. At first, Brown was getting goods produced by a local sporting store which printed basic Naughty T-shirts. "I went through every catalog he had from baby bibs to pins and put the logo on it," says Brown. "It totally upset his business. When we first started, I was getting a certain price from him. It was just basic embroidery and screen printing. Then, when he was supplying the whole store of nothing but goods, it totally upset his business and he de-prioritized his core customers for me. It got to a point that he had to charge me more. By the time I had to charge the people, the pricing was just ridiculous."

Brown hired childhood friend Kevin Jackson to manage the Naughty Gear store. It was Jackson who was then sent to the MAGIC show in Las Vegas to assist Brown in obtaining a licensing deal. There, Jackson met designer David Sierra who was working for an apparel manufacturer that would take on the license. According to Brown, the brand had unfortunate timing. The licensing deal came to fruition in 1997 just when the group members of Naughty by Nature were at odds with each other. At this time, the success of a hip hop artist was directly tied to an apparel line's success. Both were inseparable. Naughty Gear did not do as well at wholesale as anticipated while other hip hop artists and acts like Fat Joe (FJ560) and Wu-Tang Clan (Wu Wear) were checking well at retail. "They had a stronger sell-through than us," admitted Brown. "Some of those brands were in the same stores as us, but because the groups were more current and hotter, their goods sold through faster than ours and our goods started coming back." Although Naughty Gear did $1.2 million in sales at the MAGIC show in 1998, Brown's stay in the apparel and retail business was short-lived.[1] He began carrying other brands in his store and ultimately shut down his shop in 1999. "I was hemorrhaging with losses," admitted Brown. "All of that stuff was so brand new to me and I had no formal training. Coming off the block, there's no overhead on the product you sell or on the block."

Brown admittedly made poor decisions early on in his business career. Pressured to make his store's grand opening, he hired about 16 teens from the block for a shop that was not even 1,000 square feet. His first year in salaries alone averaged $160,000. "Coming from the hood you think you make a few million dollars and you can save the world," Brown says. "But those few million dollars are only going to help you raise your family and send your kids to college. I lost over $2 million doing the retail store. I lost so much money I couldn't take it anymore." Brown continued to sell concert merchandise and in 2005, launched a new Naughty by Nature site where he sold Naughty memorabilia online. Brown is also a partner in a screen printing business and works with several companies to get his boxers and shirts made.

Naughty by Nature was not the only rap group to attempt a venture into wholesale and retail. Executive producer Oli "Power" Grant envisioned a Wu-Tang Clan clothing empire after the Wu dropped its first album, *Enter the Wu-Tang (36 Chambers)* in 1993. Like Naughty by Nature, Wu-Tang had a catalog business that would eventually expand into a wholesale and retail operation, according to Alfaro Clark, former manager of Wu Wear stores in Staten Island and Philadelphia and childhood friend of the Clan. Clark grew up with Grant, Raekwon, U-God, and Inspectah Deck in Staten Island. "Our first year in junior high school (1981), that's where Wu-Tang was started," Clark remembered. "It was I.S. 49 in Stapleton." Clark took on the job of going out on tour with the Clan and selling clothes out of minivans. When the time came, he worked in the mail order department and later, was promoted to manage several Wu stores. The store in Staten Island, located at 61 Victory Boulevard, became the first to open followed by two stores in Virginia, one in Atlanta, and the last in Philadelphia at 610 Third Street. The stores all sold Wu Wear exclusively from key chains, cups, sweatbands, lanyards, shoes to denim. Prices ranged from $1 for a keychain to $550 for leather outerwear. "Wu Wear was a shirt before we even built the stores," says Clark. "It was a T-shirt. Everything started with that."

Clark confirmed that the Wu stores hosted in-store signings with Wu-Tang members and other artists including Mobb Deep, Fat Joe, Big Pun, Ray Diggaz, Shaheem, and Heather B. Publicity were the responsibility of Cynamin Jones, who was an FIT student. She had applied for a job at Wu Wear after seeing a job posting on a FIT bulletin board. "I called up the store and Cleve (Clark), who was the manager at the time, told me to come up for the interview," recalled Jones. "I went up there with my resume and he was like you are hired." Jones started working sales in 1995 at the Wu store in Staten Island. Working retail less than a year, Jones was transferred to Wu Wear's Manhattan office, located inside the Fashion Atrium building at 463 Seventh Avenue. Wu Wear had a men's line at the time and was in the middle of doing a women's line.

Jones then switched roles to publicity, a job for which she did not have any prior experience. "I didn't know what P.R. was. I never went to school for it," admits Jones. She credits *The Source's* editor in chief Carlito Rodriguez for putting her on. "I told him in a ruthless manner that he needed to put my clothes in the magazine," she says. "He came to the store and met me. He was like 'ok, let me teach her' cause he said I acted like we [were] supposed to do something." Rodriguez ended up writing a story about Wu Wear and told Jones how the fashion editorial process worked. "I caught a niche and I started contacting all the magazines by going through the fashion pages," Jones says as she recalled sending out over $30,000 worth of samples for editorial placement. *The Source* became her first editorial placement followed by *Paper*, *XXL*, and *Sportswear International*. "We never had a budget. My budget was clothing. If you wanted to do something for us I would give you a hoodie. It was a trade off." Wu-Tang's 1996 single "Wu-Wear" was also a catalyst for putting the Clan's fashion business on the map. Shortly after its release, Macy's selected Wu Wear's "killa bees" shirt to be displayed on its windows. "It was the shirt that almost didn't make it," recalled Jones. "It was overseas and something happened with the boat."

Long before writing his book on sneakers, *Where'd You Get Those?* (2006), Puerto Rican deejay, writer, and entrepreneur Bobbito Garcia had an affinity for sneakers and fashion. An avid sneaker collector,

Garcia opened his shop called Bobbito's Footwork in the East Village in 1996 and later, opened another shop in Philadelphia. It became a go-to spot for all the things he loved—unique vinyl, kicks (sneakers), and gear. It was the same year veejay Ralph McDaniels decided to open his own store as an extension of Phat Fashions, a fashion show extravaganza that he produced at various New York City venues like Club Exit, The Supper Club, and the Javits Convention Center. Uncle Ralph's Urban Gear was located at 1622 Bedford Avenue in Crown Heights, Brooklyn.

Opening a store made sense for McDaniels, who through *Video Music Box*, was always being approached by people pitching their fashion lines. He remembers, "Whether it was some kind of hat, T-shirt, sweatshirt, or jeans, it was 'Ralph, can you wear them on *Video Music Box*?' or 'Can you put it in this music video?' and we were like, 'Yeah, no problem.'" McDaniels also saw an opportunity to help the designers that were participating in his fashion shows. "The majority of the stuff you saw in the show, you couldn't get anywhere," recalled McDaniels. "You could only get it at that particular place. So we said, let's open up a store where you can sell this stuff." Karl Kani and FUBU were among the first brands he carried in the store. "Karl, I'm opening a store and I know nothing about opening a store," McDaniels remembered telling the designer. "He helped me out and FUBU was just probably starting to get it together and they helped me out."

McDaniels selected the store location with the help of his friend and retail business partner, Dominique. The spaced leased was inside the co-op building where Dominique lived and McDaniels was able to secure a good price. "That's why we picked it," he explained. "We really couldn't afford Manhattan. We knew we could in Brooklyn, in the hood, because those were the people who were buying it." And because it was located around the corner from Eastern Parkway, it also meant that the store was in a good traffic location.

It was both the best and worst time to open a hip hop specialty store. For McDaniels, fashion designers who were coming up in the early 1990s reminded him of the hip hop artists coming up in the early 1980s. "It was the same feeling I got. I was whipped. I couldn't wait to see what the next design was gonna be. I couldn't wait to see what they were gonna do with a sweatshirt. I couldn't wait to see what kind of jeans they were gonna do. I couldn't wait to see that leather that people was gonna put out. It was like waiting for a next Eric B. and Rakim record. It was the same energy to me," he recalls. However, hip hop fashion's sudden popularity in 1996 meant that competition would now include department stores like Macy's. The downfall of Uncle Ralph's Urban Gear occurred as the designers got larger and more popular, the exclusively of brands for local retail shops went out the door. "All these different people were buying stuff that we had exclusively at one point," he says. "Then bootlegging came about. So people were buying knock offs/bootlegs for half the price. We were doing straight business and we were getting screwed. We couldn't compete after a while. Sales began to drop and that was when we got out of the retail business."

Launched by music moguls Damon Dash and Jay-Z in 2000, Rocawear became the second most popular music-inspired brand after Sean John. The streetwear-based brand spoke volumes to its music fans that were looking to emulate the luxurious lifestyle of multiplatinum artist and entrepreneur Jay-Z. In 2002, Rocawear got its first windows at Macy's Herald Square, its major New York City billboards as well as its entrance into several Bloomingdale's doors including the location in the Mall of America, the largest mall complex in the United States. While longtime business partners Dash and Jay-Z would eventually part ways, Rocawear went on to become one of the leading urban sportswear brands. The brand was eventually sold to Iconix Brand Group, Inc. for $204 million in 2007.[2] Jay-Z stayed on board in charge of product development, marketing, and licensing.

A WOMAN'S WORTH

Until the early 2000s, the celebrity clothing business had been solely a man's game. But female trendsetters from Jennifer Lopez, Eve, and Beyoncé Knowles to Gwen Stefani have now joined the ranks and the playing field. When Eve decided to host her fashion inaugural party in 2003, she celebrated in style. Using the Las Vegas restaurant/nightclub Prana as the backdrop, she hosted a private dinner for the fashion industry's elite followed with a night of entertainment courtesy of deejay Biz Markie for the likes of urban fashion pioneer Karl Kani and

Naomi Campbell wearing J. Lo Clothing. (Ronnie Wright)

Kobe Bryant. With her line Fetish, the 24-year-old Philadelphia rapper joined the ranks of celebrity clothing designers such as Jennifer Lopez (JLO), identical twin sisters Mary Kate and Ashley Olsen (who exclusively sold their apparel line to Wal-Mart), supermodel Kimora Lee Simons (who represented Baby Phat until August 2010), Beyoncé Knowles (House of Dereon), and Gwen Stefani (L.A.M.B.). Starting a clothing line added another dimension to Eve's career, with music and television already added to her credits. Fetish consisted of urban activewear, denim, and separates in fabrics including velour, satin, cotton, spandex, stretch poplin, corduroy, and denim. The Los Angeles-based Innovo Group Inc., a multidivisional sales and marketing company, designed and distributed the Fetish apparel.

Multiple Grammy Award-winning hip hop artist Nelly, who made his fashion debut with his men's line Vokal in 2002, announced the launch of Apple Bottoms in the summer of 2003. This line of female clothing openly addressed the curves of women in all shapes and sizes. Nelly kicked off the launch with a six-city tour (New York, Miami, Atlanta, St. Louis, Houston. and Los Angeles) searching for the perfect "Apple Bottoms" girl. The signature of the line is the Apple Bottoms jean, which features a colorful back pocket shaped like "big juicy" apples.

As time went by, it seemed, consumers did not even have to like the artist or even know their music or movie credits to wear their clothes. The success of the celebrity brand had more to do with the lifestyle it emulated and perpetuated. As consumers liked the way a celebrity looked and stood for, it became matter of following their lead. Sean Combs would soon be a prime example of this new celebrity businessperson.

CHAPTER 10
Urban Luxe—A Sean John Story

I just basically wanted to look good, man. To be perfectly honest, I was just like looking in my mother-fucking mirror, looking at myself and saying "Boy, God damn, you look good." You know. I just wanted my pants to drape perfectly over my combat boots. I just wanted to walk down the street like I was Shaft or John Travolta. I just wanted to feel what it would feel like to be one of those super bad, super fly, mother fuckers.

—Sean "P. Diddy" Combs' introduction to his fall
2001 7th on Sixth show

While music impresario Russell Simmons became the first music mogul to launch a clothing line in 1992, six years later it was Sean "P. Diddy" Combs who decided to follow in his footsteps and change the urban fashion landscape. A individual with an innate passion for success, drive, and determination, Combs's career had demonstrated time and time again that whatever he sets his mind to do, he could accomplish. Having successfully mastered music and acting, fashion was also right up his alley. A fashion trendsetter and tastemaker early in his life, it was Combs who was behind the looks of Uptown Records acts such as Jodeci and Mary J. Blige. He understood the connection between the image of an artist and the story that needed to be sold to the public. Like everything Combs has ever done, his clothing line Sean John was created with the intent of being untraditional. From its inception in 1998, the brand Sean John set a precedent that other youth fashion brands would find difficult to follow.

The Sean John brand had flair, sophistication, and most importantly, P. Diddy's personal style all over it. No question, the urban marketplace was ripe for a brand like Sean John. At the time, the market had been experiencing a mundane feeling by existing brands such as FUBU, which had begun to saturate the marketplace. Companies such as Enyce, Ecko, and BET's Exsto (later became defunct in 2000) had laid down the groundwork for which Sean John would later get credit. Its predecessors had placed a heavier emphasis on better fabrications and design. Unfortunately, their spearheaded efforts were not enough to convince retailers who continued to pigeonhole urban fashion. While independent startup companies began to pop up in enormous numbers, the sentiment of retailers was that they would fail and that the urban fashion market was quickly becoming oversaturated with meaningless brands. Local and regional retailers, the backbone of the youth fashion business, had patiently waited for a new brand that could have glitz, glam, and most importantly, staying power. And Sean John ended up delivering all they had hoped for.

The idea of a clothing line came to Combs in 1998. Over the years, he had witnessed firsthand the emergence and explosion of urban brands. A young Combs had been featured in the early ads of Karl Kani, one of the first streetwear brands to find retail success during and after the Cross Colours' phenomenon. As urban brands began to flourish and product placement became prominent in hip hop videos, Combs and his protégés were among the many artists who benefited from free clothes for a chance to receive brand exposure. It would make perfect sense then to see Combs, who was always known for his impeccable style, join the ranks of hip hop celebrities who had introduced their own clothing lines. Like any smart mogul, Combs did his homework by talking to all the right people in the fashion industry before taking the leap into a business somewhat unfamiliar to him.

Combs enlisted Jeffrey C. Tweedy, a seasoned fashion executive, who had a knack for developing celebrity-driven apparel lines and a long history in the urban fashion business, as his "right hand." Tweedy's fashion vision and credentials spoke volumes. Player haters in the urban fashion game would always trash-talk about Tweedy, labeling him a dreamer and very few of his peers took him seriously as a key executive because of his hit-and-miss track record. (His robust attitude did not exactly help him either, something he shares in common with Combs.)

Film director Spike Lee's Spike's Joint was a hit, Kani was a mega success, but Los Angeles Lakers' Shaquille O'Neal's TWIsM was the ultimate flop. All and all, it was just a matter of time before Tweedy could rub in the face of disbelievers that he did possess the Midas touch. Tweedy was among the few black executives that stood out to Combs in the fashion industry. He began his fashion career in his hometown of Washington, D.C. as a stock boy and later, as a manager of Neiman Marcus in Chevy Chase men's department. It was there where he met Ralph Lauren, Alexander Julian, Calvin Klein, and Jeffrey Banks. "I had the opportunity to speak to Mr. Lauren and I told him my dreams and aspirations to be in the fashion industry and one day live in New York City. Within six months, he and two gentlemen by the name of Michael Winter and Stuart Chrystler, who at the time were president and vice president of Ralph Lauren, helped me get into FIT overnight," recalls Tweedy.

Tweedy worked for Lauren as a "gofer," from fetching Lauren's lunch, pulling racks up and down Seventh Avenue to cutting swatches. He moved from Ralph Lauren to Bidermann, which housed Yves St. Laurent, which he worked for, and Calvin Klein. "I winded up going back to Ralph Lauren as an East Coast regional sales manager. I was the only African American person at the time that reached that level. I worked my way up to vice president of sales and then I met an interesting gentleman by the name of Spike Lee," remembers Tweedy. In 1986, he started working for Lee as his executive vice president of 40 Acres and a Mule clothing line.

Tweedy would eventually move to the West Coast and make a transition from working for a celebrity to becoming president of Karl Kani while under the Cross Colours' umbrella. It was actually at Kani where Tweedy and Combs first met. Combs, a bubbling music executive then simply nicknamed Puff, had posed for urban fashion pioneer Kani in his ads. Both would continue to run into each other at various industry events and they would speak on occasion; but their meeting in 1998 would prove to be most noteworthy. At the time, Tweedy had left Mecca USA and was in discussion with FUBU executives about joining their company. He wanted to relocate to the East Coast to be closer to his ill mother in Washington, D.C. During this same time, Combs was developing his brand and considering investors including FUBU and Tommy Hilfiger.

Tweedy said, "Puffy was like why do I need partners when I have my own money? He had just received a check from Arista for about $59 million. So he really didn't need partners at all." He met Combs to discuss the possibility of working with him one night at the Trump Hotel by Central Park in New York City. Combs informed Tweedy about his vision. Although most people in his shoes would jump at the opportunity, he took three to four months to make his decision to join Combs. "I wanted to be on cruise control when I moved back to New York. FUBU would've put me in cruise control because they were already established," Tweedy remembers. Ultimately, it was Combs' passion that convinced Tweedy to come on board as executive vice president of brand development and licensing at Sean John. Tweedy notes, "I liked his vision, I liked what he was talking about, now it was just a matter of how do you put it together, and make it different and capitalize on the market."

At the time, Combs was at the height of his music career and was looking to add to his entrepreneurial credentials. Combs applying his business sense with his intrinsic trendsetter abilities, he decided to venture into the apparel business and utilized a seasoned $100-million private label manufacturer to make the clothes. Strategically, Tweedy decided to have news of the line break in the men's fashion trade *DNR* about a month before the MAGIC trade show in Las Vegas. Combs was given a banner on the front cover of the paper and he and Tweedy provided the exclusive details about the brand, revealing the Sean John scripted logo on some basic T-shirts and baseball hats. Combs' initial vision was to provide a clean, sophisticated urban brand that did not resemble the big logo and baggy brands associated with urban fashion. "The market at the time was hot, but with noncelebrity brands," recalled Tweedy. While brands such as Wu-Tang Clan's Wu Wear, Naughty by Nature's Naughty Gear, and Fat Joe's FJ560 existed, none had achieved acceptance by the elite fashion guard and the streets. Combs was on a mission to conquer both and he did.

Combs took complete creative control of his brand which other entertainers, with the exception of Russell Simmons, had failed to due in the past. This might have had something to do with the fact that Combs actually owned his brand, as opposed to owning a percentage of the line like some of his music counterparts. Instead of giving his brand a name with the words "gear" or "wear" attached, Combs decided to take a completely different approach from some of his predecessors. He chose to name his line after himself and utilized his first and middle names as its brand moniker. A white embroidered Sean John signature logo on a black T-shirt became the first of many product offerings found in the line. "Our key wasn't that we wanted to be a celebrity brand. We never pitched that. That's why we used [the name] Sean John as oppose to Puff Daddy. We wanted [the brand] to be based on great product," explains Tweedy.

Combs, who had grown up in the 1970s and 1980s in the suburbs of Mount Vernon, New York, the streets of Harlem, and the campus of the historically black Howard University in Washington, D.C., gave new meaning to the return of dress-up for youths. Out went what had been traditionally stereotyped and baggy and sloppy and in came a more refined look of luxurious classics. Like other urban brands before, Sean John offered button-front shirts (commonly called button-downs), polos, denim, and velour sweatsuits. However, what made Sean John stand out from the competition was that the brand mimicked Combs' personal sense of style. He brought sexiness into urban brands—he was a modern-day Calvin Klein. Infusing Comb's fashion sense meant a cleaner fit, better fabrications, and overall star power.

After a year in the fashion business, Combs faced the scare of his life as he would be charged with gun possession and bribery in connection to a shooting inside Club New York with then girlfriend/fiancée Jennifer Lopez. Three people were wounded and rumors began to swirl that Combs had attempted to bribe his limo driver with Lopez's $50,000 ring. After a grueling seven-week trial, Combs was acquitted of all charges. (Rapper Shyne, who was with Combs at the time of the shooting, would be found guilty and sentenced to 10 years in prison.) The incident, however, did not tarnish Combs' budding designer reputation. The following year, he received accolades from the mainstream fashion community, something past urban designers had not experienced. Combs received his first nomination from the Council of Fashion Designers of America Award for Designer of the Year in 2000, the same year the company reported sales of $100 million.[1] It would take a total of three consecutive nominations before Combs would actually be deemed a winner. Nonetheless, getting a nomination was an indication that urban fashion could be viewed by some as having longevity, even if it was partly due to a celebrity connection.

Looking to build his brand's maximum exposure, Sean John made its 7th on Sixth debut in fall 2001 and appropriately themed the show "Revolution." It was apparent then, as it is now, that Combs was strategically making a statement of sorts. For one, he knew how to work his celebrity status as *E! Entertainment* Television network aired a two-hour television show that highlighted behind-the-scenes of one of the most anticipated fashion shows to hit the runway at The Tent in Bryant Park. Combs also used the runway show as his platform to debut his collection of three-piece suits in windowpane and pinstripe styles with Faith Evans, Jacob the Jeweler, and Bloomingdales' Kal Ruttenstein in the audience. Jacob the Jeweler had provided seven to twelve carat custom-made dog tags for the show as well as diamond buckles, priced from $12 to $18,000 each.

By this point, Sean John had grown through an initial "limited distribution" strategy. Its first account was Up Against the Wall in Washington, D.C. while Macy's became its first major department store alongside other major retailers like Belk's, Carson Pirie Scott, Bernini, Bloomingdale's, and Fred Segal on Melrose. "Back then [limited distribution] meant you could not find it everywhere like you could with some of the other brands. We made sure we sold one guy on 145th Street and one guy on 125th Street and we picked our spots. We wanted to right next to where Polo was being sold, where Timberland was being sold, where Nautica was being sold. That's what our focus was," says Tweedy. The brand had been reluctant to start using Combs' image until the company's third year of operation to avoid being pigeonholed as a celebrity-driven brand. "We wanted people to naturally like the product and by the way, it's by Puff Daddy," stressed Tweedy. In 2001, Sean John took over the Tommy Hilfiger billboard overlooking New York's Fashion District in Herald Square. The 30' by 70' board, operated by outdoor company Van Wagner, sits atop 1239 Broadway at 31st Street and has one of the highest daily effective circulations at over a million. The billboard had been Hilfiger's since October 1998.

Four years after the club shooting incident, Combs faced public scrutiny in 2003 with sweatshop labor allegations put forth by the National Labor Committee (NLC). Combs took on a "zero tolerance" and "pro-worker" approach and quickly dissolved the controversy. Nonetheless, it also meant that although Combs was a glorified designer, he also had to mind his ship as tight, if not tighter, than other designers due to his celebrity fame. In 2006, Sean John was again in the headlines. This time, the controversy was about the brand's faux-fur claim on two

Mercedes-Benz fashion week, fall 2008, Sean John runway, pictured Tyson Beckford, P. Diddy. (JP Yim/Wire Image)

particular styles of jackets. The Humane Society of the United States found that the particular Sean John jackets being sold at Macy's were made from "raccoon dog." (Jay-Z had a similar incident with Rocawear in 2007.) The styles were immediately pulled off Macy's shelves. That same year, Sean John moved into fragrances with a partnership with

Estée Lauder. Its signature men's fragrance, Unforgivable would become a top-seller in department stores. Its feminine counterpart, Unforgivable Woman would launch a year later and in 2008, Combs would strike with another popular fragrance appropriately called I Am King.

The year 2008 illustrated Combs' eye for brand expansion. He purchased Enyce from Liz Claiborne that summer, a brand known for its better fabrications and design sense. Founded by the same men who were once behind Mecca USA, its name stemmed from the phonetic spelling of New York City. Sean John acquired the brand to offer quality fashion at a more reasonable price through another brand extension; similar to the idea to what Cross Colors wanted to do but never had the chance. "We thought why not take this brand that people love and hasn't been tainted and take it to mid-level which is specialty store. Instead of [Sean John] jeans being $70, they are $32 and $30 [at Enyce]," says Tweedy. While Enyce became the first brand acquired under the Sean John umbrella, there are hopes that other brands would follow suit. Unlike its forefather Cross Colors, Sean John will license the brands it acquires rather than taking on brands in-house. "It's very few companies that can do that successfully without cannibalizing the other brand they have," added Tweedy.

As specialty stores began selling out and closing due to the sluggish economy after the events of 9/11, retail opportunities on the specialty store level, once the "bread and butter" of urban fashion distribution, have deteriorated. One by one, lifestyle brands began to disappear from PNB Nation to FUBU; only a handful of brands have managed to survive the economic downturn in the United States and the world. And Sean John has been one of them. Having changed its distribution pattern once specialty stores in the hood began to lose momentum, Sean John continued to play in the big leagues with a department store distribution strategy. Taking a page from Tommy Hilfiger's business model in 2010, Sean John and Macy's, Inc. signed an exclusive distribution deal that would put Sean John in 400 Macy's stores across the country as well as to be sold online at macys.com. "Macy's was a retailer that has been with us for a long time," says Tweedy. "They have been with us since the inception of the line and it was the right relationship that Puff and I had with Macy's."

With annual sales of $525 million, it was the perfect union for the contemporary sportswear company and the popular U.S. department retailer.[2] The exclusive sportswear line would now sell its woven sport shirts, knits, sweaters, T-shirts, denim, outerwear, and sport coats at the retailer which has identified with urban sportswear for over 20 years. As part of the deal, Sean John would include placement in flagship stores at Macy's Herald Square in New York, Union Square in San Francisco, State Street in Chicago, Dadeland in Miami, and South Coast Plaza in Costa Mesa. Sean John fragrances, tailored clothing, shirts and ties, lounge and underwear, leather goods, boy's, women's, and other product categories would also have increased visibility in Macy's stores. With the creation of this unique destination shop at one of the country's leading department stores, Sean John marked a great triumph for urban wear which was originally seen as a passing fad by the fashion industry.

CHAPTER 11
They Got Fashion Game

Both [basketball] athletes and [hip hop] music artists come from an environment where there are humble beginnings. Both didn't require more than just two things—talent and a dream. The difference is one picked up a mike and another, a hoop. The circumstances surrounding their rise to fame and what it took to achieve that are basically identical.
—Erin Patton, Founder of The Mastermind Group

The legendary 1991 University of Michigan's Fab Five consisting of Chris Webber, Jalen Rose, Juwan Howard, Jimmy King, and Ray Jackson could also be considered the equivalent of the Wu-Tang Clan for college basketball. Bringing a unique hip hop style and swagger to college basketball, these five freshman players at the time advanced to the NCAA Tournament championship while donning their fashion trademarks of long baggy shorts, black socks, and sneakers. Their hip hop camaraderie brought them into the spotlight like the Georgetown Hoyas faced in the mid-1980s when they first had their love affair with Nike Dunks, a basketball shoe that evolved from Air Jordan.

College and professional basketball players' affinity for hip hop therefore should come as no surprise. "All this is relative to cultural collisions that take place within the context of the urban experience, which is what makes it so dynamic and makes it a true renaissance," says Erin Patton, founder of The Mastermind Group, a brand management firm. Patton was instrumental in the most notable footwear product launches in history including the Jordan Brand and Stephon Marbury's Starbury and its $14.98 sneaker partnership with national retailer Steve & Barry's. "Both [basketball] athletes and [hip hop] music artists come from an environment where there are humble beginnings. Both didn't require more than just two things—talent and a dream. The difference is that one picked up a mike and another, a hoop. The circumstances surrounding their rise to fame and what it took to achieve that are basically identical," says Patton. From Patton's perspective, sports and music are two very obvious ways to bypass the traditional route to success. As the rapper Talib Kweli noted, both share the "beautiful struggle."

From Antonio Gray's perspective, a buyer for the Maryland-based chain DTLR (Downtown Locker Room), when hip hop became really popular, hip hop artists started wearing athletic clothing and the urban teens followed. "It was about taking your Adidas track jacket worn by Run-D.M.C. or Adidas shoe or Le Coq Sportif USA sweatsuits seen on LL Cool J," he says. Athletic brands were thought of as authentic, colorful, and comfortable. For athletes, hip hop signified a badge of credibility in helping some athletes maintain an allegiance to their fans and culture as they faced the daily challenge of "keeping it real." Many basketball players have taken that same MC swagger and used it to define themselves as they stepped into the professional arena. Some even tried their hand at rhyming such as Shaquille O'Neal, Kobe Bryant, Ron Artest, Jason Kidd, and Allen Iverson.

Former Los Angeles Lakers center Shaquille O'Neal also took a shot at the apparel game in the 1990s. At that time, athletic endorsements were the norm for basketball athletes and many times, they included apparel. However, the seven-foot-one O'Neal was among the first to think outside the box. Signed to Reebok to endorse his footwear line in the mid-1990s, O'Neal desired to move into entrepreneurialism with the launch of both a record label and an urban clothing line. TWIsM, an acronym for The World Is Mine (and also tattooed on O'Neal's arm), started as a mentoring program for children and later branched out into music and fashion. "[Shaq] really didn't plan it to be a fashion line, but he really did it for the kids," says Jeffrey Tweedy, who once headed TWIsM as its executive vice president. "That's why his record company was called TWIsM. It was really to show kids that the world is theirs and do whatever you want and be as big as Shaq and be as powerful. That was the real message."

O'Neal struck a joint venture deal with Cyrk, a Gloucester, MA-based manufacturer which developed a young men's urban line of T-shirts, tops, jeans, and outerwear. At first, it was not easy for O'Neal, who had a conflict of interest as he was signed to promote Reebok while wanting to brand his own line of apparel. Eventually, Reebok and O'Neal worked things out leaving him to use his likeness for his own brand and opening the doors for other athletes to follow in his footsteps. The line was initially well-received, but it encountered obstacles at retail. For example, it is hard for a big man to sell clothes especially in the young men's market. The youth fashion brand went through several hiatuses through the late 1990s and became short-lived.

On the East Coast, former New York Knick shooting guard John Starks would also try his hand at urban fashion with a line called Original Man Wear, Inc. (OMW) in the late 1990s. The activewear meets streetwear line consisted of jeans, outerwear, T-shirts, and tops and donated a portion of the licensed proceeds to his John Starks Foundation. The young men's business was also short-lived for Starks who decided to stay with what he knew best—activewear. In 2007, he co-founded a new apparel company called Zipway, created around zipper-infused active apparel which has since been successful.[1]

Athletes have also dabbled with hip hop and starting their own design labels. However, the National Basketball Association (NBA) has had another take on the matter of hip hop and fashion statements made by its professional athletes. In 1997, the NBA fined the Minnesota Timberwolves and the Portland Trailblazers a total of $67,500 for violating the league's dress code. The Minnesota Timberwolves' Kevin Garnett and Stephon Marbury, at the time, were also fined for the same infraction—wearing baggy shorts.[2]

However, nobody comes close to former Chicago Bulls Michael Jordan and his relationship to hip hop and fashion. When Nike captured Jordan from Adidas in 1984, no one could have ever imagined the cult-like status that this basketball superstar would soon acquire. When Jordan decided to wear his Air Jordan warm-up suit to the 1985 All-Star Game as a rookie instead of the standard All-Star warm-up suit, it not only signified a power move, but it was also a defiant hip hop moment. It quickly became evident that Jordan, who earned six championship rings during his professional basketball career, had the Midas touch from basketball to selling footwear and later, apparel. He became a true modern-day superhero. As the book *Young, Black, Rich, and Famous: The Rise of the NBA, the Hip Hop Invasion, and the Transformation of American Culture* (2003) points out, "The soul of basketball, however, remains at least for the time in urban America." Like the man himself, the Air Jordan's popularity defied all expectations. "The cool thing about brands is that as much

Athletic wear has always been popular in hip hop fashion. Flavor Flav in Nike Jordan tracksuit and Chuck D in a Chicago Bulls jersey. (© Ernie Paniccioli. Used by permission.)

we as keepers of the brand like to think that we are driving consumer behavior at our very best, we are only reacting," says Patton. "Jordan is one of those rare examples where the consumer was reacting to the brand instead of creating a shift that the brand was reacting to. This was really a real-time relationship between brand and consumer."

Erin Patton was on both sides. He started as an early adopter, growing up in inner-city Pittsburgh in the late 1980s and coming of age in high school when the Jordans were elevated to iconic status. Patton, part of the sneaker culture and a self-admitted sneaker head, worked for Nike to help decode the code Jordan consumers lived by. He was the consumer as well as a seasoned and skilled marketer. His marketing strategy kept both of those things in mind. "We talked a lot about how we could make it feel like an insider brand because so many consumers were gravitating to brands literally being birthed from the music and the culture," Patton says. He understood the importance of getting the community's support so his strategy included going to urban New York specialty stores such as Jimmy Jazz and Dr. Jay's for feedback on the new Jordan sneakers. When brand Jordan launched as a separate brand in 1997, Patton was given the mantle to carry and move the brand to a unique position in the marketplace. He did mix tapes with the sneaker release and a sneaker release party with *Vibe* magazine with a performance by Mos Def (Yasiin) to help brand positioning within the hip hop market.

With the success of brand Jordan, athletes moved beyond traditional endorsement deals and made their moves to promote their own apparel brands. It seemed like a natural progression for these athletes in an attempt to gain more financial control of their identity. Former NY Giant Carl Banks also knows all too well the connection of sports, fashion, and hip hop.[3] Banks's interest in fashion and his New York Giants connection proved to be a winning combination for them both. He recognized a lack of quality and oversized apparel, so he took to the drawing board and designed outerwear for several teammates and friends in the NFL in the late 1980s. After receiving positive reviews in 1989, Banks applied for an NFL license to distribute his outerwear to retailers. In 1992, he joined G-III Apparel Group as its director of licensing and today serves its vice president. While Banks became well known in the apparel business for his various professional sports licensees, he also dabbled in urban fashion business. In the summer of 1999, the NFL and BET Design Studio, LLC (a joint venture owned by G-III Apparel Group, Ltd. and Black Entertainment Television, Inc.) teamed up to launch the BET Sports Collection. The collection featured knit tops, velour sweatsuits, fashion jerseys, outerwear, T-shirts, and polar fleece targeted to the urban fashion consumer. At the time, BET Design Studio was producing and distributing sportswear under the labels Exsto XXIV VII and Exsto Black Rivet Uniform Denim. Unfortunately, the Exsto brand was short-lived.

At a moment in time in the late 1990s/early 2000s, it seemed that everybody was chasing their own young men's apparel brand. Even world-famous boxing promoter Don King joined in with his Only in America line. Targeting mid-tier retailers like Sears and J.C. Penney, his goal was to seize the moment and capture some of the exploding urban fashion scene though his connection to urban fashion. It seemed almost anybody and everybody with some name recognition would become an apparel maker. This, in turn, helped create clutter in the urban fashion market. Athletes, looking to cash in on their image, saw a unique opportunity to take their popularity and fan base to create a unique brand concept. But the apparel business requires a significant amount of time and resources, not just a famous name and likeness. Even star athletes and star millionaires are not exempt from the economic challenges of sourcing, manufacturing, and finding proper distribution channels. Athletes, therefore, had to look at the apparel industry and its business model like hip hop artists did with the launch of their own record labels. Athletes could just be a commodity, a paid endorser, or take part in the equity by becoming real partners in fashion. It is apparent that there will eventually be more athletes who will look at the sneaker and fashion industries as a way to capitalize on their brand equity. What athletes need to do is figure out ways to create true equitable partnerships.

The urban fashion business was not only limited to professional athletes. Fila USA, a classic name in hip hop due in part to its sneakers and velour warm-up suits in the 1980s, went after the urban fashion business in 1997 when it teamed up with members of the Mecca USA camp including Lando Felix, Tony Shellman, and Evan Davis. The former Mecca executives proved to have the magic touch. Launched in spring 1997, the Enyce (the phonetic spelling of New York City) provided design and design inspiration to a market that they felt was lacking both. Known for its focus on quality fabrications and small strategic logo placements, the brand today is housed under the Sean John umbrella of brands.

THE LOVE AFFAIR WITH JERSEYS

Credit must be given to film director Spike Lee for putting jerseys in the forefront of his film to generate thought, dialogue, and conversation. Before rappers and A-list celebrities made wearing jerseys fashionable, it was Lee who strategically used jerseys as cultural statements to help better portray central and supporting characters. Movie audiences first saw a Jackie Robinson (#42) Brooklyn Dodgers baseball jersey and a Larry Bird (#33) Boston Celtic basketball jersey in his 1989 film *Do the Right Thing*. Mookie, a pizza deliveryman who is a die-hard Brooklynite from Bedford-Stuyversant (Bed-Sty), played by Lee, wore the symbolic Dodgers jersey. The apparel item played a pivotal role in the film deemed "culturally significant" by the U.S. Library of Congress. It helped define Lee's character beyond the obvious. The film explored topics of racial tensions, police brutality, institutional racism, stereotypes, and prejudice in New York City. It received a number of accolades and awards as it equally received criticism. Robinson, the first black major league baseball player made his debut with the Brooklyn Dodgers in 1947. He was also the first black player instrumental in bringing an end to segregation in professional baseball. Mookie's jersey paid homage to his superhero much as did the Larry Bird (#33) Boston Celtics jersey worn by the white character in the film.

In both cases as well, the jerseys were used to represent the places the characters were from—Brooklyn and Boston—as well as a particular mindset. The Boston Celtics were primarily a white team during the years Bird played so he could be viewed as a white person's modern-day super-hero much like Jordan was for people of color in the late 1980s. Athletic jerseys would later sporadically appear in television shows such as Bill Cosby's *Different World* on Dwayne Wayne and on the police drama, *New York Undercover*. Michael DeLorenzo, who played Detective Eddie Torres in the New York City-based show, would frequently be seen chasing the bad guys wearing hockey and baseball jerseys.

It really was not until the 1990s that throwback jerseys became all the sensation. The phenomenon of the throwback jersey was started in Philadelphia by a sales associate who observed the sales of the classic sports jersey at his store Mitchell & Ness Nostalgia Co. The store was founded in 1904 by former tennis and wrestling champ Frank P. Mitchell and Scottish golfer Charles M. Ness. The sporting goods store initially specialized in selling tennis and golf goods. Over the years, the store expanded into designing and manufacturing uniforms for high school, college, semi-pro, and pro teams. In 1983, Mitchell & Ness began creating vintage jerseys after a customer asked to have two game-worn jerseys repaired. In 1988, the sports retailer received exclusive permission to make player number jerseys from Major League Baseball (MLB) for its Authentic Cooperstown Collection. Soon, Mitchell & Ness received licenses from the National Basketball Association (NBA), the National Football League (NFL), and the National Hockey League (NHL).

By the late 1990s, Mitchell & Ness found tremendous success with its vintage throwback jerseys as a result of its popularity among hip hop celebrities and entertainers. By noticing what types of jerseys stylists were purchasing, the store incorporated this information into their company's product and design strategy. Mitchell & Ness of Philadelphia and Stall and Dean in Brockton, Mass. became overnight sensations with celebrities and hip hop fans as the two leading suppliers of the $200+ jerseys. These two athletic manufacturers held licenses for old-school jerseys for NFL, MLB, and NBA teams. The who's who of hip hop donned their throwback jerseys. Thank rapper Fabolous for making throwback jerseys part of his everyday wardrobe regiment, followed by Outkast, Fat Joe, Ludacris, Sean "Puffy" Combs, Jay-Z, Cam'Ron, Jermaine Dupri, DJ Clue, and Big Tigger. Former fashion stylist Roger McKenzie recalled Jay-Z promoting Carolina blue, "We put Mya in a jersey dress for his video. We took one of the Carolina blue jerseys and we made them cut it down and make it into a dress for her."

It seems that the more obscure the jersey, the more appealing it was to the customer. The logic behind purchasing a jersey fell into a few categories—pick a jersey on a player no one in the hood ever heard of or match the jersey colors to the latest and most popular sneaker. Urban fashion companies like Mecca USA, Maurice Malone, FUBU, and Willie Esco would also jump on the jersey trend. Mecca became known for its soccer jersey; Malone for his hockey jersey; and FUBU for its NBA licensed basketball jersey while Willie Esco obtained the MLB license for a baseball jersey. In 2002, RTB Apparel launched Rap Throwbacks. The jerseys featured the original artwork and song titles of various rappers. Numbers on the front and back of the jersey commemorated the year the song was released. Created by the husband-and-wife team, Rodney and Knia Bonds, the jerseys were classified by four classifications of rap music. They included "Classic," which focused on the pioneers like Kurtis Blow, Grandmaster Flash and the Furious Five, and the Cold Crush Brothers; "True School," which focused on 1980s rappers like Big Daddy Kane, Stetasonic, and MC Lyte; "Commemorative," which paid homage to deceased artists like Jam Master Jay, Left Eye, and Tupac Shakur; and finally, "The Cutmasters," pioneering deejays like Afrika Bambaataa, Kool DJ Red Alert, DJ Chuck Chillout, Jazzy Jay, DJ Jazzy Jeff, and AJ Scratch. Unfortunately, the throwback jersey trend would not last. It became a passing fad thanks to the shift in urban dress by the likes of Kanye West and a more mature hip hop mogul Jay-Z. When Jay-Z went from throwback jerseys to button ups almost overnight, there went the phenomenon with it.

CHAPTER 12
White Behind the Brands

When Tommy [Hilfiger] started coming into the fashion world, he was larger than life. Snoop Dogg on *Saturday Night Live* made a huge impact.

—Carrie Harris, former vice president of men's and children's at Directives West

Diversity has not always been something the fashion industry has excelled at from a design, modeling, or even specific target market perspective. But when hip hop music started generating money beyond record sales, it became evident that fashion could also capitalize on this emerging trend. While black designers were the first to come to mind with the development of hip hop brands, there are a number of white designers and apparel manufacturers who have hip hop to thank for some, if not all, of their success. "Race is a hot-button issue [in fashion]," states style expert Lloyd Boston, a regular style contributor on NBC's *Today Show* and author of several fashion books. "Whenever it comes down to categorizing color, heritage, race, as it relates to a product, it becomes a sensitive subject. Fashion is no exception."

Hip hop's influence quickly spread beyond the black fashion world in the 1980s as it graced the runways of high fashion. Realizing the potential dollars of urban consumers white designers decided to join in—some shouted it out while others took a more subdued approach. In 1984, Norma Kamali showed her collection in a hip hop influenced video. Chanel followed in 1987 with a hip hop-infused collection that included gold door-knocker earrings, oversized baseball jackets, and Kangol cap-like replicas. By the 1990s, the influence of hip hop moved beyond imitating style. Hip hop celebrities such as Mary J. Blige, Treach, and Mos Def graced the runway on behalf of Tommy Hilfiger and Marc Ecko while many hip hop personalities became permanent fixtures in the front rows of the most desired fashion shows. Lil' Kim, Beyoncé, Eve, Jay-Z, Mary J. Blige, and J.Lo, for example, would become familiar faces during Mercedes Benz Fashion Week in New York. Hip hop music saw the power of the white rap artists with a variety of acts over the years including the Beastie Boys, Vanilla Ice, 3rd Bass, Markie Mark (better known as Mark Wahlberg), Kid Rock, and Eminem. Therefore, it would only be natural to see a similar evolution take place in the fashion world. Like the music, the fashion industry saw a void in the market for white designers who catered to a black audience. White designers and their closeness to the market varied. On one extreme were U.S. designers with sportswear roots who catered to the hip hop clientele such as Tommy Hilfiger while on the other extreme, were hip hop purists and entrepreneurs such as Camella Elhke.

TOMMY HILFIGER AND HIS HIP HOP SWAG

It was not until the 1990s that Tommy Hilfiger became a household name and the influence of hip hop had made all the difference. Much credit to Hilfiger's hip hop success must be given to his younger brother, Andy, who for many years handled marketing and public relations for Tommy Jeans. A musician at heart, Andy made his way into fashion through his brother Tommy as a teen working at his hippie shop, People's Place in Elmira, New York, which sold predominately bell bottoms, incense, and records.

Tommy became involved with fashion as a teen while still in high school. An entrepreneur at heart, the young Hilfiger opened up his own chain of stores with the intent of bringing New York and London fashion to upstate New York.[1] Andy would head to the store on Saturdays to fold jeans at the age of 12 and to also attend sample sales in New York for great finds to take back to Elmira. "We would go to the cool shops, the punk rock shops and we would buy $100 pair of jeans that were like unheard," recalls Andy. "We would also go to sample sales and buy jeans for $1 and sell them for $10. Those trips were great because at night, Tommy would take us to the clubs even though we were 14 and 15 years old. We would see all these bands like the Ramones, the Talking Heads, and the Plasmatics. We saw their style and we liked it so much that we adapted that style into the store."

Tommy moved to New York City in 1979 and closed the upstate stores as he began to freelance design for different companies including Jordache. By 1985, he was able to launch his own collection with limited classic American sportswear basics like chinos and oxford shirts. A clever billboard developed by advertising guru George Lois (among his famous ads include the "I want my MTV" campaign campaign) that read "The Four Great American Designers" in Times Square compared the then unknown Tommy Hilfiger to design heavyweights Calvin Klein, Ralph Lauren, and Perry Ellis. The ad featured just the initials of each designer with dashes for viewers to fill in the black. The last designer was TH, with the necessary spaces to spell out Tommy Hilfiger's name. At the bottom of the ad was featured the Hilfiger red, white, and blue logo known today with the words "This is the logo of the least known of the four" alongside it. Instantly, this "seemingly outrageous" campaign that some may even call obnoxious helped Tommy obtain a newfound notoriety.[2] He would go from an unknown to a fashionista virtually overnight. His brother Andy would join him five years later and market the Tommy Hilfiger brand into a hip hop designing superstar.

A T-shirt and jean type of guy, Andy resembled one of the Ramones. He began working on projects for his brother to make extra money between his music gigs. At the time, Andy played in rock-and-roll bands in a number of venues including CBGB's in New York and toured for clubs all over the country. He also had experience working in film and video. "I met this guy who owned cameras, lights, and stuff. He asked me if I could drive a truck and being that I was from upstate New York, we drove everything," recalls Andy, who remembers working on Run-D.M.C.'s *Tougher than Leather* as a truck driver and grip. "It was $100 a day. I drove the truck and I started doing all the hip hop videos," he says. When Andy starting receiving calls from hip hop stylists requesting wardrobe, product placements in hip hop videos seemed like a no-brainer.

Tommy Hilfiger received a lyrical plug by Brand Nubians' Grand Puba on Mary J. Blige's song "What's the 411?" in 1992 before his big break with Snoop Dogg on *Saturday Night Live* in 1994. According to his brother, the lyrics "Girbaud's hanging baggy, Tommy Hilfiger top gear" were done organically. "That just happened. Coincidentally, I worked on a video for Brand Nubians, but not that song," says Andy. Upon hearing the lyrics, he went to his brother's house in Greenwich, Connecticut to share the good news. "When played the cassette for Tommy, he was floored with excitement," recalls fashion expert Lloyd Boston who served as the former vice president of art direction at Tommy Hilfiger. Boston says, "He told Andy and me to reach out to Grand Puba—his crew and dress them." Once the video went into production, Andy Hilfiger placed the Tommy Hilfiger brand in the rap video that plugged his brother's clothing line. The rest is hip hop history.

Tommy first met Brand Nubians in 1993 while flying back from Hong Kong on a trip to look at clothing samples. Landing in Los Angeles and taking the "redeye" to New York City, the Hilfigers met the rap group at John F. Kennedy Airport. "I saw these guys dressed in Tommy," recalls Andy. "They were waiting for their luggage and we were waiting for ours. It happened to be Grand Puba and the Brand Nubians. We invited them up to the showroom. The next day, they came up to the showroom and we gave them wardrobes full of the newest, latest and greatest [gear]."

A year later, the Hilfigers went to the Grammy Awards. While at the Natural Museum of History for an Atlantic Records party, they met Snoop Doggy Dogg. The next day, Andy received a voicemail from the Dr. Dre protégé. Taking the Hilfigers up on their invitation to get clothes, Snoop Dogg brought the Dogg Pound to the Hilfiger showroom. "He wanted the pinstripe banker suits, they were pimp suits to him, so I hooked him up," recalls Andy. A week later on a Friday night at about five o'clock, Andy received a call from Snoop Dog, who needed clothes for his upcoming performance on *Saturday Night Live*. Andy was to meet Snoop Dogg at Hotel Macklowe (153 West 44th Street) at 9:00 P.M. "I stayed in the office, walked over to Hotel Macklowe in the pouring rain with two shopping bags," remembers Andy. Unfortunately, Snoop's Dogg Pound crew also wanted clothes so Andy went back to his showroom where he undressed the showroom mannequins and took the clothes back to the hotel. While Snoop assured Andy that he was going to wear his clothes for the show, it was something that Andy took lightly. "To me, it was like that's cool if he does and if he doesn't," he says.

The next night, Saturday night, Andy received a call from his brother Tommy around 11:30 P.M. telling him to tune into *Saturday Night Live*. Snoop Dogg went on the show wearing a Tommy Hilfiger red, white, and blue rugby. That Monday, Andy started getting calls from the Tommy Hilfiger salespeople and remembers, "They were getting calls from the stores saying 'Where is that rugby?' That thing sold out that day." Carrie Harris, former vice president of men's and children's of West Coast-based Directives West (a trend forecasting company now part of trend forecasting firm The Doneger Group) agrees. "When Tommy [Hilfiger] started coming into the fashion world, he was larger than life. Snoop Dogg on *Saturday Night Live* made a huge impact."

While the Grand Puba Tommy Hilfiger plug set the brand on fire within the hip hop community, it was the Snoop placement that turned Tommy Hilfiger from a preppy, American classic company to a preppy, American, classic, *cool* company because Snoop brought coolness to the brand. "It was un-strategic and very magical," admits Andy. "From then on, the stores went crazy with it. Anything Tommy Hilfiger was cool to wear." Tommy started seeing an increase in sales on his logoed items. Ultimately, the company launched Tommy Hilfiger Jeans, a new jeanswear division aimed at both men and women. Andy would then create an ad campaign that would feature Kidada Jones, Quincy Jones's daughter; his nephew, Michael Fredo; and deejay Marc Ronson, among others. That campaign was then followed by one featuring the sons and daughters of famous people. Aaliyah, who was on Atlantic Records, became part of the infamous shoot. "My sister Jenny and I styled the shoot with Kidada [Jones]. We took men's and we made women's out." Tommy Hilfiger Jeans wardrobed the film *The Faculty* which featured Usher and Rosario Dawson. Hilfiger was strategic to embrace hip hop culture. "We were the first commercial, corporate, mainstream apparel company to advertise in a black publication," says Andy, referring to *Vibe* and *The Source*. "We had gatefolds with race cars in it. It was a whole lifestyle thing."

Tommy Hilfiger later became the target of rumors claiming to have been on *The Oprah Winfrey Show* and expressing that he did not want black people to wear his clothes. In 2000, Andy left Tommy Hilfiger Jeans to launch Jennifer Lopez's Sweetface Fashion Company and rumors soon began to link J.Lo with Andy. Eventually, Andy went back to work for

Tommy in late 2000s and in 2009, left again to start his own company called Star Branding.

AVIREX

Long before Avirex made a name for itself with hip hop heads, the brand took pride in its long history with the military. Founded by pilot and airplane collector, Jeff Clyman, the brand "took flight" in 1975. Clyman was particularly fond of his father's aviator jacket from World War II and would frequently receive compliments about it which, in turn, sparked the idea for Avirex as an apparel and outerwear company. The company began as a mail order catalog business and expanded to traditional retail outlets by the late 1980s. In 1986, Avirex created aviator jackets for blockbuster film *Top Gun* and the demand for the brand globally took off. Cylman and his wife Jackie then opened The CockPit, a specialty store in SoHo whose interior resembles that of a giant authentic aircraft. Conveniently located near the Hot 97 (radio station) offices, the Cockpit became a frequent destination of rappers and A-List celebrities. Fans of Avirex included The Notorious B.I.G. (Biggie Smalls), Big Pun, Fat Joe, Puff Daddy, Jermaine Dupri, and Ludacris. In 2006, Clyman sold Avirex and its trademark to Marc Ecko Enterprises. Today, he operates Cockpit USA, a military-inspired apparel line, the Cockpit boutique, and is president of the American Airpower Museum at Republic Airport in Farmingdale, NY, which houses operational WWII aircraft and vintage planes.

PELLE PELLE

With no formal garment training, Marc Buchanan began designing hippie clothes as a way to finance his art school studies. From the age of two, he had had his heart set on being an artist as he enjoyed painting, sculpting, and ceramics. However, it was fashion that would embark Buchanan into his destined career path. Self-taught, he learned pattern drafting from books and started making clothes for himself in high school. "I started making stuff for myself and drew simplistic patterns and start alternating them from whatever designs I wanted in the late 1960s," recalls Buchanan. An entrepreneur at heart, he launched his first apparel company called Gandolf & Company in 1971 and sold it five years later to explore other interests. Simultaneously, Buchanan pursued design and art. He began freelance design while taking sculpture classes. "By the 1970s, my involvement in leather business overtopped my art career and it took over." In 1978, he launched Pelle Pelle (*pelle* means leather in Italian), which has become a hit with hip hop fans who adore attention to detail like studs and rhinestones on soft leather.

TRIPLE FIVE SOUL

Cool white girl Camella Ehlke just wanted a space to make clothes, throw parties, and show some art. That was 1989 and the platform she used was called Triple Five Soul. One of the few pioneering female hip hop designers, Ehlke started a retail and wholesale business on Lafayette Street in New York City and named it after a popular telephone party line. The brand, which had an underground hipster feel vibe, quickly expanded internationally. The streetwear brand grew both its whole and retail operations simultaneously, making it stand out among its competitors. In 2003, Ehlke sold her company's shares to then business partner Troy Morehouse to pursue other endeavors. Today, no longer in the apparel business, Elhke, with Marlon Aitcheson, runs and operates Breathe Inn, a bed and breakfast in Lanesville, NY and the Picnic Country Store, a boutique café and sandwich shop in Brooklyn.

SLIM SHADY

The multitalented rapper turned actor Eminem became the most sought after artist by fashion executives with the hope of launching a clothing line in the early 2000s. In 2003, Slim Shady Ltd. was launched through an exclusive license with Nesi Fashion Brands, headed by garment designer Vincent Nesi Sr. (co-founder of the famous 1980s brand Bugle Boy and who later built a name for himself in the urban apparel industry with Rocawear junior's and School of Hard Knocks). Slim Shady was off to a great start as Macy's announced it would place the brand in 90 of its locations.[3] Unfortunately, the Detroit native did not experience the same type of explosive apparel success with Slim Shady as did some of his fellow rap predecessors.

ED HARDY

The Ed Hardy brand, a lifestyle extension brand from the legendary tattoo artist Don Ed Hardy, did shake up the industry. Launching in 2004, the success of Ed Hardy was reminiscent of that of FUBU, which catapulted sales to record-breaking heights. French fashion designer Christian Audigier was behind the brands' explosive growth (and some say demise) as the tattoo-inspired brand had a strong five-year run with products in just about every category from T-shirts, bedding, and cologne to scarves and bottle warmers. Prior to Ed Hardy, the savvy Audigier was chief designer for Von Dutch Originals, where he popularized the modern trucker hat which sold for close to $50. Von Dutch became Ed Hardy's "training wheels." Like Von Dutch, Audigier built Ed Hardy through celebrity product placement and licensing. The brand, known for its studded garments, repeated artwork, and embellishments grew a celebrity following that included Madonna, Dennis Rodman, and David Beckham. The brand became a hit within the urban community for its affiliation for tattoos, rock-and-roll, and a cool lifestyle. The Ed Hardy brand grew quickly, but its popularity had fizzled by 2008. *Business Week* reported that sales were a little over $100 million at that time. In 2011, Iconix, the same company who also owned brands such as Mossimo, Mark Ecko, and Rocawear, purchased the master license in 2011 for $55 million plus a $7 million earn-out.

CHAPTER 13
The Ecko, The Rhino, and the Empire That Marc Built

Graffiti, which was suppose to be some gateway to crime was actually some gateway for me to recognize that I was creative. I could express myself in this kind of creative way that was the extreme sport of art. For me, it was a gateway into entrepreneurialship, into a lifestyle.
— Marc Ecko, chief creative officer, Marc Ecko Enterprises

Raised in the New Jersey suburbs of Lakewood, Marc Ecko grew up in a diverse neighborhood that consisted of a large Orthodox Jewish, Latino, and black population. It was this diverse upbringing that would influence him both personally and professionally. Born Marc Milecofsky, Ecko identified with hip hop early on. "Being this white kid, Jewish kid, in a town that was really ethnically diverse, I didn't really identify myself with my Jewishness. There was a big Jewish population there and my parents grew up as reformed Jews. [Hip hop] was a gateway for me to socialize with my peer group and have some kind of unique look to bring to the party," recalls Ecko.

Ecko grew up as a heavyset kid and became very conscious of what he wore as early as sixth grade. It was then he started to recognize that hip hop and the influence of black culture on popular culture was something that was part of his experience. "I wasn't very athletic so dressing was kind of my way to smooth it out," he says. "I could express myself through dressing." Ecko, who won "Best Dressed" in eighth grade, considered himself to have "mashed up" style as a result of early MTV's influence on pop culture. He felt "white on the outside, black on the inside, kind of identifying with black popular culture and hip hop, while at the same time very aware of the downtown skate and BMX scene." He always seemed to lean a little more street and hip hop

Designer Marc Ecko attends the 2010 Emery Awards at Cipriani. (Joe Corrigan/Getty Images)

because of the influence his hometown had on him. Ecko says, "I remember listening to Slick Rick talk about Polo cologne and that was the first time I became aware of a brand. When he started rhyming about Polo cologne, I needed Polo cologne. So that was a rite of passage for me, going to the Ocean County Mall to a Macy's and getting the smallest-sized bottle of Polo as a gift from my grandmother and wearing way too much of it and dousing myself in it and thinking I smelled like Slick Rick."

Becoming fashionable was just one way Ecko became connected with his peers while an alternative vice was his art. "Graffiti, which was suppose to be some gateway to crime was actually some gateway for me to recognize that I was creative. I could express myself in this kind of creative way that was the extreme sport of art. For me, it was a gateway into entrepreneurialship, into a lifestyle," says Ecko, who avidly practiced graffiti in the late 1980s throughout the New Jersey/New York area on everything from notebooks, community walls, and subway cars to bridges. His tags would eventually evolve like many other graffiti artists from walls and subway cars to a clothing canvas jumpstarted by T-shirts. "I was painting on T-shirts and denim jackets by the middle of eighth grade," remembered Ecko, who started turning his craft into a business in his freshman year at Lakewood High School. "It was slightly exotic, being in Lakewood and being someone who could airbrush," he says. "Everyone wanted them. So, there was a demand."

Ecko did not have much "business acumen at the time," but he credits his parents for pushing him into his entrepreneurial stride. "My parents knew that I was going to get an air compressor and airbrush and I was going to save up for that. They didn't want it to go unkempt like some dusty, old piano that you buy for your kid and then never use. They made a fuss. 'If you are going to do something with [airbrush equipment] than you are going to have to sell T-shirts. You are going to work to make good on this,'" remembers Ecko. It was expected of their son to have a job by his freshman year of high school so he took on airbrushing as his alternative means of traditional work. Ecko made airbrushed denim outfits out of his parent's garage as a way to make extra money. He says, "I was going to make good on the promise of delivering on the $100 investment made to get the Sears air compressor and the Paasche BL3 airbrush. I definitely felt I was obligated to do something with it."

By the time he graduated high school in 1990, Ecko was forced with the decision to go to college and pursue a career. During his high school years, Ecko saw making T-shirts more as a passion than as a full-time profession. It also did not help when his school guidance counselor posed the question, "Do you really think you are going to feed the mouths of kids painting T-shirts?" that Ecko could not answer. Under unnecessary pressure to choose a traditional career, Ecko went with one that was familiar to him—pharmacology. His father had studied pharmacology at Rutgers University so following his footsteps and entering a five-year program seemed like the thing to do at the time. The irony was that his father actually ended up disliking the profession, but that did not deter Ecko from giving it a try. "He had left it when I picked it up," recalled Ecko. "I think it was like a badge of honor or something because I was pretty good at math and at left-brain skills. As much as I excelled with the right-brain side exhibiting leadership skills—I was class president from eighth grade all the way through my senior year—for whatever reason, it wasn't enough to give me confidence to take a leap [of faith]."

As hip hop started to merge and validate itself commercially in the world, Ecko began to see his career path more clearly. After completing three years of pharmacy school, he realized that his art could be his profession. That magical year became 1993—a good year for hip hop and the eureka moment for the 20-year-old Ecko. East Coast artists A Tribe Called Quest released their historic third album, *Midnight Marauders* (Jive Records) and Shaolin's Wu-Tang Clan broke ground with *Enter the Wu-Tang Chambers* (Loud Records). On the West Coast, Snoop Doggy Dogg made his debut with *Doggystyle* (Death Row Records) and hip hop fans continued to be exposed to the genre with a Latino twist with the release of Cypress Hill's second album, *Black Sunday* (Ruffhouse/Columbia Records). This also became the year that Ecko experienced the practice of pharmacy, the promise of that career, and what it was going to look like. He recalls, "I started to meet people that were one, two years out [of pharmacology school]. I just figured to myself I am going to be fucking miserable doing that. That's when I took the leap."

Ecko's airbrush designs had caught the attention of his eventual business partner Seth Gerszberg (he had met him the previous year through a friend of his whose mother was Ecko's high school art teacher) who gave him a loan for $5,000 and who took on the role of president, business development and strategic planning. Ecko focused on the vision behind the brand and had his twin sister Marci Tapper provided organizational assistance in the areas of finance, sales administration, customer service, and shipping. Interestingly enough, the trio did not have prior garment experience, but what they lacked in familiarity, they made up for with determination, drive, and ambition. Ecko drafted his business plan and called it ECHO: Educating Change to Heal and Overcome. The acronym E-C-H-O was Ecko's nickname, which stemmed from his days in his mother's womb. As Ecko tells it, his mother was pregnant with twins, but did not know it at the time. The obstetrician back in 1972 was puzzled by a recurrent echo sound in the sonogram. Not until delivery and a surprise second baby did it become apparent that the "echo" was, in fact, Marc. The Echo nickname stuck for obvious reasons and it began common practice for people to call him by that name—from family to friends and customers. Ecko also made it his graffiti moniker, which would lead him to his incorporated business name, Echo Unlimited, years later.

Targeting trendsetters between the ages of 16 and 26, Echo Unlimited started by selling six graffiti-inspired T-shirts on consignment (in which the retailer gets paid after the goods are sold) and quickly grew into a full-scale cut-and-sew business. According to Ecko, early attempts to find financing led him to pitch his small T-shirt company to several well-known celebrities including Michael Bivins of New Edition and Bell Biv Devoe fame and indirectly, to film director Spike Lee. Bivins was a logical pitch for Ecko, who was among the first celebrities to admire his work. Ecko had airbrushed a denim jacket for him in the past as a way to pitch his friend's demo tape. A note strategically placed in the left-hand pocket of the jacket had Ecko's telephone number along with a cassette demo tape made by Cale Brock (today a preacher). According to Ecko, his clever approach got him a 3:00 A.M. wake-up call. Subsequently, that call led to a meeting and it got Brock a record deal. Ecko recalls of that time, "All of a sudden at a very young age [19 years old], I started to get a taste of this world. The next thing I know, I'm at college taking intro to biology and all these chemistry classes, but on the weekends, I'm in a room with Q-tip, Grand Puba and Red Alert is spinning. I'm at the Jodeci party. I see Puff running around. I was the white boy in the corner with the Echo airbrushed hat." Shout-outs by deejay Red Alert on the radio to Ecko and Lakewood made him a local celebrity.

It seemed that all the stars were aligned. "This became the genesis that gave me the confidence to take the leap," Ecko says.

Ecko took advantage of any and every opportunity that came his way and he made sure to seize the moment. For example, take his initial attempt to chat with director Spike Lee. Ecko discovered Lee was to speak at Rutgers University, so he figured that he could take his business plan to him and at the very least, get his products carried in Lee's Brooklyn shop. Weeks prior Lee's Rutgers University speaking engagement, Ecko "meticulously crafted" a Mars Blackman/Michael Jordan T-shirt and sent it to Lee. While Ecko received a "form letter" thanking him for his support, it was just enough to make Ecko "delusional" for thinking he had an opportunity to approach Lee with his idea. He says, "I was going to be like, remember the Mars Blackman T-shirt you got? I'm the dude that sent it to you." Ecko managed to approach Lee at the Rutgers event only to be turned down and directed to Jeffrey Tweedy who ran Lee's Dekalb Avenue store and who would later work for Cross Colours, Karl Kani, and Sean John.

Shortly thereafter, Ecko, along with his friends Terrence Jackson and Brock, headed to Brooklyn by train with a business plan in hand. "He [Tweedy] basically gave me the door. I bought a couple of books, a hat and felt kind of defeated," Ecko recalls. That became a "thread into Spike," but none of those experiences deterred Ecko from moving forward with his master plan. From the beginning, he saw that launching a clothing company was not going to be an easy task. "It was quite complex to make tees," recalled Ecko, who attributed his early challenges to the cost of getting the right printing technology for his art. "You would send out your file to a place called Sera Chrome and they would cut your art into transparencies to burn screens from. They charged like $1,500 just to do C-M-Y-K." Technological breakthroughs in the early 1990s more than doubled the cost of the process. "A $1,500 set would cost you $3,500, $4,000 just to get the separation," he says.

A month after officially launching his company, Ecko received his first television plug on *Good Morning America* as the "summer's hottest T-shirt line." However, Ecko credits one of his big breakthroughs at his first MAGIC trade show in 1994 when he met Eighth Day, a marijuana-themed T-shirt company that utilized photo printing techniques. A casual conversation turned into a bartering situation and with Ecko mastering the printing technique himself.

> "I traveled with an ounce of weed," Ecko admitted. "It was the first and last time I exported dope. I had checked my bag, like an [idiot] and I packed it among unwrapped Certs and mint Certs. I figured the dogs would never get it. A cop comes around with a dog and the world just disappeared before my eyes. I see my mom yelling at me, my girlfriend who eventually became my wife would leave me, my sister saying 'I told you so,' Seth saying 'what are doing jeopardizing our business.' All of a sudden, the bag comes off and I see the dog starting to go towards it. The dog starts to walk away and I take that bag and got the fuck out. That was the first and last time I transported an illegal cargo."

It was a close call, but the trip was well worth it as Ecko got a tower PC (sold to him) out of it, bootleg copies of Photoshop and Adobe Illustrator, and an "amazing" one-week lesson on color separations. "That was our first big T-shirt where I printed photo real on a dark base." says Ecko "What could've cost me $3,500 to enter in terms of the color separation costs, now cost me my time, a flight, and an ounce of weed. That was a major breakthrough for me because all of a sudden, I became that T-shirt company."

Also in 1994, Ecko designed a logo for Sony Records, Epic Street Division and moved the Echo Unlimited offices to a 5,000-square-foot space. The next two years proved to be vital for Ecko's business growth. He entered into a nonequity joint venture with King Wear in 1995, who acted as agent and financier. The arrangement allowed Ecko the ability to produce its first line of clothes overseas. By then it became time to give his company a recognizable icon; the rhino was chosen to honor his father who was avid miniature wooden rhino collector. With financing in place, Ecko was able to start his first aggressive advertising campaign in 1996 with ads placed in *The Source*, *Slap*, and *Thrasher*. It was the same year that marked both the assassination of The Notorious B.I.G. and the retail boom of urban fashion at the department store level. Ecko incorporated Sweat Equity Laboratories as a design and marketing extension of his company. He was becoming equally known for his innovative marketing and design strategies early on as he was for his wares. It was this multifaceted approach to design that would garner Ecko a unique space in the fashion community and in business, overall.

Music clients were a natural fit for Ecko, who distributed Underground Airplay, complimentary hip hop mix tapes as a form of branding and promoting his company. He initially pressed 10,000 of the 44-minute promotional tapes which were distributed with each purchased T-shirt and featured some of the best of hip hop's underground scene. Both signed and independent artists were included from Cella Dwellas, Problemz, 80FF the Assassin, Mad Skillz, Craig Mack, The Notorious B.I.G., O.C., The Beatnuts, and Common. With the release of its Volume V1 in 1997, the company production totaled over 250,000. It would come as no surprise with his direct connection to hop hop music that Ecko would service music clientele such as Columbia Records, Loud/RCA/BMG Records, and Elecktra Records with his creative services. Projects varied from logo design to designing and producing brochures and collateral for the 1996 Rap Roast (created to honor those who had made significant contributions to hip hop).

There seemed to be no industry Ecko could not tackle as film clients became another avenue to grow his design portfolio. Universal Studios and DreamWorks Studios hired Ecko to design pieces for the motion picture *Jurassic Park 2: The Lost World* and Universal ended up hosting an Echo Unlimited fashion show for 500 of its worldwide licensing partners in an Universal Studios soundstage. Ecko would garner other film clients over the years to include designing 20 pieces for Steven Spielberg's *The Lost World*; providing the wardrobe to music director Hype Williams' directorial film *Belly*; and teaming up with Lucas Films for a special edition *Star Wars*-inspired apparel line in 2007. Retail design became another avenue to show off Ecko's artistic skills. In 1996, Ecko was contracted to design Yellow Rat Bastard (YRB), a 4,000-square-foot shop in SoHo, which he is also helped name (inspired by comic book writer/artist Frank Miller's comic "Sin City"). Slowly but surely, Ecko was building a name for himself in various aspects of design which gave him a clear advantage over his fashion competitors in the hip hop, skate, and snowboard markets. By the time he presented his spring 1997 collection at two notable fashion trade conventions—Action Sports Retailer (ASR) and MAGIC—the company had booked approximately $6 million for that season alone.

With financing in place and increasing sales, Echo Unlimited launched a $1 million celebrity advertising campaign in 1997. It was the year of the good and the bad for Ecko. He was legally forced to change his company's original "Echo" name and had no choice but to change it to its current "Ecko." With its name dispute settled and international trademarks secured, Ecko would tackle its next challenge, the famous 7th on Sixth show, then sponsored by the Council of Fashion Designers of America (CFDA). Founded in 1993, 7th on Sixth is an event management company known for producing designer runway shows which catered specifically to the trade industry and press. By participating in such a prestigious event, Ecko went from being a budding urban sportswear company to entering the major leagues of fashion. According to Ecko, he made the decision after reading *DNR*, seeing the announcements for show's dates, as well as reading about a men's sportswear company named Boing, known for its stretch products. "The guy who started that business somehow knew Seth [his partner] and ended up in South River at our office," Ecko says. "He started getting in my ear about runway show. I looked at as a platform to validate myself as a designer. I viewed myself as this illustrator, artist, and designer. It gave me something to work towards."

By producing several 7th of Sixth shows, it afforded Ecko to work directly with one of the people he most admired, the filmmaker Spike Lee. The two formerly were re-introduced at the Ecko showroom by the company's publicity point person Bernadette Gist. "We really hit it off," Ecko says. "It was a professional ambition of mine to work with him." Over the years, the two worked together on a variety of projects. Ecko hired Spike/DDB, the ad agency between Lee and DDB Needham as its agency of record. Through this unique partnership, Lee was able to lend his expertise in a number of ways. Lee produced a "mockumentary" and Ecko Unlimited's 7th on Sixth runway show in 2000, which featured actress Rosario Dawson, poet Sarah Jones, rapper/actor Mos Def, and Ray Lucas of the New York Jets. By this point, Ecko's domestic sales reached $150 million, with another $30 million in revenue arriving from foreign markets in Canada, Australia, the United Kingdom, Western Europe, and Japan.[1] The lasting relationship between the two creative geniuses even afforded the opportunity for Ecko to develop a limited apparel

Ecko Unltd fashion show male model. (Ronnie Wright)

collection for Lee under the 40 Acres and a Mule label. "The runway show gave me the forum," says Ecko. "I remember feeling somewhat avant-garde."

Over the next 15 years, Ecko Unlimited would go through a series of highs and lows. It would become the first company to replicate its 7th on Sixth show at a national tradeshow, bringing 15 models and a 30-foot runway to Las Vegas during the MAGIC show. It would dissolve its non-equity joint partnership with King Wear and begin using its own agents to organize and supervise production and later contract Scope Imports to act as a P.O. financier and fulfillment center. Ecko Unlimited expanded its distribution channels to include Macy's East and West, obtaining Macy's West windows, and participating in the televised Macy's Passport Show. "I would go to the department stores and I would see Ralph, Nautica, and Tommy and I was like, I want some of this," Ecko admitted. "I want some of this action. I want to make that product. I want to make it like that. I want to present it like that. I want a shop." However, with rapid growth came company headaches. In 1999, the company fell on hard times and rumors quickly spread that the company was financially struggling. Ecko, who can be argued as making some of the best fashion comebacks, was resuscitated by restructuring the company.

Ecko was able to get himself back in the black and by 2000, the company had licensing agreements with Playboy Enterprises, Marvel Comics, and the NFL. In addition, he held unique relationships with key entities including videogame powerhouse EA SPORTS. "I always thought that if Ralph could do paint than I can do video games. So that was a very huge hurdle to get over," says Ecko. It shared its nationwide street team with EA SPORTS as well as becoming an integral part of several of its virtual video games to include Knockout Kings 2000 and Madden, which launched in 2001. Knockout Kings 2000, a virtual boxing game, offered players interactive features including the ability to choose their own fashionable character. Donning specially-designed Ecko Unlimited's red rhino logos, players were given the option to box as designer Ecko. In Madden, Ecko had its own playing field and team called Physical Science, after Ecko's NFL collection.

Nevertheless, rumors continued to plague Ecko to include unofficial reports of overspending and taking on more projects than the company could handle. Once again in 2001, whispers resurfaced that the company was nearing extinction. But each time, Ecko seemed to make a valiant comeback. The following year, Ecko ventured into the publishing business with the launch of *Complex* magazine. The zine was unique for the times and the publishing space overall. Its audience was young men who were obsessed with clothes, women, technology, comics, and everything cool. It targeted trendsetter consumers very much like the profile of an Ecko shopper which was very different from what existed in the marketplace; think one part *Maxim* with some

Lucky with a twist. "For three years, we promised *Complex*. And for three years, people sent us hundreds and thousands of addresses. We manually logged them in and that was the basis of our first 100,000 subscriptions," says Ecko. By 2011, *Complex* boasted about 350,000 subscribers and its core website received 3.5 million unique views. Rumors of bankruptcy continued to afflict Ecko in 2009 although in 2007, the company boasted that it had generated more than $1.5 billion in global retail sales according to its official Web site.

"We had bought along the way some companies that we had sold as the market went through hiccups," admits Ecko. "We went through interruptions in the economy just overgrowing and overexpanding, bad governance and we thought we could walk on water and took on too many brands." The company ended up downsizing and selling celebrity brands including 50 Cent's G-Unit Clothing Company and Eve's Fetish as well as outerwear/sportswear brand Avirex while retaining skate brand Zoo York. However, Ecko has never been short of innovative marketing strategies like participating in the Macy's Thanksgiving Day Parade in 2003 with his iconic rhino float. It was 2005, however, that proved to be Ecko's most pivotal year. He became the youngest member inducted into the Council of Fashion Designers of America (CFDA); had an Indian baby rhino named after him (appropriately named Ecko) at the San Diego Zoo; his video game Getting Up won "Best Wireless Category" at the Spike TV Awards; Sweat Equity, an after-school design program for underserved teens was launched; and perhaps most intriguing, he took on New York City Mayor Michael Bloomberg and the City of New York.

Not too many people can say that they have gone toe-to-toe with Mayor Bloomberg and won and Ecko definitely earned his bragging rights. Bloomberg, who was looking to prevent Ecko from organizing a street festival that would feature graffiti artists at work and coincided with the release of Ecko's video game Get Up, did not realize that Ecko would soon be a thorn in his side.[2] From that moment on, Ecko became the poster child for graffiti advocacy and a defender of artistic expression and most importantly, of the First Amendment. After fighting Bloomberg and winning the first battle, the two clashed again the following year. Bloomberg signed into New York City law the prohibition of selling graffiti-like paraphernalia such as broad-tip markers and spray paint cans to individuals under age 21.[3] Standing proudly behind seven artists who actually brought the case against Bloomberg, Ecko proved yet again that artistic expression prevailed. Unfortunately his friend—writer, artist, publisher, and graffiti historian/advocate Alain Maridueña, known as Alan Ket, did not have the same luck in his legal battles the following year.[4]

On September 15, 2007, Ecko once again made the headlines—this time for purchasing San Francisco Giant Barry Bonds' record-breaking 756th homerun ball hit in on August 7, 2007 while playing against the Washington Nationals (surpassing Hank Aaron's homerun record in U.S. baseball history). The historic ball, caught by 21-year-old New Yorker Matt Murphy, was auctioned by Sotheby's/SCP Auctions online. Paying the hefty price of $752,467 for the famous ball, Ecko then created a Web site to determine its fate. Launching www.vote756.com, Web viewers were given three choices to select from: (1) they could send the ball to the Baseball Hall of Fame in Cooperstown; (2) they could place an asterisk (for Bonds' alleged steroid use) on the ball and send it to the Baseball Hall of Fame; (3) or they could send it into outer space. The ploy recorded over 10 million hits and with 47 percent of the vote favored the branding/Cooperstown option.[5] However, *The New York Daily News* reported in 2008 the ball never made it to Cooperstown as a result of the conditions of the gift changing into a loan.

Despite a variety of business ventures and brand expansion projects Ecko continued to make, he could not avoid biting off more than he could chew. In 2009, Ecko sold controlling interest of its portfolio of brands (Ecko Unlimited, Marc Ecko, the rhino logo, and Zoo York) to Iconix Brand Group, Inc. which owns licenses and markets a variety of brands including Rocawear, which it purchased in 2007 for $204 million. Iconix garnered 51 percent controlling interest through a newly formed joint venture company, IP Holdings, Unltd LLC. Iconix paid $63.5 million in cash and the joint venture company obtained $90 million in financing for a total purchase price of $109 million. "It was clear that we were at a place being where we very much overleveraged ourselves cause we expanded at retail," admitted Ecko. "We went from 60 retail stores to 100, 115, and 120 in a span of about 18 months. You can imagine the capital expenditures of building all those stores, the leases, pre the Lehman's crash, pre the real estate crash, pre the Simon's mall crashes, not to mention the cost of acquiring all the fixtures and inventory." The negatives outweighed the benefits in Ecko's mind who considered becoming heavily involved in the retail business as a "necessary evil." While opening retail stores (operating 90+ in 2011) overstretched his company from a credit position, Ecko claims he would not have changed the course direction one degree.

CHAPTER 14
Dollars and Sense

In the beginning stages [of urban fashion] at the specialty store level, it all came from the street. We would watch videos [and read] *XXL*, *The Source*, and *Stress*. As retailers, we would just get whatever the customers wanted.

— Sneaker Steve Patino, apparel executive and former retailer

It might be hard to imagine a time when youth retail was devoid of celebrity-driven apparel brands, featured no eye-catching displays or flat-screen televisions, or even lacked music in the background creating that inviting environment that we have all come to know. The dynamics of youth-oriented retail in the twenty-first century have all these elements needed to draw in adolescents, their parents, and anyone in search of fashionable gear. Shoppers can thank, in part, the hip hop phenomenon for some of those retail innovations.

Prior to hip hop, youth retail was dominated by the department stores. These stores generally tucked away their young men's section somewhere in the back with little attention paid to developing a section that catered to the generation's needs and spirit. The look and feel of the young men's floor was similar to its older men's counterpart (the main floor). Youth fashion was classified into two categories—classifications and collections. Classifications, a category still in existence today, is considered to be an item-based business and is based on price. Examples of classification categories include knit shirts and denim. Unlike classifications, the collections area focuses on brands. "Half of the floor was designated for classification and the other half for collections," recalls Carrie Harris, the former vice president of men's and children's of West Coast-based Directives West, a trend forecasting company now part of trend forecasting firm, The Doneger Group. Seattle, Washington became young men's sportswear heaven with popular 1980s brands like Generra and Unionbay leading alongside West Coast brands like Bugle Boy Industries Inc. and surf labels like Quiksilver and Gotcha. Generra offered paisley fashions, Unionbay offered classic, contemporary styles while Bugle Boy became famous for its parachute pants, khaki cargo pants, and jeans with its famous ad tagline "Are those Bugle Boy jeans you're wearing?"

In 1986, Seattle-based specialty store Zebra Club was opened by the late Michael Alesko of Brittania Bay Sportswear and International News fame. With close to 4,000 square feet, the unique concept store served as a test market for popular brands such as International News, B.U.M. Equipment and Unionbay, and Code Blue. "Seattle came up with this concept called Preline where it actually decided to break individual lines," says Seattle native and Filipino American Lando Felix, who co-founded urban sportswear company Enyce and worked as a teenager at Zebra Club. Seattle Preline, which started in the mid-1970s, was created with the intent to have a cross section of retailers critique new merchandise. It was important enough for all the major buyers—Chess King, Miller's Outpost, and The Bon Marché—to attend. Felix worked at Zebra Club before moving to New York and becoming an assistant buyer for the now-defunct New York specialty boutique Canal Jean Co. Located at 504 Broadway in Greenwich Village (today located in Brooklyn), this trendy thrift shop once stood where Bloomingdale's is now located. Founded in 1973, its owners also operated a warehouse-like specialty store also located on Broadway called Unique (the location is now a McDonald's just a few blocks from New York University). Both Canal Jeans (as it was commonly called) and Unique were the place to get Levi's, trendy brands, vintage clothes, and airbrushed carpenter jeans, overalls, and jean jackets as well as garment-dyed knitwear in any color. "Canal Jean Co. was American Apparel before American Apparel existed," states Felix. The store would buy a lot of blank bodies whether it was T-shirts, basic carpenter jeans, or overalls and then dye them in a variety of colors. Back then, youth brands were not associated with a celebrity or music mogul and also did not represent any part of an ethnic group.

A shift in youth retail occurred when the business started to reflect the changing demographics which local mom-and pop-stores were also aware of. It became a cemented trend when the sales dollars started adding up. "Retailers began seeing the personalization of the youth culture," remembers Harris, today a career advisor at the Fashion Institute of Design and Merchandising in Los Angeles. "Groups embraced their personal say on how to put together a look." The 1980s became a critical decade for youth retailers who were introduced to lifestyles. On the West Coast, surf and skate dominated the playing field although urban fashion styles were being worn in Los Angeles, San Francisco, and other West Coast inner cities. The urban momentum naturally became East Coast-driven due to the West Coast's strong ties to action sports. Trade shows like MAGIC International saw the explosion of urban fashion firsthand when urban labels began taking more booth spaces within its exhibition halls. Emil Wilbekin of essence.com recalls attending MAGIC in the early 1990s before the hip hop fashion explosion. "It was just junior clothing, very bland American designer clothing with sprinkles of hip hop," he says. "Two years later, you started to see whole community of urban sportswear growing."

MAGIC, which was very much a buyer's market about editors and advertisers going to see clients, almost overnight turned into a hip hop festival equipped with blaring hip hop music, stripper girls dancing in the booths, and celebrities with their entourages. When one walked into the urban section, all of a sudden the music got louder, the aisles became more crowded, and people seemed to be having more fun. "You could really feel the energy of urban music and urban culture," says Wilbekin, who also once served as fashion editor and editor in chief at *Vibe*. This hip hop magazine decided to get into the fashion trade show business in October 1998 when it partnered with the existing men's tradeshow called NAMSB, a once powerful trade show in the men's business which was losing momentum and looking to *Vibe* as its salvation.

Vibestyle married urban sportswear, athletic wear, and skate wear on the viewing floor of the Javits Convention Center for about 10,000 to see. The idea was not to only have the buyers there, but to have brands show their lines and bring the culture and lifestyle to Midtown. The show featured a basketball court, skate ramps, and a celebrity-driven fashion show. Getting into the fashion trade show business seemed to make sense for *Vibe* at the time, which had a successful run with its Vibe Music Seminar, a music trade show which had previously featured a celebrity fashion show by Tommy Hilfiger. One major problem Vibestyle faced was the fact that it competed with the goliath West Coast-based trade show MAGIC. The other problem it had was timing. Held in October and March after MAGIC market periods in August and February, buyers already had orders placed so the purpose of attending Vibestyle would become a "see show" rather than a trade show in which orders were placed. While Vibestyle provided a cool environment, it never picked up the way it should have and *Vibe* eventually let it go and stuck to publishing. As urban brands continued to exhibit at trade shows, it was obvious that these brands were targeting consumers who were ignored by everyone else. Urban would soon change the way brands were sold in the United States.

Early urban fashion retailers did not always resemble the stores seen carrying the merchandise today. Akademiks' sales executive Peter Mintz (who has been in the urban business for over 20 years) recalls that the first stores on the East Coast to carry urban fashion were Army/Navy shops. Each borough, city, and state had its own version of Army/Navy shops. Other local shops carrying urban-inspired styles included Dr. Jay's in New York, Walter's in Atlanta, Harold Pener's Mens Wear in Kansas City, and Breyers LLC in Chicago. Damaris Vega-Bennett, who began her urban fashion retail career in summer 1991, landed her first retail job with Dr. Jay's after passing by its windows and asking to work there. For the next 10 years, Vega-Bennett, along with her buying counterpart Sharon Pattishaw, were considered the dynamic duo of urban fashion retailing. They had an advantage over most buyers, particularly department store buyers, because they were also the customer they wished to target. In the early days of buying, Vega-Bennett, who is Dominican American, admits that she would give most brands a try because there was such a void in the marketplace. She closely monitored television shows and music videos for her merchandising cues. They were easy to catch if one had an urban eye. Every Friday on *Hot Traxx*, one could spot Run-D.M.C. in a coordinating Adidas black sweatsuits or Heavy D in a Coca-Cola shirt.

Like Vega-Bennett, former buyer Sneaker Steve Patino kept his finger on the pulse by keeping his ear to the street. A Columbian American, Patino worked double-duty at this; he ran a small apparel and sneaker shop called Sprint II in Elmhurst, Queens while producing his own urban athletic brand called GAWSIE (Great Ancient Wisdom

Strengthen Individual Enlightenment). "We would watch videos [and read] *XXL*, *The Source*, and *Stress*. As retailers, we would just get whatever the customers wanted," he says. As Patino noted, the launching of urban brands provided consumers with choices from designers that represented a different nationality than the Anglo status quo. Urban brands promoted the good life and the idea was to make the consumer look and feel like a hip hop celebrity. "It affected the swagger or emotional experience of the consumer," Patino says. "I didn't know how to look like Ralph Lauren, but knew how to look like Jay-Z and my idols of the street." Lisa Blumenthal, today vice president of sales at Rp55 Group and a former urban fashion retailer, agrees with this assessment. Since urban designers were influenced by aspirational brands like Polo, Tommy Hilfiger, DKNY, and Calvin Klein, the urban designers needed to up their designs and fabrications to compete. Urban brands were not afraid to push the envelope with color, mixing fabrics and different textiles together, and offering larger silhouettes. It was no secret that early urban fashion brands did not always make the best product, but apparel makers knew the consumer was compulsive and related luxury with a high-ticket price tag.

Major retailers located in urban areas would eventually follow suit. Mall-based chains Oaktree and Merry-Go-Round, both defunct today, were some of the biggest players to enter the urban arena. "The noise was too loud to ignore," admits Harris, formerly of Directives West. Even if large specialty chains and later, department stores wanted to ignore this emerging trend, they could not as it came down to sell-throughs. The word on the street became "urban's in and surf is dead." Like a domino effect, major retailers began experimenting with urban during the next three decades. According to the International Council of Shopping Centers (ICSC), the 1980s saw an unparalleled period of growth in the shopping center industry, with more than 16,000 centers built between 1980 and 1990.[1] The ICSC reported that this was also the period when superregional centers (malls larger than 800,000 square feet) became increasingly popular with shoppers. A 1990 Gallup poll found that people shopped most frequently at superregional malls and neighborhood centers with Americans averaging four trips to the mall per month according to the ICSC. Carl Jones, co-founder of Cross Colours, recalls the late 1980s/early 1990s as a time when the youth retail landscape was rich with accounts. "I remember

Miller's Outpost. It was a $4 million account for me. I didn't sell [midtier retailers] Sears, JC Penney's, or Burlington Coat Factories at the time. I really didn't need to. Merry-Go-Round was a big consumer of our goods. It had 1,400 stores and then what started took the wind out of their sales when they bought Chess King, another 1,000. Edison Brothers was another 1,200 chain."

Derek Tucker was president of Oaktree during the heyday of the young men's urban business. He was one of a few African Americans to run a national youth apparel chain during that time. Today an entrepreneur and owner of a consulting and licensing company, Tucker started his retail career with Edison Brothers Store, Inc. (the parent of Oaktree) just out of high school. He later worked for JW Jeans West and became a manager for one of its San Francisco locations. Tucker eventually was promoted and moved to St. Louis, Missouri, working his way up to buyer, a divisional merchandise manager, a general merchandise manager, and eventually president of Oaktree by age 32. The then 213-store chain was designed and manufactured like The Gap's of the world. It was considered to be a predominately private label business, housing its own labels although consumers thought they were buying actual brands. Tucker, originally from San Francisco, was always entrenched with the black consumer and inner city fashions. The code name for this type of fashion was "ethnic," recalls Tucker, who always felt confused by the name. "Every time we talked about ethnic fashion, we were really talking about black people," Tucker explains. "This particular type of fashion was driven by black folks. It [later] became ok to say the 'b' word."

In the early 1980s, it came apparent to Tucker that lot of fashion was more progressive out of Detroit and Chicago. For Oaktree, malls like Evergreen Plaza Shopping Center in Chicago and Northland Center Mall in Detroit, dictated fashion. The so-called "ethnic" consumer was buying brands like Major Damage and Get Used, which were being produced by nonethnic designers. Oaktree found its own urban success with its private label called U Men, which sold as a national brand. Interesting enough, at one point, Cross Colours' co-founder T.J. Walker designed U Men which later played a key role in getting Cross Colours into the Oaktree chain. It was not the company's policy to carry brands, but Cross Colours became the first brand it carried in that magnitude. "I took a lot of heat for carrying it," admits Tucker.

"It probably represented no more than 15 percent. The impact was far greater than that. Those bright colors made a statement. It was very, very powerful." Born and raised in Maryland, Antonio Gray, buyer for the Maryland-based chain DTLR (Downtown Locker Room), got his retail start as a stock boy for the now defunct Ames Department Stores, Inc. and later moved to Merry-Go-Round Enterprises, Inc. "It dictated the fashion of the day. It owned pop culture and lifestyle," says Gray, who worked at Merry-Go-Round an assistant manager at age 18. Merry-Go-Round did both a private label and branded business; it also eventually carried its private label IOU and urban brand predecessors like Major Damage (known for its rips and tears) and Get Used to Cross Colours.

Urban breaking into department stores was another matter because department stores may know numbers, but not product. "For a long time department stores were a bubble no one could break," says designer Maurice Malone, who fought against the stigma of being classified just as an urban designer. "We would constantly call and the buyers wouldn't even see us. They were doing lots of Tommy Hilfiger business and the hip hop guys are what made his business. They made him a lot larger than what he would have been. We couldn't break in." Jeffrey Tweedy, who ran Karl Kani in the 1990s, could empathize with Malone. "The [department] stores didn't accept it at all. They were afraid of it," he remembers. "Department stores didn't embrace it. To be blunt with it, they didn't want this consumer in their stores. This customer was being watched, followed, all those things. Department stores didn't understand this type of clothing and attempted to come up with names for it from gang wear, rapper's clothing, ethnic clothing, urban to eventually streetwear." In the mid-1990's, most department store buyers were not watching hip hop videos, reading hip hop magazines like *The Source*, and were certainly were not visiting urban brands at their showrooms. Old-school retail buying meant going with safe brands like Calvin Klein, Nautica, and Polo Ralph Lauren—the brands that worked for their consumers at the time.

The tipping point for urban brands happened with the success of FUBU, which demonstrated to major department stores that its consumer base had tremendous spending power. At its peak, FUBU reached $350 million in sales.[2] Thanks to this brand, other urban fashion brands were able to break through the glass ceiling of doing department store business. A leader behind urban fashion in department stores was Federated Department Stores, now known as Macy's, Inc. While its stores like Macy's had experimented with Karl Kani in the early 1980s, it was not until the mid-1990s that Federated became committed to expanding its floor and shelf space. In 1996, *DNR*, the trade newspaper of men's fashion, reported Federated's rumored urban push. Carmine Petruzello, today president of Buffalo David Bitton, was formerly the vice president of men's collections, young men's and boy's for Federated/Macy's at the time. Born and raised in the Bronx, Petruzello's experience in youth retail included Chess King and Merry-Go-Round before joining Federated/Macy's. He began his retail career in the late 1970s at Steinbach, a small department store chain with stores throughout the Tri-State Area.

Chess King was among the first major young men's specialty stores in the country. It catered to a young consumer between the ages of 15 to 21 years of age and carried about an 80–20 product assortment mix of private label versus brands like Guess and Z. Cavaricci Couture (known for its big, baggy parachute pants). According to Petruzello, the urban customer always existed, but major retailers were only "nibbling" at it. Cross Colours became the first urban brand to give specialty retailers a "taste." Looking to promote destination brands on the young men's floor, Petruzello decided to go after urban business in a big way some years into his post at Federated. By this time, Cross Colours had imploded, but Petruzello saw enormous potential in the market due to the success of mega-brand FUBU and the popularity of hip hop music. Prior to 1996, major opportunities across the country were not being capitalized on as department stores only carried urban in a small way. Petruzello starting seeing the impact hip hop music had on fashion through the eyes and fashion sense of his 13-year-old son. Petruzello, who was living in the suburbs in Westchester County, saw the shift towards urban firsthand. The traditional brands of the times like Polo Jeans, Tommy Jeans, and Nautica Jeans, all of a sudden were replaced by brands like Wu Wear and FUBU which were taking market share. "You just saw that this consumer was latching on to something that was made specifically for them," he says.

The first generation of urban fashion designers (in the 1980s) brought really exaggerated fits, colors, and logos, which made industry experts predict the look to be a passing fad. However, with the second generation of designers in the 1990s, the fashion industry had to recognize the urban brands as a legitimate business because of their volume. Urban brands in the 1990s were booking orders of a few million from the beginning as what once took companies years to obtain, were done in one season for some urban brands. This might have also been due, in part, to urban apparel lines having better merchandise and manufacturing capabilities. Despite these benefits, Petruzello's idea was initially met with hesitation. "There was fear of shrinkage implications," he says. "My comment was if you are worried about the shrinkage implications than that means its desirable product. That's what we are trying to get." Petruzello also argued that it did not help that usually the young men's department was tucked in the back area of a store with limited staff.

Petruzello did in fact get the green light and went after FUBU, which had Samsung backing and a great rags-to-riches tale behind it; Mecca USA, produced by Seattle-based International News; and Wu Wear, the apparel extension of the multiplatinum rap group Wu-Tang Clan. "The idea was if we are having some success with one brand, what would happen if created a department store with four to five brands. We wanted them to have own area and be adjacent one another," says Petruzello. Department store branches rolling out the urban concept included Macy's East, Rich's/Lazarus/Goldsmith's, Burdines, and The Bon Marché. While Wu Wear had a very strong logo and brand recognition, it never had the proper production or sourcing structure to make it happen on a large department store scale. FUBU was the complete opposite story of Wu Wear for Federated Department Stores; it performed extremely well at retail and came with notable spokesperson LL Cool J for some Macy's in-stores. What made FUBU somewhat less desirable for department stores like Federated was that the brand sold all distribution tiers (mom-and-pop stores, regional and national specialty chains; high, mid, and eventually mass retailers). From a department store perspective, it is all about exclusivity. Mecca USA was well-merchandised and designed and was able to perform at retail.

Two years later, Petruzello added more urban lines including Ecko Unlimited, which had New Jersey roots and Enyce, which had Fila backing at the time. He did find that traditional brands had strengths in regional markets. For example, Petruzello says Guess had strengths in Miami, New York, and the West Coast in the mid-1990s. However, he found that urban was the first category that worked right across the entire country. This was part of the urban fashion phenomenon which happened thanks to the power of MTV and hip hop magazines. With Federated going after urban fashion aggressively, it spoke volumes to the fashion world; one of the largest department stores in the country was recognizing that this was an important market. Once Federated aggressively jumped into urbanwear, it became a domino effect as one by one other department stores began to infuse urban fashion into their stores.

"When [specialty stores] were the only guys inside the mall. you had Macy's starting to enter in to the urban business," recalls retail consultant Stephen Chase, who has worked in the urban retail arena for 20 years buying brands. "Macy's killed our business. They would do their 15 percent off on Wednesday plus their extra get a Macy's card, then automatically the mom who was buying the goods went to Macy's and got a Macy's card."

By 2000, department stores and young men's specialty stores were carrying the same brands. This was a far cry from the way urban

Macy's Herald Square. (Amanda Hall/Getty Images)

business was originally conducted. Mom-and-pop, regional, and national chains had dominated the urban distribution strategy from urban fashion's inception. Ironically, department stores would reclaim the youth business they had once dominated several decades ago. However, once that paradigm changed, specialty stores felt it the most. All of a sudden, mom-and-pop stores found themselves unable to compete with the big department stores. Specialty retailers were no longer getting merchandise at the best price; therefore, the best deal could not be passed down to the consumer. As the popularity of urban brands began to dwindle due to market saturation and later, the recession, urban brands shifted their distribution channels to mid-tier and eventually mass merchants, which were once taboo. "The stigma back in the day was that you had to be hard to get to be cool, so your distribution had to be tight," recalls Chase.

The recession affected the urban business as fast fashion (value-oriented) has become the future. When the urban business matured, department stores were able to quickly compensate by shifting dollars around because this market represented a small percentage of its overall business. For specialty stores, it represented 100 percent so the impact was greatest. Some stores transitioned better than others while many began to sell out, merge, file for bankruptcy, and eventually close. West Coast-based Pacific Sunwear closed all of its 154 hip hop-inspired Demo Clothing Stores; Coda Clothing's 155 stores were sold by Edison Bros. during its bankruptcy to Coda Acquisition Group, Ltd. and was later liquidated four months after the acquisition; all 63 Colorado-based Mr. Rags stores also went out of business; Against All Odds based in New Jersey filed for bankruptcy; and Man Alive, once a family-owned business was sold to a new owner. The urban stores that survived did so because they listened to the consumer. It became obvious that urban brands which expanded their distribution to include department stores would ultimately hurt the very stores that built them—specialty stores. "At some point we were less special simply because the things we had weren't completely different than the things found in department stores," says Antonio Gray.

A problem urban brands faced was determining the proper distribution mix. Department stores brought in larger orders but that came with a price—chargebacks (markdown allowances). Growing one's business with the department stores also meant hurting their existing relationships with specialty stores. Many urban brands felt they had to choice but to pick one over the other. Brands that went after department store dollars ultimately hurt their specialty store relationships and business, in essence, biting the hand that once fed them. The more distribution a brand sought, the more it took away from the cache of the brand. "Everybody wants to feel that they are the only one in the world that has that shirt because they just bought it," says Gray. "As the department stores gets on it and the discount stores get on it, then you got guys like us, specialty stores guys we got to find something else that's special." Specialty retailers were not getting the merchandise at the best price; therefore, the best deal could not be passed down to the consumer. At the same time, business at the specialty store level became stale. All of the sudden, local mom-and-pop stores could not compete and began to close.

The urban success at Federated sparked shops like those seen with mainstream designers. Department store business in bed with urban was great for several years until the market started slowing down around 2005. Then, the chain letter went out in 2006 that urban was dead. Abercrombie & Fitch infiltrated areas that it had not been before and brought the notion of better pricing to surface. As urban brands began to lose steam, they moved their business to mass merchants, once considered a taboo move. The recession affected the urban business as fast (value-oriented) fashion has become the future. The stigma was that you had to be hard to get to be cool, so your distribution had to be controlled. The youth consumer also slimmed down when skatewear infiltrated urban wear to create skurban, with celebrities like Pharrell Williams, Lupe Fiasco, Gym Class Heroes' Travis McCoy to skaters Styeve Williams and Marcus McBride donning the look. A shift towards the rocker trend bought in part to the success of Von Dutch and its head designer Ed Hardy, had urbanites wearing slim jeans as their Pharrel and Lil Wayne counterparts. Rocker-inspired brands like Seven and True Religion replaced urban denim brands and it became acceptable to pay $160 for jeans. These brands became the new attainable status brands. Skurban later morphed into the category of streetwear. A Rocawear or Crooks & Castle button-front shirt could be paired with a pair of True Religion jeans. Traditional urban specialty retailers and sporting goods stores had to adjust to the fashions of the time—skurban and streetwear. At the same time, other youth specialists led the way in carrying innovative product centered on streetwear culture. Streetwear got its support from specialty retailers like Union, Undefeated, DQM, Downtown Locker Room, Foot Action, Goliath, Kamaloop, Dr. Jay's, Vinnie Styles, Brooklyn Projects, Suru, Leaders, Shoe Gallery, Villa, Jimmy Jazz, S & D, Ubiq, St. Alfred's, Bodega, Michael K, Transit, and others across the United States. The media outlets to obtain fashion direction also changed. Every retailer in the South and Midwest played BET and 106 & Park, which replaced MTV as the source of fashion trends. *Complex* replaced *The Source* as the ultimate young men's fashion reference guide. Talk shows in 1990s became the reality TV of today while Jerry Springer empowered the common persona and denominated the celebrity. Now it has become Facebook, Myspace, and Twitter that has allowed common folks to get responses for being themselves and becoming celebrities in their own right.

The original urban fashion customer has since grown up and started a family of his/her own while becoming more price-conscious and making dollars stretch at a time where the economy is slow. Today's urban consumer is also not just listening to hip hop music and his/her vast musical preference impacts his/her wardrobe decisions. There is no question that technology has cut into the business. Other factors to consider were the economy and the lack of innovativeness on the part of urban designers. Styling cues once found on MTV, music videos, and hip hop magazines were now coming from the Internet, bloggers and online retailers. A lesson that could be learned from the urban fashion phenomenon is that one cannot dismiss a particular consumer or trend based on preconceived notions. When the fashion was categorized as ethnic and urban, it became an initial term to dismiss the potential of the market. But it became so much more than that; this was product made for the musical phenomenon called hip hop.

Inside the castle-like museum, 50 medieval trumpet players played upon each step taken until we reached the event's main entrance. With an instant sigh of relief, I saw a familiar face in the cocktail area as celebrities made their grand entrance and greeted one another. It was Emil Wilbekin, editor in chief of *Vibe* magazine at the time, now managing editor of essence.com. He had received his invitation from Donatella Versace and like me, Wilbekin was scanning the crowd for a recognizable face. The moment we made eye contact, we immediately walked towards each other, embraced and said, "Am I glad to see you here." Simultaneously, we whispered into each other's ears, "I can't believe that we're here!"

At the very moment, it was clear that we were witnessing fashion history in the making and were also a part of it. The event symbolized multiple meanings to our lives. For one, it made us aware of our power, respect, and growth in our respective fields. But more importantly, it meant that urbanites could socialize with the elite, hip hop had indeed crossed over, and urban fashion had made significant inroads in pop culture. Absent from the crowd was P. Diddy himself, who had gone to Miami to get a break from the negative media attention about his involvement in a Club New York shootout on December 27, 1999 while with then girlfriend Jennifer Lopez. (He would later be cleared of illegal gun possession and bribery charges.) Taking his place was his mother Janice, who was accompanied by celebrity music stylist Derek Khan (who was jailed and deported years later); Sean John Vice President Jeffrey Tweedy; music pioneer Russell Simmons and his then wife, supermodel Kimora Lee. Simmons traded his Phat Farm jeans and pink argyle sweater for a tux that night, while Lee opted for a slinky Roberto Cavalli dress. However, a black-tie affair could not keep Simmons from donning his pair of shell-top Adidas sneakers (he had not invented Phat Classics yet) and a plain baseball cap to complete his outfit. Our table was across from that of Von Furstenberg, Galiano, and Mrs. Clinton who played catch-up with the couple by making sure to see the latest pictures of their daughter Ming Lee (daughter Aoki wasn't born yet). Even more fascinating was witnessing Tweedy and Simmons sitting at the same table—together, direct competitors in the multibillion urban fashion game and united to prove a point—the fact that African American designers can play with the "big boys" of fashion. The Jacqueline Kennedy exhibition and dinner ceremony received worldwide media attention for weeks thereafter, but the story I just provided you went unwritten. Until now!

A few years after the Jacqueline Kennedy event, the once exploding urban fashion market crashed. Doneger trend analyst Tim Bess had declared that "urban was dead." It was a statement that was synonymous with Queen's rapper Nas's provocative eighth album, "Hip Hop Is Dead." The initial statement made by Bess took the urban community by surprise, although insiders had been talking about this quietly among themselves, but they never voiced it out loud. Pioneering urban designer April Walker attributed the implosion to the urban fashion market to being "severely exploited by the oversaturation of manufactured force-fed hits versus the organic process of designers that were creating lifestyle brands of quality products. There was only limited real estate space."

At its peak in 2002, the urban fashion industry represented a $58 billion business according to The NPD Group. Despite the numbers, most urban designers were not able to reach substantial sales volume as there were more business failures than there were successes. Designer Marc Ecko also believes urban designers were not able to break through certain challenges. "There's still this reluctance to view this category as authentic design voices—that the designer [title] is some other, means something else. It's representative of a different ethos," says Ecko, whose expanded his fashion empire to $600 million in annual sales and does not need the fashion community to dictate what he supposedly is.

In February 2010, the MAGIC International trade show, once held in the Las Vegas Convention Center, moved the men's portion of the show to the Mandalay Bay Resort and Casino on the Las Vegas Strip. It had been the first time that I had attended the show since my transition into academia and it was very different from what I remembered. The MAGIC International Show, which was once the best place to see urban brands, was to be very different in 2010 than from what I remembered in the mid-1990s and early 2000s. For a brief second, I had thought it would be a reunion for urban fashion old-timers; Daymond John, co-founder of FUBU, announced on Facebook that he was attending MAGIC for the first time in 15 years and Marc Buchanan's Pelle Pelle was making a return to the show after sitting out for a year.

Unfortunately, the energy on the floor was not the same. "Urban as we knew it is dead," Navell Shorter, a longtime urban sales representative had told me a year prior to visiting the trade show. I was in disbelief. How could it be? Like many industries, the urban apparel business is now in a stage of flux. There is no question that the economic recession has also made its impact on the industry. Many of the people who originated this new business have moved on. For example, April Walker now sells her own line of dog food. Daymond John is now an author and television personality seen regularly on ABC's *Shark Tank*. Russell Simmons has passed the torch to brother Rev Run and nieces, Vanessa and Angela Simmons, with Pastry. What was once considered to be leading the youth market has shifted to what is now being labeled the "streetwear" market, a mixture of many different consumers and styles. Streetwear encompasses the culmination of urban fashion with its roots in hip hop, skatewear with its roots in 1980s punk, and skateboarding culture and other actions ports, along with causal sportswear. The look which has roots on the West Coast would be later adopted to Toyko, Japan before growing into the next international counterculture. W. Zak Hoke, retail and brand experience designer of www.Addicted-To-Retail.com, says "The youth market today has hundreds of streetwear brands. Important elements include vintage-style/retro sneakers and graphic tees." WeConnectfashion.com, an online network that offers fashion forecasts and trend analyses, reports that streetwear represented a half-billion dollar segement of the industry in 2007 and hit the $1 billion mark a year later. Since then, WeConnectfashion.com reports that the market has tripled in size.

The market once dictated by the East Coast and that used to belong to Sean John, Ecko, Phat Farm, and Rocawear is now being driven by West Coast influences and occupied by streetwear brands such as Crooks and Castles, Hundreds, Diamond, Stussy, Supreme, Mishka, 10deep, Rocksmith, PAM, bathing Ape, Kidrobot, LRG, Staple, Neighborhood, BBC, Alife, Sixpack France, Carhart, and many others. The youth momentum once found at MAGIC has now been captured and replaced by its sister event The Project Show, a bi-annual trade show in New York and Las Vegas housing directional and streetwear brands. Online and specialty store retailers have taken the business back from the department store-driven arena (and rightfully where directionally youth fashion should be). Indeed, the market is going through a transition. Many designers had relied on a formula of design and advertising that no longer applies.

The hip hop lifestyle is also now shopping in Zara, Forever 21, and Hollister. Youth fashion has entered an item-driven cycle. These types of retailers have a much broader appeal and the consumer has far more choices in terms of brands and styles to choose from. "You have to keep in mind that people were dictating what urban was," Jeffrey Tweedy reminded me out of the Sean John showroom. "Urban is not that, it's a lifestyle." Urban fashion was once dictated that it had to be baggy; it had to be bright colors; it had to be in certain stores and in a certain mall. It had to be in this certain block or a certain section of the store. Urban is not that anymore as the consumer is now transcultural. Urban fashion is not anymore dead than some of the urban cities going through reinvention. The urban style and inspiration now represents a much stronger, bolder idea with a specific microfocus on the microconsumer. Reinvention is mode of survival and the urban fashion industry has to reinvent itself. It will be the designers who can change their game plan who will be able to stay relevant in the future.

Notes

The primary resource used for this manuscript was over 60 firsthand interviews. Secondary text sources were used to supplement historical account and details. In citing references, short descriptions have been used. Please refer to the Bibliography for their full identifications.

AUTHOR'S NOTE

1. Hip hop has been deemed to start when Clive "Kool DJ Herc" came to New York from Jamaica in 1967. Alex Ogg and David Upshal, *The Hip Hop Years* (Fromm International: New York, 1999), p. 13.

2. Figures quoted by Marshal Cohen, chief industry analyst of The NPD Group in Black Enterprise's "Rags to Riches" article in the September 2002 issue. Cohen became one of the only fashion analysts to track urban fashion sales when it was bubbling.

CHAPTER I: A CENTURY OF STYLE

1. Fanny Lou Hamer was instrumental in organizing the Mississippi Freedom Summer for the Student Nonviolent Coordinating Committee (SNCC).

2. Kente cloth is a multicolored, basketweave-effect fabric composed of alternating warp-and-weft-faced fabrics, produced by the Ashanti of Ghana. Originally made from European silk that had been carefully unraveled for the reuse of its thread and worn by the elite of the 18th century Ashanti court. *The Fairchild Encyclopedia of Menswear*, p. 203.

3. Cheryl L. Keyes, *Rap Music and Consciousness* (Chicago: University of Illinois Press, 2002), p. 40.

4. Ibid.

5. Cesar Miguel Rondon. *The Book of Salsa* (Chapel Hill: The University of North Carolina Press, 2008), p. 17.

6. Sidney Lemelle and Robin DG Kelley. *Imagining Home* (London: Verso, 1994), p. 109.

7. "Classification" is a term used for an item-based business determined by price such as that of knits or denim. Collection refererd to brands sold head to toe from a designer.

CHAPTER 2: FRESH DRESSED

1. The hip hop generation is referred to as black Americans born from 1965 to 1984, but the term should include all U.S. youth born in that time period. Bakari Kitwana (*The Hip Hop Generation*, New York: Basic *Civitas* Books, 2002), p. 4.

2. The following reports were used to obtain statistical data: *Current Population Reports, Income, Poverty, and Health Insurance Coverage in the United States*: 1990; The U.S. Bureau of the Census, *Current Population Reports, Characteristics of the Population Below the Poverty Level*: 1980; The U.S. Bureau of the Census, *Population Reports, Poverty in the United States:* 1990; and The U.S. Bureau of the Census, *Current Population Reports, Income in 1970 of Families and Persons in the United States*. See the Bibliography for complete citation.

3. The "Is Hip Hop History?" Conference was founded by adjunct professors Elena Romero and Warren Orange in 2010. The annual conference brings together academic and members of the hip hop community for the purpose of engaging dialogue and knowledge enrichment. Rodriguez spoke at the first conference held at the City College Center for Worker Education on February 20, 1010.

4. *American Skin* by Leon E. Wynter.

5. Ibid., p. 172.

6. Ibid., p. 172.

7. Ibid., p. 173.

CHAPTER 3: THE REVOLUTION WILL BE PUBLICIZED

1. Ibid, p. 34.

2. Will Smith was a rapper in the 1980s before going into television in 1990 with *The Fresh Prince of Bel-Air*. The *NBC* show aired from 1990 to

1996. The sitcom was loosely based on the life of its co-producer, Benny Medina. Unlike Medina who is from East Los Angeles and went to live in Beverly Hills with a white family, Smith's character was a street-smart teen from West Philadelphia and was sent to live with his wealthy relatives in Bel-Air. Actor/comedian Arsenio Hall had his own variety/late night talk show in syndication from 1989 to 1994.

3. *In Living Color* was a sketch comedy series, which aired on FOX from 1990 to 1994. The show's content had a strong emphasis on black subject matter. *Soul Train*, created by Don Cornelius, ran from 1971 to 2006. The black version of Dick Clark's *American Bandstand*, it featured R&B, Hip hop, and soul as well as funk, disco, and occasionally gospel artists and music.

4. Born in Brooklyn to Jamaican parents, Special Ed becomes known in the early 1990s for hits including "I Got It Made" and "The Magnificent." MC Hammer rose to fame in the late 1980s/early 1990s. He became known for hits like "U Can't Touch This" and for his trademark Hammer pants, which were baggy pants tapered at the ankle and ballooned on the sides.

CHAPTER 4: SOLIDARITY IN CROSS COLOURS

1. Carmine Petruzello began his retail career at Steinback Department Stores. His retail background includes Chess King, Merry-Go-Round, and Federated/Macy's. On the apparel side, Petruzello has served as president of Guess Kids, senior vice president of sales and merchandising at Tommy Hilfiger, president of Cut and Sew at Mark Ecko Enterprises, and president of Liz Claiborne's Enyce division. He is currently president of Buffalo David Bitton, U.S. Division.

2. Bethann Hardison is a former model, agent, writer, and businesswoman. She broke ground as an African American model in the 1960s and 1970s. Later as a modeling agent, Hardison made the careers of several supermodels including Veronica Webb and Ralph Lauren spokesmodel Tyson Beckford. She is also the mother of Kadeem Hardison, who played Dwayne Wayne in 1990's hit television show *A Different World*.

3. Jeffrey C. Tweedy is a pioneer in the urban apparel game. His experience includes Spike Lee's Spike's Joint, Karl Kani, Shaq's TWIsM, Mecca USA, and most recently Sean John.

4. Touki Smith's acting credits include playing Sheena Easton's assistant on *Miami Vice* and Eva Rawley, *227's* artist-in-residence. Smith also has two sons with actor Robert De Niro.

5. Otis-Parsons was once affiliated with New York's Parsons School of Design. Its full name was the Otis Art Institute of Parsons School of Design. In 1991, it became independent and known as Otis College of Art and Design.

6. Datsun's were first introduced in 1932 by the Dat Motorcar Co. Two years later, Nissan Motor Co., Ltd. took control of Dat Motorcar Co. in 1933. Nissan phased out the Datsun brand in 1986.

7. The Super Show is the world's largest sports product, apparel, footwear, and accessories trade event. Originally housed in Atlanta, the show moved to Las Vegas in 2001. NSI produced the NAMSB Show twice a year at The Javits Convention Center in New York. The show was sponsored by the National Association of Men's Sportswear Retailers, a not-for-profit membership association of men's retailers. Launched in 1976, Surf Expo caters to manufacturers from the surf, skate, water sports, swim, and resort industries. It houses about 2,000 booths and received about 15,000 attendees that include retailers and press. MAGIC International is the world's largest and most widely recognized organizer of trade shows for the apparel industry. The show moved to Las Vegas from California in 1988. Ten years later, Advanstar announced its largest acquisition ever, the $234 million purchase of MAGIC International, Inc. MAGIC, which had revenues of $40 million, put on shows in Las Vegas twice yearly under the names "MAGIC," "WWDMAGIC," and "MAGIC Kids."

8. Merry-Go-Round Enterprises consisted of 1,450 stores, including Merry-Go-Round, DeJaiz, Cignal, and Chess King. It filed for bankruptcy in 1994 and went out of business in 1996.

9. Djimon Hounsou's notable films include *Amistad* and *Blood Diamond*. He also has a child with his wife, fashionista Kimora Lee Simmons.

10. Black Expo was launched in 1989 as a traveling trade show for African American businesses to come face-to-face with their customers. At its peak, it hit 16 cities and attracted almost 500,000 attendees annually. It filed for Chapter 11 bankruptcy in 1997.

11. SEHM is an acronym for Salon International de l'Habillement Masculin. It is the largest men's trade show in Paris.

12. Merry-Go-Round Enterprises consisted of 1,450 stores, including Merry-Go-Round, DeJaiz, Cignal, and Chess King. It filed for bankruptcy in 1994 and went out of business in 1996. St. Louis-based Edison Bros. declared bankruptcy in 1995.

13. Private label refers to manufacturing done by a company for itself or for another brand under a different name. This is not an exclusive practice to fashion. Private labels occur in a variety of industries including food to web hosting.

14. Chess King was founded in 1968 by the Melville Corporation. It grew to over 500 stores in 1980 before the chain was sold to Merry-Go-Round Enterprises (MGRE) in 1993. MGRE filed for Chapter 11 bankruptcy protection the following year and shut down its Chess King chain in 1995.

15. Modisch was launched in 1999 as a contemporary, sophisticated sportswear brand with urban appeal. German for avante-gard, Modisch stayed in business for about a year.

CHAPTER 5: BROOKLYN'S FINEST

1. Starett City was renamed Spring Creek Towers in 2002.
2. The Nation of Gods and Earths, the Five-Percent Nation, or Five Percenters is a religious organization founded in the 1960s in Harlem. It has been seen as an offshoot of The Nation of Islam.

CHAPTER 6: TAILOR-MADE

1. Putnam, Pat. "Now The War at the Store," *Sportsillustrated.com*, June 13, 2011. http://sportsillustrated.cnn.com/vault/article/magazine/MAG1067694/index.htm

CHAPTER 7: HIP HOPRENEURS

1. There were a few white exceptions like graffiti artist turned fashion designer Marc Ecko and downtown girl Camella Ehlke of Triple 5 Soul.
2. Statistics were taken from the Shabazz Fuller interview conducted on March 10, 2010.
3. Patrick Robinson used his middle name for his urban brand called Xctasy Patrick Clark. His impressive fashion resume includes working for Giorgio Armani, Anne Klein, and Perry Ellis International. Today, he serves as executive vice president of design at The Gap. He joined the company in 2007.

CHAPTER 8: HOW FUBU CHANGED THE WORLD

1. Statistics provided by Daymond John during July 30, 2002 interview at FUBU headquarters.
2. Statistics from "Gift of Garb" article, which appeared in *People* magazine on March 3, 1997, vol. 47, issue 10.
3. Statistics were according to an article I wrote for *DNR*, "Macy's East Pushes Fubu to the Fore" on June 9, 1997.
4. The $70 million statistic is according to the *Adweek* article, "Fubu Starts Talks with Shops" in 1998. The 2,500 retailers statistic was from my article, "Fubu to Spend Cool Million on TV Campaign" in *DNR* on May 30, 1997.
5. These figures came from my article in *DNR*, "Fubu gets Ball Rolling with NBA License" on January 25, 1999.

6. The breakdown of sales was reported in *The Chicago Tribune* in an article by Patrick Cole, "Fubu's Ultra-Hip Clothing Hops from Niche to Mainstream."

7. *Shark Tank* features aspiring entrepreneurs and their sales pitches to the show business moguls with the intent of having one of them invest into their idea and company. John sits alongside real estate tycoon Barbara Corcoran, educational software guru Kevin O'Leary, technology wizard Robert Herjavec, and informational king Kevin Harrington.

CHAPTER 9: HIP HOP HOORAY

1. Statistics were extracted from an in-person interview conducted with Vinnie Brown of the rap group Naughty by Nature on May 12, 2010.

2. Iconix Brand Group, Inc. is a powerhouse brand management company that licenses brands to retailers and manufacturers. Among its urban staple of brands includes Ecko and Eminem's Slim Shady.

CHAPTER 10: URBAN LUXE—A SEAN JOHN STORY

1. The statistic was provided by Jeffrey C. Tweedy in an in-person interview on October 18, 2010.

2. Current apparel statistics obtained from the Sean John Web site. For more information, go to: http://www.seanjohn.com/blog/2010/05/macys -and-sean-john-ink-exclusive-distribution-deal/

CHAPTER 11: THEY GOT FASHION GAME

1. Information found on http://www.zipwayusa.com/JohnDocument.pdf.

2. In October 2005, the National Basketball association commissioner David Stern implemented a mandatory dress code for all NBA and NBA development players. The NBA became the first major sports league to do so. The code states that all players must dress in business or conservative attire while arriving and departing scheduled games, while on the bench when injured and conducting NBA official business (press, events, etc.) The dress code bans many styles associated with hip hop culture such as large jewelry including chains, pendants or medallions, and work boots. To learn more about the NBA dress code, go to http://www.nba.com/news/player_dress_code_051017.html.

3. Information about Carl Banks was found in his bio, G-III website, http://www.g-iii.com/.

CHAPTER 12: WHITE BEHIND THE BRANDS

1. Background information on Tommy Hilfiger was collected from the Tommy Hilfiger biography found on his Web site, http://company info.tommy.com/#/company_profile/tommy_biography

2. George Lois and Tommy Hilfiger were both featured in the film *Art & Copy*. They both talked extensively about the campaign that helped promote Hilfiger to stardom. In this advertising documentary, Lois discusses how advertising must at times be "seemingly outrageous" for it to do what it is intended to do. His approach to introducing Tommy Hilfiger and his red, white, and blue logo were no different.

3. Macy's announced in a press release the launching of the Slim Shady line in its doors in 2003. See link for further details, http://www.rain makercomm.com/collateral/Eminem-Shady%20release%20final.pdf

CHAPTER 13: THE ECKO, THE RHINO, AND THE EMPIRE THAT MARC BUILT

1. The statistics were found in Ecko Unlimited press materials.

2. A favorable decision was entered on Friday, August 19, 2005 in favor of designer Marc Ecko against New York City Mayor Michael Bloomberg and the City of New York in the United States District Court, Southern District of New York. As a result, Ecko's street festival, which was held in August, would feature ten 48-foot-long by 8-foot-high replicas of the legendary NYC transit blue-bird subway cars, which were transformed into contemporary urban works of art by 20 renowned graffiti writers. The work was later donated to The Point, a nonprofit organization dedicated to youth development and the cultural and economic revitalization of the Hunts Point section of the South Bronx. The fair coincided with the release of Ecko's video game "Getting Up: Contents Under Pressure."

3. Under a law signed by Mayor Michael Bloomberg, no one under 21 could possess "an aerosol spray paint can, broad-tipped indelible marker, or etching acid." A First Amendment lawsuit (*Vincenty vs. Bloomberg*) was filed against New York City Mayor Michael Bloomberg, Councilman Peter Vallone, Jr. (Dem.-Astoria), and the City of New York in the United States District Court in 2006 by seven artists under the age of 21. The suit was backed by Marc Ecko with attorney Dan Perez representing the case. According to Perez, a federal trial court entered an injunction enjoining Mayor Bloomberg and the City of New York from enforcing the law; that decision was subsequently upheld by the Second Circuit Court of Appeals.

4. Alain Maridueña of Ecuadorian and Cuban descent founded *Stress* magazine in 1995. Within the magazine's five-year run, it provided a fresh voice documenting the hip hop movement. Maridueña went on to work for Marc Ecko in 2000 and helped him with the launch of *Complex* magazine. He later consulted urban fashion brands Azzure Denim and Indigo Red through MarAlaining and Advertising in addition to serving as a graffiti consultant to Ecko's "Get Up" Atari graffiti video game. In 2005, Maridueña founded From Here to Fame LLC, a book publishing company, content development, and art agency. That same year he curated Ecko's street festival, which New York City Mayor Michael Bloomberg attempted to stop. The highly publicized event eventually took place after court battles and the next year, it was Maridueña who faced legal woes. In October 2006, a Special Investigations Unit of the New York City Police Department obtained a search warrant and raided Maridueña's home office. He was later charged with 12 felony charges for criminal mischief for conducting subway graffiti in three boroughs (Manhattan, Queens, and Brooklyn). In addition, Maridueña was charged with one misdemeanor count of possession of graffiti tools, Maridueña was facing three to seven years for each felony count. In a 2007 plea deal, Maridueña agreed to one count per borough and was also ordered to do a public mural within a three-year period approved by the DA office. While he did not have to serve time in prison, Maridueña did have to pay several thousand dollars in fines and restitution.

5. According to *New York Times*. "Asterisk to Mark Bonds' Record Ball" by Mike Nizza. September 26, 2007.

CHAPTER 14: DOLLARS AND SENSE

1. Statistical research on retail malls was found on the International Council of Shopping Centers (ICSC) Web site, where it discussed the "Impact of Shopping Centers." For more statistics on this subject, go to http://www.icsc.org/srch/about/impactofshoppingcenters/briefhistory.html

2. Statistic provided by Daymond John during in-person interview on May 19, 2010.

Bibliography

INTERVIEWS CONDUCTED BY AUTHOR

Adams, Bryan, New York, New York, April 7, 2010.
Bennett-Vega, Damaris, Telephone, November 22, 2010.
Bess, Tim, New York, New York, March 23, 2010.
Blumenthal, Lisa, Telephone, July 17, 2010. Boston, Lloyd, Telephone, April 21, 2010.
Brown, Carl, New York, New York, July 30, 2002.
Brown, Vinnie, New York, New York, May 12, 2010.
Buchanan, Marc, Telephone, July 29, 2010.
Byerson, Terrence, New York, New York, July 27, 2011.
Campos, Rueben, New York, New York, March 31, 2010.
Chase, Stephen, Telephone, March 30, 2010.
Clark, Alfaro D., Telephone, July 27, 2010.
Ecko, Marc, New York, New York, September 8, 2010.
Ezrailson, Stuart "Izzy," New York, New York, March 31, 2010.
Felix, Rolando, New York, New York, March 18, 2010.
Fuller, Shabazz, Email and Telephone, March 10, 2010.
Gray, Antonio, New York, New York, March 23, 2010.
Green, John, Las Vegas, Nevada, February 16, 2010.
Green, John, New York, New York, March 19, 2010.
Hardison, Bethann, Telephone, November 4, 2010.
Hardy, Don Ed, Las Vegas, Nevada, February 17, 2010.
Harris, Carrie, Telephone, July 17, 2010.
Haussan, Telephone, November 11, 2010.

Hilfiger, Andy, New York, New York, August 10, 2010.
Hoke, "Zak" W., New York, New York, December 2, 2011.
Hoke, "Zak" W., Email Interview, January 4, 2012.
John, Daymond "The Shark," Telephone, October 1, 2002.
John, Daymond "The Shark," New York, New York, July 30, 2002.
John, Daymond "The Shark," New York, New York, May 19, 2010.
John, Daymond "The Shark," New York, New York, August 31, 2010.
Jones, Carl, New York, New York, August 4, 2010.
Jones, Cynamin, New York, New York, March 22, 2010.
Joseph, Bobby, Telephone, October 14, 2002.
Kani, Karl, Telephone, March 3, 2010.
Malone, Maurice, Telephone, July 19, 2010.
Malone, Maurice, Telephone, August 25, 2010.
Martin, J. Alexander, New York, New York, July 30, 2002.
McDaniels Ralph, Telephone, November 17, 2010.
McDaniels, Ralph, New York, New York, August 5, 2002.
McHayle, Shara, Telephone, January 26, 2011.
Mckenzie, Roger, New York, New York, August 26, 2010.
Mintz, Peter, New York, New York, March 15, 2010.
Mossberg, Neil, Telephone, March 3, 2010.
Patino, Steve, Telephone, March 6, 2010.
Patton, Erin, Telephone, December 13, 2010.
Pennix, Sybil, Email, March 22, 2010.
Perrin, Keith, New York, New York, July 30, 2002.
Peterson, Kianga "Kiki," Brooklyn, New York, September 24, 2002.
Petruzello, Carmine, Telephone, November 30, 2010.
Pratt, Ertis, New York, New York, March 26, 2010.
Reynolds, Ralph, Telephone, May 25, 2010.
Rodriguez, Carlito, New York, New York, March 18, 2010.
Rowan, Dave, Email. January 4, 2012.
Sacasa, Ed, New York, New York, September 13, 2010.
Shellman, Tony, New York, New York, March 31, 2010.
Shorter, Navell, New York, New York, April 6, 2010.
Stennett, Davide, Telephone, November 4, 2010.
Tucker, Derek, Telephone, November 9, 2010.
Tweedy, Jeffrey C., New York, New York, October 18, 2010.
Walker, April, New York, New York, April 6, 2010.
Walker, Erich, New York, New York, March 15, 2010.
Walker, T.J., Telephone, September 2, 2010.
Wilbekin, Emil, New York, New York, April 24, 2001.
Wilbekin, Emil, Telephone, August 25, 2010.
Williams, Gary, New York, New York, March 31, 2010.

Wood, Guy, New York, New York, April 15, 2010.
Wood, Sharene, New York, New York, April 15, 2010.

NEWSPAPERS, MAGAZINES, AND OTHER SERIALS

The Daily News Record, DAILY NEWS RECORD (New York, New York)
The New York Daily News (New York, New York)
The New York Times (New York, New York)
Sportswear International
Vibe
Women's Wear Daily, WWD (New York, New York)
XXL

FILMS AND VIDEOS

Martinez, Elena & Steve Zeitlin, Prod. *From Mambo to Hip Hop: A South Bronx Tale, DVD.* Dir. Henry Chalfant. Perf. Colon, Willie. City Lore and Public Arts Films, Inc.: 1990.

Tovares, Joseph, Prod. *Zoot Suit Riots.* Dir. Joseph Tovares. PBS Video American Experience, WGBH Educational Foundation: 2001, Web. Aug 26, 2011. http://www.pbs.org/wgbh/amex/zoot/index.html. Greenway, Jimmy & Michael Nadeau, Prod. *Art & Copy*, DVD. Dir. Doug Pray. The One Club: 2009.

GOVERNMENT PUBLICATIONS

DeNavas-Walt, Carmen, Bernadette D. Proctor, and Jessica C. Smith, U.S. Census Bureau, Current Population Reports, P60-238, *Income, Poverty, and Health Insurance Coverage in the United States: 2009*, U.S. Government Printing Office, Washington, D.C., 2010. http://www.census.gov/prod/2010pubs/p60-238.pdf (accessed 08/26/2011).

Fendler, Carol. U.S. Bureau of the Census, Current Population Reports, series P-60, No. 133, *Characteristics of the Population Below the Poverty Level: 1980*, U.S. Government Printing Office, Washington, D.C. 1982. http://www2.census.gov/prod2/popscan/p60-133.pdf (accessed 08/25/2011).

Littman, Mark S. U.S. Bureau of the Census, Population Reports, Series p-60, No.175, Poverty in the United States: 1990, U.S. Government Printing Office, Washington, D.C., 1991.

Sotomayor, Sonia M. "Sonia Sotomayor Personal Data Questionnaire," 1997, William J. Clinton Presidential Library. http://www.clintonlibrary.gov/_previous/Documents/Sotomayor/NLWJC-Sotomayor-Box0001-Folder000 03.PDF (accessed 08/26/2011).

Spiers, Emmett F. U.S. Bureau of the Census, Current Population Reports, Series P-60, No. 80, *Income in 1970 of Families and Persons in the United States*, U.S. Government Printing Office, Washington, D.C., 1971. November 4, 1971. http://www2.census.gov/prod2/popscan/p60-080.pdf (accessed 08/26/2011).

WEB SITES

Advanstar Communications, Inc. International Directory of Company Histories. 2004. *Encyclopedia.com*, August 10, 2010. http://www.encyclopedia.com/doc/1G2-2846100011.html

"WeConnectFashionResearch." USA Streetwear Market Report. *Weconnectfashion.com*. January 4, 2012. http://weconnectfashion.com/fido/getpublication.fcn?&type=research&searchstring=usa+streetwear+market&id=737870st0000937&start=1&tr=1

http://www.marceckoenterprises.com

www.breathe-inn.com

www.crosscolours.com

www.danperezlaw.com

www.fundinguniverse.com

www.nike.com

www.seanjohn.com

www.vote756.com

www.wikipedia.org

www.youtube.com

ARTICLES

Adams, David. "Judge Orders Marc Ecko Event to Proceed." Ps2.ign.com, June 8, 2011. http://ps2.ign.com/articles/644/644233p1.html

Amandolare, Sarah. "Sagging Pants Shunned at Morehouse." *Finding Dulcinea*. December 8, 2008. http://www.findingdulcinea.com/news/Americas/2008/December/Sagging-Pants-Shunned-at-Morehouse.html

Bailey, Lee. "A Spike Lee Joint Venture." *Daily News Record*. Highbeam.com, June 8, 2011. http://www.highbeam.com/doc/1G1-148760747.html

"Barry Bonds' 765th Home Run Ball to Be Auctioned." Associated Press. Foxnews.com, June 8, 2011. http://www.foxnews.com/story/0,2933, 294016,00.html

"Barry Bonds' 756 Home Run Ball Won't Land in Cooperstown." The *Associated Press*. Nydailynews.com, June 8, 2011. http://www .nydailynews.com/sports/baseball/2008/07/01/2008-07-01_barry_bonds_756th _home_run_ball_wont_lan.html

"Benny Medina Proves that Hollywood Life Can Be Stranger than Hollywood Fiction." *Ebony*, April 1991.

Best, Tamara. "He's Dog's Best Friend." *The New York Times*, July 31, 2009. http://fort-greene.thelocal.nytimes.com/2009/07/31/hes-dogs-best-friend/

"Bomb the City." Nypress.com, June 8, 2011. http://www.nypress.com/ article-13440-bomb-the-city.html

"Bonds New King of Swing after 765th Home Run." Associated Press. Nbcsports.msnbc.com, June 8, 2011. http://nbcsports.msnbc.com/id/ 20169917/

Boswell, Tim. "Akademiks Brand to Celebrate 10 Years with 'Ultimate 10 Tour.'" www.ballerstatus.com, July 13, 2010. http://www.ballerstatus .com/2010/07/13/akademiks-brand-to-celebrate-10-years-with-ultimate -10-tour/

Bowers, Katherine and Lisa Lockwood. "J. Lo, Hilfiger Join Forces in Megadeal." *Women's Wear Daily*, April 17, 2001: 2, 13.

Branch, Shelly. "Carl Jones Changes Colours–Threads 4 Life Corp., Parent of Cross Colours and Karl Kani, Drops Clothing Manufacturing for Licensing." *Black Enterprise*, March 1994: 14–16.

Branch, Shelly. "How Hip-hop Fashion Won Over Mainstream America–Threads 4 Life Corp." *Black Enterprise*, June 1993: 111–20.

"Break Dancing the Night Away." *Newsweek*, August 22, 1983: 72.

"A Brief History of Shopping Centers." Icsc.org, June 8, 2011. http:// www.icsc.org/srch/about/impactofshoppingcenters/briefhistory.html

Bronson, Cory. "NBA Breaks Mold with Urban Apparel Deal." *SGB: Sporting Goods Business*, September 14, 1998, vol. 31, issue 15: 12.

Bryan, Robert. Fashion: The Last 10 Years. *Men's Wear*, November 23, 1973: 60–68.

Chappell, Kevin. "Fubu the Collection." *Ebony*, Oct. 1999, vol. 54, issue 12: 108.

Chin, Brian. "Break-dancing Breaks Out all over H'Wood." *New York Post*, June 5, 1984.

"CODA Acquisition Group Obtains Majority of CODA Stores." *Business Wire*. Highbeam.com, December 7, 2010. http://www.highbeam.com/doc/ 1G1-55333977.html

"CODA Acquisition Group Obtains Majority of CODA Stores: James 'Jimmy Jazz' Khezrie to Head up New Venture." *Business Wire*, August 3, 1999. *Highbeam Research*. December 7, 2010. http://www.highbeam.com.

"Designer to Brand Asterisk on Ball; Hall of Fame to Accept It." *Associated Press*. Espn.com, June 8, 2011. http://sports.espn.go.com/mlb/news/story?id=3036756

Dini, Justin. "Fubu Starts Talks with Shops." *Adweek* Western Edition, Oct. 12, 1998, vol. 48, issue 41: 81.

The Editorial Board. "The Latest in Law Enforcement: The Pants Police." NYTimes.com, http://theboard.blogs.nytimes.com/2008/07/14/the-latest -in-law-enforcement-the-pants-police/

"Editor's Choice of the Year Awards." *SGB: Sporting Goods Business*. December 15, 1998, vol. 31, issue 18: 11.

Feldman, Elane. *Fashions of a Decade: The 1990s*. Facts on File, Inc., 1992: 20, 29.

"Follow the Leader." Xxl.com, June 9, 2011. http://www.xxlmag.com/features/2009/09/feature-follow-the-leader/

Furman, Phyllis. "Music Stars Legal Eagle Bed-Stuy Product a Big Hit on Urban Scene." *The New York Daily News*, January 3, 2000. http://www.nydailynews.com/archives/money/2000/01/03/2000-01 03_music _stars__legal_eagle___b.html

Garland, Sarah. "Graffiti Bill Is Written to Foil Free Speech Suit." nysun.com, June 8, 2011. http://www.nysun.com/new-york/graffiti-bill-is-rewritten-to-foil-free-speech/57229/

Gellers, Stan. "Pietrafesa Files Chapter 11, Loses FUBU License." *Daily News Record*, June 14, 2000.

"Gift of Garb." *People*, March 17, 1997, vol. 47, issue 10: 62.

Gipson, Brooklyne. "Jacob the Jeweler Released from Jail." *XXL*, April 5, 2010. http://www.xxlmag.com/news/latest-headlines/2010/04/jacob-the-jeweler-released-from-jail/

Goldstein, Laura. "Urban Wear Goes Suburban." *Fortune*, December 21, 1998, vol. 138, issue 12: 169–72.

Gray, Geoffrey. "Wild Style with Peter Vallone Jr." *New York Magazine*, June 8, 2011. http://nymag.com/news/intelligencer/31542/

"Green awarded $45,000 in Tyson Case." *Los Angeles Times*, October 16, 1997. http://articles.latimes.com/1997/oct/16/sports/sp-43467

Haberman, Clyde. "Can Obama Help Kill Baggy Pants Look?" *The New York Times*, November 14, 2008. http://www.nytimes.com/2008/11/14/ny region/14nyc.html

Hartocollis, Anemona. "In Plea Deal, Artists Admits to Subway Graffiti in 3 Boroughs." Nytimes.com. June 8, 2011. http://www.nytimes.com/2007/10/05/nyregion/05graffiti.html?_r=2&ref=todayspaper&o ef=slogin

"Has the Hip-Hop NBA Become a Thug League?" Therx.com, June 8, 2011. http://www.therx.com/blog_has-the-hip-hop-nba-become-the-thug -league.php

Hundreds, bobby. "The 50 Greatest Streetwear Brands." *Complex*, June 21, 2011. http://www.complex.com/style/2011/06/the-50-greatest-streetwear -brands#51

"Iconix Buys Rocawear for $204 Mil, with Jay-Z Remaining." Marketwatch.com, June 8, 2011. http://www.marketwatch.com/story/ iconix-buys-rocawear-for-204-mln-with-jay-z-remaining

Itzkoff, Dave. "Comeback Planned for *Vibe* Magazine." *The New York Times*, August 13, 1990. http://artsbeat.blogs.nytimes.com/2009/08/13/ comeback-planned-for-vibe magazine/

James, George. "Willi Smith, Clothes Designer; Creator of Vivid Sportswear." *The New York Times*. April 19, 1997.

Jones, Gwen. "Black Power: Is the Black Market Really Gray?" *Men's Wear*, May 9, 1975: 31–32.

Kennedy, Helen. "'Jacob the Jeweler' sentenced 30 months in prison in drug case." nydailynews.com, June 8, 2011. http://www.nydailynews.com/ news/national/2008/06/24/2008-0624_jacob_the_jeweler_sentenced_to_30 _months.html

Kenon, Marci. "Fashion Firm Fubu Starts Label Backed By Universal." *Billboard*, December 23, 2000, vol. 112, issue 52: 4.

Kenon, Marci. "Fubu Promotes 'The Goodlife.' " *Billboard*, July 28, 2001, vol. 113, issue 30: 28.

"Kimora Lee Simmons Ditching Baby Phat Line." *New York Post*, August 24, 2010. http://www.nypost.com/p/pagesix/shedding_phat_isQbcJaBkB TrmjSrqvpfdM

"Kimora Lee Simmons 'Dumped' from Baby Phat." *New York Post*, August 25, 2010. http://www.nypost.com/p/pagesix/phat_blindsided _kimora_oySW8hmUnOZmu4Fd86AiyL

Krupnicki, Barbara. "Dancers Break Their Way into Licensing." *Daily News Record*, November 16, 1984: 15, 18.

Lazaro, Marvin. "Hip Hop Home." *Home Textiles Today*, April 1, 2002: 1, 14.

Lelinwalla, Mark. "Mark Ecko Defends Graf Artists, Files Lawsuit Against NYC. *Vibe*. Thefreelibrary.com, June 8, 2011. http://www.thefreelibrary .com/Marc+Ecko+Defends+Graf+Artists%2c+Files+Lawsuit Against +NYC-a01611417049

Liepmann, Erica. "Marc Ecko Launches 'Unlimited Justice' Campaign to End Corporal Punishment in Schools." Huffingtonpost.com, June 8, 2011. http://www.huffingtonpost.com/2011/03/09/marc-ecko-corporal punishment _n_833623.html?awesm=awe.sm_5H25f

Lippman, John. "'Arsenio Hall Show' Given Pink Slip after Low Ratings Television: Some Network Affiliates Swung away from Syndicated Program When David Letterman Joined CBS." *Los Angeles Times,* April 19, 1994. http://articles.latimes.com/1994-04-19/business/fi-47760_1_arsenio-hall-show

Lucas, Sloane. "For Us, Forever." *Adweek* Eastern Edition, October 11, 1999, vol. 40, issue 41.

Mariotti, Jay. "Once Again, Fab Five Prove They're No Fad." *Chicago Sun-Times,* April 4, 1993, p. 2, sports section.

Martinez, José. "Courtney Love Sued by Disgraced Celeb Jeweller for Losing Borrowed Diamond, Earrings." nydailynews.com, June 8, 2011. http://www.nydailynews.com/gossip/2010/11/22/2010-11 22_courtney_love_sued _by_disgraced_celeb_jeweler_for_losing_borrowed_diamond_chains.html

McKinney, Jeffrey. "Rags to Riches." *Black Enterprise,* September 2002: 99–104.

McLaughlin, Mike. "It's a Wrap: Filmmaker Spike Lee's Fort Greene HQ for Sale." *The Brooklyn Paper,* April 12, 2008. http://www.brooklynpaper.com/stories/31/15/31_15_its_a_wrap_filmmaker.html

"Men's Custom Tailor Shot to Death." *Daily News Record,* December 3, 1996. *Highbeam Research.* November 12, 2010. http://www.highbeam.com.

"Merry-Go-Round to Close Third of its Stores, Including Chess King." *Bloomberg Business News,* November 14, 1995.

Middleton, Diana. "Urban Retailers Struggle to Keep up with Brands." www.specialtyretail.com. January 29, 2008. http://www.specialtyretail.com/news/2008/01/urban_retail_clothing.

Middleton, Diana. "Urban Retailers Struggle to Keep up with Trends." Jacksonville.com. specialtyretail.com, June 7, 2011. http://www.specialtyretail.com/news/2008/01/urban_retail_clothing

Moessel, Andrew. "Graffiti Kids File Suit against Vallone, City." Queenstribune.com, June 8, 2011. http://www.queenstribune.com/news/1146179924.html

Newborne, Ellen and Kathleen Kerwin. "Generation Y." *Newsweek,* February 15, 1999: 81–88.

"New NBA Dress Code Bans Most 'Hip-Hop' Fashions." Sports.yahoo.com, June 8, 2011. http://sports.yahoo.com/nba/news?slug=nbadresscode

Parker, Erik. "Hip-hop Goes Commercial." *Villagevoice.com,* June 3, 2011. http://www.villagevoice.com/2002-09-10/news/hip-hop-goes-commercial/

Randolph, Laura. "The Real-Life Prince of Bel-Air: Television and Recording Tycoon Benny Medina Proves that Hollywood Life Can Be Stranger than Hollywood Fiction." *Ebony,* April 1, 1991: 30, 32–34, 38.

Randolph Laura. "Who Is Toukie Smith and Why Are People Talking about Her?" *Ebony,* May 1990.

Reed, Shaheim and Sway Calloway. "Jay-Z, Nelly, Fabolous Seek Uniforms that Don' Conform Oldest, Most Obscure Jerseys Sought by Style-conscious Rappers." Mtvnews.com, June 9, 2011. http://www.mtv.com/news/articles/1450431/ballers-players-suit-up-like-ballplayers.jhtml?headlines=true

"Retail's Lost Generation–Clothing for Teenage Boys–AM Apparel Merchandising." *Discount Store News*. FindArticles.com. June 8, 2011. http://findarticles.com/p/articles/mi_m3092/is_n17_v32/ai_13257169/

Rishin, Steven. "Throwback Hip-hop Style Points." November 4, 2002. http://sportsillustrated.cnn.com/vault/article/magazine/MAG1027299/index.htm

Roberts, Frank Leon. "What Not to Wear at Morehouse." *The Daily Voice*, October 9, 2009. http://thedailyvoice.com/voice/2009/10/new-dress-code-for-a-famous-bl-002336.php

Romero, Elena. "Avirex Has Altitude." *Daily News Record*. Businessweek.com, June 9, 2011.http://www.businessweek.com/innovate/content/jun2008/id20080618_440297.htm

Romero, Elena. "Breaking Out of the Urban Mold." *Daily News Record*, February 10, 1997: 12.

Romero, Elena. "Federated May Hop on Hip-Hop YM Trend." *Daily News Record*, December 18, 1996: 1, 8.

Romero, Elena. "For Them, By U.S." *Daily News Record*, October 1997.

Romero, Elena. "Fubu Adds Entertainment to Its Roster." *Daily News Record*, January 26, 2001.

Romero, Elena. "Fubu Gets Ball Rolling With NBA." *Daily News Record*, January 25, 1999.

Romero, Elena. "Fubu Gets Fatty." *Women's Wear Daily: Flash*, September 20, 2001: 17.

Romero, Elena. "Fubu Pays Tribute to Muhammad Ali." *Daily News Record*, December 17, 2001.

Romero, Elena. "Fubu Signs Development Deal for Film, Television." *Daily News Record*, April 19, 2000.

Romero, Elena. "Fubu Sponsoring Race Car for Indy 500." *Daily News Record*, May 12, 1999, vol. 29, no. 56: 1.

Romero, Elena. "Fubu to Spend Cool Million on TV Campaign." *Daily News Record*, May 30, 1997.

Romero, Elena. "Get Money." *Vibe*, March 1999.

Romero, Elena. "Herald Square Hip Hop." *Daily News Record*, February 7, 1997, vol. 27, no. 17.

Romero, Elena. "Hip Hop Hopping on N.Y. Catwalks." *Daily News Record*, February 3, 1997, vol. 27, no. 15.

Romero, Elena. "Hip-Hopping into Fashion." *Daily News Record*, February 26, 1997: 6–7.

Romero, Elena. "Hip YM Retailers See Federated Hitting Bumps Hopping Into Area." *Daily News Record*, January 2, 1997.

Romero, Elena. "Hoop Dreams." *Daily News Record*, July 22, 2002: 1.

Romero, Elena. "Macy's East Pushes FUBU to the Fore." *Daily News Record*, June 9, 1997, vol. 27, no. 69: cover, 2.

Romero, Elena. "Macy's West Boards Urban Bandwagon." *Daily News Record*, September 15, 1997.

Romero, Elena. "News in Brief." *Daily News Record*, March 25, 2002.

Romero, Elena. "O Lucky Daymond." *Daily News Cord*, March 22, 2000: 40.

Romero, Elena. "Patrick Robinson to Enter Young Men's Market." *Daily News Record*, highbeam.com, June 3, 2011. http://www.highbeam.com/doc/1G1-64789759.html

Romero, Elena. "Ready to Wear." *Vibe*, March 2003: 148.

Romero, Elena. "Still Standing." *Savoy*, November 2002: 7884.

Romero, Elena. "Stitching One's Claim to Fame." *Daily News Record*, October 18, 1999: 7.

Romero, Elena. "Supreme Snags Hip Brand PNB Nation." *Daily News Record*, May 11, 1998.

Romero, Elena. "Urban Shuffle: When Money Talks, Execs Walk." *Daily New Record*: 1, 14.

Romero, Elena. "Urban Steals Thunder in MAGIC's Young Men's Area." *Daily News Record*, August 27, 1997.

Romero, Elena. "Urban Wave Now Crashes Across Suburban Heartland." *Daily News Record*, February 9, 1998: 46.

Romero, Elena. "Young Men's Market Goes Loco over Logos." *Daily News Record*, October 16, 1996: 2, 4.

Rovell, Darren. "King of Bling Gives NBA a New Face." Espm.com, June 9, 2011. http://sports.espn.go.com/espn/page3/story?page=jacobjeweler/rovell

Royal, Leslie E. "Hip Hop on Top: Urban Fashion Designers Rule." *Black Enterprise*, July 2000: 91–94.

Rozhon, Tracie. "Dressing Down Tommy Hilfiger." Nytimes.com, June 3, 2011. http://query.nytimes.com/gst/fullpage.html?res=9B0DE0D711 30F935A15751C1A9629C8B63&pagewanted=3

Sales, Nancy Jo. "Is Hip-hop's Jeweler on the Rocks?" *Vanity Fair*, November 2006. http://www.vanityfair.com/culture/features/2006/11/jacob200611?currentPage=1

"Sean John were made with dog fur." MSNBC.com, February 23, 2011. http://www.msnbc.msn.com/id/16329355/

"Shaquille O'Neal's Clothing Company, TWIsM, Hires Executive Vice President." *Business Wire*. allbusiness.com, June 8, 2011. http://www.allbusiness.com/company-activities-management/board-management-changes/6959094-1.html

Span, Paula. "Spike Lee, Owner of The Joint: The Filmmaker's Store Opens in Brooklyn." *The Washington Post. Highbeam Research*, November 18, 2010. http://www.highbeam.com

Spevack, Rachel. "Shaq's Contract Puts New Twist in TWIsM." September 26, 1996. *Daily News Record*. http://www.highbeam.com/doc/1G1-18747201.html

Stack, Kyle. "John Starks Doin' Business." *Slam*, April 8, 2010. http://www.slamonline.com/online/nba/2010/04/john-starks-doin-business/

Stein, Joel and Cole, Patrick. "Getting Giggy with a Hoodie." *Time*, January 19, 1998, vol. 151, issue 2: 71.

Strom, Stephanie. "Melville to Sell Chess King to Merry-Go-Round Chain." *The New York Times* (March 18, 1993).

Strom, Stephanie. "Merry-Go-Round Files for Bankruptcy Protection." *The New York Times*, January 12, 1994.

Strong, Nolan. "Rap Throwback Jerseys Launched." Allhiphop.com, June 8, 2011. http://admin.allhiphop.com/stories/news/archive/2004/02/16/1812 8793.aspx?Ajax_Callack=true&Ajax_CallBack=true&Ajax_CallBack=true

Ten, Michelle. "Akademiks' Emmett Harrell: Family Business." *XXL*, November 11, 2010. http://www.xxlmag.com/lifestyle/2010/11/akade miks%e2%80%99-emmett-harrell-family-business/

TMZ Staff. "Jay-Z Accused of 'Faux Fur' Fraud." TMZ.com, June 6, 2011. http://www.tmz.com/2007/01/16/jay-z-accused-of-faux-fur-fraud/

"Top 5 Urban Apparel Companies." *SGB: Sporting Goods Business*. November 11, 2001, vol. 33, issue 15: 22.

United Press International. "Fashion Designer Willi Smith Had AIDS, His Attorney Says." *Los Angeles Times*, April 24, 1987.

Walden, Amy. "Neighborhood Report: Fort Greene; The Marquee Remains but Spike's Joint Is Closed." *The New York Times*, December 14, 1997.

Walker, Chezik. "Jay-Z, Nelly, Fabolous Seek Uniforms that Don't Conform." mtv.com, June 8, 2011. http://www.mtv.com/news/articles/1450431/ballers-players-suit-up-like-ballplayers.jhtml

Watson, Margeaux. "Skurban Legend." Entertainment Weekly (April 13, 2007). http://www.ew.com/ew/article/0,,20034823,00.html

White, Constance, C.R. "Spike Lee Rolls out a Pair of Unisex Lines for Fall Intro. (Movie Director Spike Lee's New Clothing Lines, Spike's Joint and Joints by Spike Lee)." *Women's Wear Daily*, June 9, 1992. http://www.highbeam.com/doc/1G1 12313135.html

White, Gayle. "Morehouse Takes on Sagging Pants, Cursing." *The Atlanta-Journal Constitution*, December 7, 2008 http://www.ajc.com/services/content/metro/atlanta/stories/2008/12/07/morehouse_saggy_pants.html?cxtype=rss&cxsvc=7&cxcat=13

White, Paula M. "End of the Road for Black Expo USA." *Black Enterprise*, April 1997: 15.

Wieberg, Steve. "Fab Five anniversary falls short of fondness." *USA Today*, March 28, 2002. http://www.usatoday.com/sports/college/basketball/men/02tourney/2002-03-27-cover-fab5.htm

Winstein, Archer. "You'll Flip for 'Beat Street.'" *New York Post*, June 8, 1984.

Wise, Daniel. "Fubu Maker Wins $6.7 Mil. over Infringed '05' Marking Public Exposure." *The Legal Intelligencer*, July 7, 2002, vol. 227, issue 11.

Wise, Daniel. "Fubu Wins Trademark Suit Over '05' Use." *New York Law Journal*, July 15, 2002.

Wolf, Alexander. "Rockin' The Retros." Sportsillustrated.com, June 9, 2011. http://sportsillustrated.cnn.com/vault/article/magazine/MAG1030920/index.htm

Wood, Gabby. "The Beautiful People." *New York Magazine*, August 7, 2005.

Young, Vicki and Elena Romero. "CODA Chain to be Liquidated by New Owners." *Daily News Record*. Highbeam.com, December 7, 2010. http://www.highbeam.com/doc/1G1-57647575.html

BOOK EXCERPTS

Bogle, Donald. *Toms, Coons, Mulattoes, Mammies and Bucks*. (New York: Continuum, 1994), 288–91, 318–23, 337–49.

Bondi, Victor. *American Decades: 1980–1989*. (Detroit: Gale Research Inc., 1995), 43–46, 62–66, 83–88, 218–30, 425–26, 435–39, 444, 627–28.

Bondi, Victor. *American Decades: 1970–1979*. (Detroit: Gale Research, Inc., 1995), 55–57, 71–74.

Chenoune, Farid. *A History of Men's Fashion*. (Paris: Flammarion, 1993), 307–8.

George, Nelson. *Blackface: Reflections on African Americans and the Movies*. (New York: Harper Collins, 1994), 61, 72–75, 94–97, 109–19.

Larkin, Colin. *The Encyclopedia of Popular Music*. (New York: Muze Uk/Oxford University Press, 1998. Vol. 4), 2540–41.

Larkin, Colin. *The Encyclopedia of Popular Music*. (New York: Muze Uk/Oxford University Press, 1998. Vol. 6), 4443.

Lurie, Alison. *The Language of Clothes*. (New York: Random House, 1981), 161–66.

McConnell, Tandy. *American Decades: 1990–1999*. (Detroit: Gale Group, 2001), 68–74, 198–213.

Null, Gary. *Black Hollywood: from 1970 to Today*. (Secaucus, NJ: Carol Publishing Group, 1993), 199–221.

Nunn, Joan. *Fashion in Costume: 1200–2000.* (Chicago: New Amsterdam Books, 1984), 211–14, 241–42.

Pendergast, Tom and Sara. *The Saint James Encyclopedia of Popular Culture.* (Detroit: The Gale Group, 2000, Vol. 4: P–T), 155–56, 175–76, 620–22.

Polhemus. *Streetstyle: From Sidwalk to Catwalk.* (New York: Thames & Hudson, 1994), 72–79, 106–8.

Rapp, Linda. "Smith, Willi (1948–1987)." *An Encyclopedia of Gay, Lesbian, Bisexual, Transgender, and Queer Culture.* (Westport, Conn.: Greenwood Press, 2002).

Rose, Tricia. *Black Noise: Rap Music and Black Culture in Contemporary America.* (Hanover & London: Wesleyan University Press, 1994), 36–41, 60–1, 170–71.

Sadie, Stanley. *The New Grove Dictionary of Music and Musicians.* (New York: Grove, 2001), 828–31.

Stegemeyer, Anne. *Who's Who in Fashion?* (New York: Fairchild, 2003), 301.

BOOKS

Agins, Teri. *The End of Fashion.* New York: Quill, an imprint of HarperCollins Publishers, 1999.

Bailey, Beth and David Farber. *America in the Seventies.* Lawrence: University Press of Kansas, 2004.

Boyd, Todd. *Young, Black, Rich and Famous.* New York: Doubleday, 2003.

Felix, Antonia. *Sonia Sotomayor: The True American Dream.* Gale Group, July 2010.

Folb, Edith A. *Runnin' Down Some Lines.* Cambridge: Harvard University Press, 1980.

Gavenas, Mary Lisa. *The Fairchild Encyclopedia of Menswear.* Fairchild Publications: New York, 2008.

George, Nelson. *Hip Hop America.* New York: Viking, 1998.

Hunter, Karen and Smith, James Todd. *I Make My Own Rules.* New York: St. Martin's Press, 1998.

Keyes, Cheryl L. *Rap Music and Consciousness.* Chicago: University of Illinois Press Urbana and Chicago, 2002.

Kitwana, Bakari. *The Hip Hop Generation.* New York: Basic Civitas Book, 2002.

Lemelle, Sidney and Robin DG Kelly. *Imagining Home.* London: Verso, 1994.

Light, Alan. *The Vibe History of Hip Hop.* New York: Three Rivers Press, 1999.

Lopiano-Misdom, Janine and Joanne De Luca. *Street Trends*. New York: HarperBusiness, 1997.

MacDonald, J. Fred. *Blacks and White TV: African Americans in Television Since 1948*. 1992. Chicago: Nelson-Hall Publishers, 1992.

Ogg, Alex and Davis Upshal. *The Hip Hop Years*. New York: Fromm International, 2001.

Okonkwo, Uche. *Luxury Fashion Branding*. New York: Palgrave Macmillan, 2007.

Ramsey, Gunthrie P. *Race Music*. Berkeley: University of California Press, 2003.

Reeves, Marcus. *Somebody Scream: Rap Music's Rise to Prominence in the Aftershock of Black Power*. New York: Faber and Faber, Inc., 2008.

Rivera, Raquel Z. *New York Ricans from the Hip Hop Zone*. New York: Palgrave Macmillan, 2003.

Rondon, Cesar Miguel. *The Book of Salsa*. Chapel Hill: The University of California Press, 2008.

Southern, Eileen. *The Music of Black Americans: A History*. New York: Norton & Company, 1971.

Steele, Valerie. *Fifty Years of Fashion*. New Haven and London: Yale University Press, 1997.

Vibe Hip Hop Divas. New York: Three Rivers Press, 2001.

Watkins, S. Craig. *Hip Hop Matters*. Boston: Beacon Press, 2005.

Wynter, Leon E. *American Skin*. New York: Crown Publishers, 2002.

Index

About the Author

Photo by Darius Vick. (Used by permission)

Elena Romero has covered urban fashion since the nineties. Her journalistic work in both trade and consumer publications helped legitimize an industry that once was considered a fad. As the author of *Free Stylin': How Hip Hop Changed the Fashion Industry*, Ms. Romero tells the untold story of a multibillion fashion phenomenon. This is her first book on the subject matter.

Ms. Romero began her fashion journalistic career as the former associate editor and a contributing editor for fashion bibles *DNR* and *WWD*. Through her work at both publications, she extensively chronicled the rise and growth of many pioneering hip hop clothing brands including FUBU, Phat Farm, Ecko Unlimited, Rocawear, and Sean John. Her work on the subject has also appeared in a variety of magazines and newspapers including *Vibe*, *Savoy*, *Giant*, *Blaze*, *Sportswear International*, *Urban Latino*, *Latina*, and *The New York Post*. She has also made television appearances on NBC's *Today Show, UPN,* and *Video Music Box* explaining the relationship between hip hop and fashion.

Ms. Romero made her transition into academia in 2002, after leaving *DNR* and *WWD*. Since then, she has been teaching fashion journalism and a variety of media courses at the Fashion Institute of Technology (FIT) and the City College Center for Worker Education. In August 2011, she co-founded the "Reading Hip Hop: Off the Records, In the Books" Lecture Series at The City College Center for Worker Education, as a vehicle to promote new and established hip hop authors. Previously, she co-founded the Is Hip Hop History? Conference at The City College Center for Worker Education in February 2010. The annual conference, held during Black History Month, aims to facilitate dialogue between the hip hop community and academics.

Ms. Romero is a member of the National Association of Hispanic Journalists (NAHJ). Her journalistic excellence and contributions to fashion journalism were recognized with an Urban Fashion Journalism Award at the Urban Fashion Awards Show at Lincoln Center in 2002. She is a recipient of the 2011 Colin Powell Center for Policy Studies at The City College of New York's Faculty Leadership Award. She holds a BA in journalism and mass communications and a MS in publishing, both from New York University. A native New Yorker of Puerto Rican ancestry, Ms. Romero resides in Brooklyn with her two daughters.

CPSIA information can be obtained
at www.ICGtesting.com
Printed in the USA
BVHW032008090722
641749BV00001B/1

9 780313 386466